SSH/HWLC

THE CHICAGO PUBLIC LIBRARY

FORM 19

THE EVOLUTION OF THE COLLEGE COMMUNITY

BY

ROBERT S. PALINCHAK

METUCHEN, NEW JERSEY

SCARECROW PRESS

1973

LB
2328
.P34

To my wife, PATRICIA

LB
2328
.P34

PREFACE AND ACKNOWLEDGMENTS

During the several years that have transpired since I felt the need to develop a story about the "new" college in higher education, too much has happened too fast. As I ventured to write a historical and developmental commentary, I realized that the institution which I was trying to develop in words had already changed in its deeds. The junior college has evolved into a community college with an amorphous identity too dynamic to capture in literary terms. Not unlike a photograph, this book can only reflect the past, however close at hand. Although I strive to relate to the future, my main purpose is to fill a void in the background of those who recently "discovered" the community college, probably in a partial vacuum. This book, therefore, forms an introductory, documentary analysis. Its purpose is to view the community college from a broad perspective within the disjointed continuum of institutional education.

I must acknowledge my debt to the many authors, publishers, and other contributors from whose research, thinking, and writing I have drawn background materials. The generosity of such contributors deserves special thanks, especially those who gave permission to quote or discuss their works in depth. While it is not practical to list each contributor here, I have attempted to do so in text and in the Bibliography. Still, I should like to acknowledge certain sources from which major portions are drawn. They include: James E. Allen, Jr., American Association of Junior and Community Colleges, American College Testing Program, Alexander W. Astin, Florence B Brawer, Eldon J. Brue and associates, The Chronicle of Higher Education, Arthur M. Cohen, Charles C. Collins, K. Patricia Cross, Kenneth T. Doran, Walter Crosby Eells, E.R.I.C. Clearing House for Junior Colleges, Norman L. Friedman, Roger H. Garrison, Edmund J. Gleazer, Jr., Donald P. Hoyt and Leo A. Munday, B. Lamar Johnson, Junior College Research Review, Win Kelly and Leslie Wilbur, Dorothy M. Knoell, Leonard V. Koos, Leland L. Medsker, Betty Read, John E.

Roueche, Hugo E. Siehr and associates, Southern Regional Education Board, Emil O. Toews, James W. Trent, Jonathan R. Warren, and Roger Yarrington.

Of course, any errors in fact or judgment are the author's.

R. S. P.

NOTE

The parenthetical citations in this study refer to bibliographical references. The bibliography is alphabetized for ease in locating sources. Parenthetical citations include the author or other identifying word(s) as listed in the bibliography, the year of publication and, where necessary, a specific page reference.

TABLE OF CONTENTS

		Page
1.	Introduction	1
2.	Historical Perspective of the Two-Year Junior College	8
	Higher Education in Transition: An Overview	8
	Discussion of Terminology	15
	Periods of Development for Early Two-Year Colleges	21
	The Carnegie Unit	31
	Reorganization in Higher Education	33
	An Upward Extension: Secondary Status	38
	The German Influence	41
	Different Organizational Formats	43
	General Education and Vocationalism	50
	Universal Higher Education	55
	A Collegiate Status	56
	Bifurcation	58
	Institutional Characteristics	61
	The Degree Structure	64
	The Conflict of Dual Status	68
	Legislative, Legal, and Judicial Influences	78
	California and Other States	78
	On Becoming a Four-Year Institution	93
	An Evolving Institutional Form	97
3.	The Community College	101
	A Break with Tradition	101
	Funding, Control, and Opportunity	107
	Growth and Uniqueness: An Emerging Philosophy	112
	Twentieth Century Land-Grant Institution	121
	Opportunities for Minorities and Disadvantaged Persons	127
	Blacks	131
	Revised Perceptions of Community	135
	The New Excellence	137
	Many Things To Many People	141
	Multi-Comprehensiveness	144
	Open Door to What?	148

	Community Service and Continuing Education	156
	Career and Occupational Education	165
	Student Personnel Services	179
4.	The Student Clientele	186
	Developing a Profile	187
	Socioeconomic Background	193
	Blacks and Minorities	195
	Interests, Attitudes, and Self-Estimates	199
	Educational Aspirations	200
	Occupational Orientation	201
	Academic Aptitude and Grades	203
	Academic Probation and Dropouts	204
	Financial Barriers	207
	In Conclusion	208
5.	The Community College Faculty	210
	The Teachers	210
	Recruitment	215
	Professional Preparation	220
	The Degree Dilemma	223
	Problems	230
	The Teaching	233
	Instruction and Learning	233
	Evaluation	236
	Grading	239
	Research: A Missing Function	244
	In Conclusion	247
6.	Summary, Conclusions, Implications	249
	Principles for Action	255
	The Institution	255
	Programs	258
	Student Clientele	259
	Faculty Preparation and Development	261
	A Need for Further Research	263
Appendix: Review of Related Literature		265
Bibliography		282
Index		349

LIST OF TABLES

		Page
1.	Comparison of Secondary School, College, and University Aims, 1924	40
2.	Sources of New Full-Time Junior College Teachers Employed in 1963-64 and 1964-65	216
3.	New Full-Time Community College Faculty Engaged to Teach in California for School Year 1967-68 Listed by Experience Level at Time of Contract	218
4.	Educational Preparation and Professional Background of Faculty Teaching Career or Transfer Courses	227
5.	Degrees Held by Community Junior College Faculty	227

Chapter 1

INTRODUCTION

The nature of the two-year college is difficult to grasp because of its elusive characteristics. The use of the generic label, "junior college," and failure to identify and differentiate among the various types of two-year institutions has brought about much confusion and inconsistency in the discussion of the two-year college and how it relates to contemporary society.

Educators generally fail to recognize the accelerated changes that have occurred in two-year college development. The complete lack of significant dialogue in this area has led to acute debilities which must be corrected. Definitive statements about the philosophy, purpose, and function of the two-year college are difficult to find. The available body of writing is often vague, platitudinous, and aimed at various factions within a larger but unrealized segment of higher education. In short, the idea of the community college is rarely examined in contemporary professional literature (Cohen, 1969a).

The evolution of the junior college has produced a contemporary institution known as the comprehensive community college. The product of a century of transition in American education, it is unique and distinct among all other institutional forms of higher education. While the community college is closely related to other two-year colleges, including the junior college, it is still quite different in philosophy, purpose, and function. Due to its impact, the community college has already brought about a new interest in improved pedagogy, nontraditional study, external degrees, credit by examination, and other developments for mass education in a technological society.

In some respects the community college is the new land-grant institution; the people's college in the truest sense. This is the promise and potential of this unique institution which has yet to be fully explored. Will it perform to expectations or will there continue to be a dysfunction between stated goals and actual practice? Can higher education be democratized? Is there evidence that this institution can adequately serve the nontraditional student? What does the community college do that other institutions fail to do or choose not to do? What makes it unique, and is there evaluative evidence to support the many claims that are made for it?

For almost a century the American system of public education has been undergoing modification and reorganization to "fit" the two-year college into the general scheme. This far-reaching reorganization is often subtle, indirect, and sometimes completely inconsistent with more dominant educational themes or plans. Nevertheless, out of unstructured growth in higher education, the comprehensive community college has evolved into a distinct postsecondary form. In less than two decades this innovation has become the characteristic educational institution of the United States.

While the community college accounts for but one segment of higher education, it is already playing a dominant role in the determination of general policy for all postsecondary education. It continues to transform the nature and composition of what we vaguely refer to as "higher education." These and other recent changes have evolved so rapidly that we find ourselves in the unique position of not only recording educational history but also giving it immediate directions that may insure a variety of desired outcomes in the near future.

It is a thesis of this book that the community college has evolved so rapidly that its present ramifications are too often and too easily misunderstood and, as a consequence, the future potential of this institutional form may well go untapped. Part of the dilemma rests on the fact that the academic profession is rarely well informed. Boards of control, students, faculty, and administrators are often misinformed or uninformed on current issues in higher education and community college developments; the academic wheel is reinvented too often. The general public is even worse off; citizens provide the funds to build an institution over which they exercise too little control and, indeed, often find themselves unable to benefit from needed services.

The community college is not a junior college--it is more. Designed to provide educational services to all people, not just the academically fit, this institution operates

Introduction

in the public interest with an equal access philosophy that is in need of further development and analysis. The community college is an institutional form with a multipurpose function and philosophy that sets it apart from other types of two-year colleges. Yet, whether for convenience or lack of understanding, all two-year colleges are discussed alike despite notable differences in philosophy and purpose.

Out of such confusion a distinct problem arises over the interpretation of what is euphemistically called the "open door" policy. There is gross distortion between written and applied policy in this area. When a "two-year" institution admits anyone and everyone, as a true open door would, it is often done with a sincere attitude of extending democracy and bringing more rights to our citizens. At this point, however, many institutions discover that they are unprepared or unable to provide adequate programs for "students" who are unconventional by all traditional criteria.

Many community colleges continue to operate as unofficial extensions of the university and literally guarantee the failure and discomfiture of nonconventional students in a conventional or otherwise traditional academic setting. All too often, we are quick to celebrate the opening of a new community college each week, but slow to recognize the dysfunction between its stated goals and actual practice. The "cooling out" function described by Clark (1960a) is still operating at a time when its appropriateness and validity should be questioned.

The community college is a direct manifestation of public will and it owes its allegiance to citizens and taxpayers. It attempts to fill an educational void not filled by other institutions and, in so doing, becomes a social agency with an open door to further the democratization of society. In trying to cope with a wide range of student interests, abilities, and aptitudes, the community college does not warrant the stigma of low prestige afforded it by elitist elements in higher education.

This nation's growing population is rapidly becoming urbanized, but the problems of man, education, and work in a technological society constitute a dilemma which American junior colleges have given less than adequate attention (Venn, 1964). A parallel situation is noted by Freda Goldman who states that "we have failed even to serve adequately the nonvocational needs of professionals and other workers by not recognizing the significance of the continuity of leisure throughout life" (Whipple, et al., 1969).

Other areas of concern require that the community college face up to providing education to minority groups and to revitalizing an inadequate system of guidance which begins in elementary and secondary schools. The need for competent and capable faculty to cope with special problems of the community college and mass education is also of utmost importance. Credentials and degrees have not proven to be satisfactory criteria in determining the potential success of community college teachers. If the college is to lay claim to being an institution of teaching excellence, it must actively aim to resolve these and related issues.

Fitting the community college into the structure of American education has proven to be difficult and confusing. There are few remaining reasons for this institution to be so amorphous that it defies description. Persons associated with the community college have a notorious record for being excessively defensive or platitudinous about its ideology. Thus, a better frame of reference and historical perspective is needed to provide a more articulate justification of this college in American education. The uniqueness of this institution is real and must be understood if it is to gain confidence and momentum to achieve unfulfilled promises.

With unstructured diversity and unnecessary competition, the American system of education is based upon a self-perpetuated hierarchy--an educational class structure. Yet, the community college continues to modify higher education so that it is now all but impossible to determine or identify levels of learning as being secondary or collegiate. Such distinctions are useless, in any case, from a pedagogic viewpoint. Current stratified levels within the hierarchy of educational institutions are artificial and serve only to enhance status and prestige. Still, education is proving to be the great social synthesizer and equalizer. The community college must now be cautioned to take advantage of its unique mission and not capitulate to the tradition and conformity of institutions which serve other purposes in higher education.

Furthermore, the organization of higher education has evolved to a point where the community college might become a major factor in extending adolescence and incomplete adulthood. The option of providing less or delayed schooling as a well-planned alternative is a problem which must be further studied. The "sheepskin psychosis" is worsening and some people are finding the community college to be a cruel

Introduction

hoax. Attending such an institution must mean more than social attainment or quasi-scholastic achievement. A reorganization or clarification of roles in higher education is needed if public confidence is to be regained.

Recognition of the importance of elementary and secondary schools as major determinants for an enlightened citizenry in a democratic society is long overdue. These schools must be strengthened and philosophically integrated with community colleges to form a continuum of educational services providing for vocational, academic, and career goals within a framework of general and liberal education.

Those who have studied the history of the two-year college agree that this institution is still in a high state of evolution. While the "junior" college can be traced back over a period of one hundred years, the "community" college is approximately twenty years old. In part, this explains why there is much misunderstanding or lack of agreement concerning its past and present role in higher education.

The effectiveness of the community college remains to be seen, as does a definitive statement of its purposes. Career and vocational programs must be reinforced as they challenge the standard-transfer-college-parallel program. The community college must stop judging its success solely in terms of those who transfer. The fact that a majority of students choose this route, while a minority attain reasonable success, is an indication of misunderstanding or misrepresentation--or both! Ways must be found to provide educational services for the disadvantaged, illiterate, unschooled, ethnic minorities, blacks, and other nonconventional students. This necessarily includes mid-career people who must advance their knowledge and skills or seek retraining for entry into new occupational areas. The new clientele will include veterans from the Armed Forces, housewives, retired people, teachers, doctors and other professionals, the aged, the blind, and any citizen who can demonstrate a need and potential to profit from further educational opportunity.

The community college is in the delicate position of dealing with various aspects of both secondary and higher education while demanding recognition as a unique institution in American higher education. While the university remains the capstone of higher education, it can never stand alone. Thus, the performance of the community college must be studied and evaluated in relation to all other educational institutions. What it does best must be determined and made visible in order to gain the necessary support and coordination to develop further. <u>Proof must be sought if the claim for excellence in teaching</u> is to be legitimately accepted.

The evolution of the community college has hardly begun, but future directions will undoubtedly be affected by the quality of present inquiries made about its uniqueness and effectiveness.

The major thesis of this book is that the comprehensive community college is unique among all other forms of two-year colleges, including the junior college. Clarification of the status of the comprehensive community college and of its philosophy and multipurpose function are major purposes here. A related thesis is that the community college concept has "peaked" at its present state of evolution and that, unless significant changes are made to preserve the philosophical tenets subscribed to earlier, the institution, like most others, will regress to a medial position heavily laden with tradition, conformity, and mediocrity.

Institutional research on the community college is at a very low level, both quantitatively and qualitatively. While this situation is slowly being remedied, comprehensive studies are needed to reconcile various attributes, past, present, and future, as they relate to the evolutionary nature of the community college. Among various social, political, and economic factors which suggest related purposes which justify this book are:

> To report the sociological, technological, and psychological factors which give rise to the demand for postsecondary educational opportunities.
>
> To clarify and articulate the philosophical nature of the community college.
>
> To differentiate the community college as a distinctly unique institution among other types of two-year junior colleges.
>
> To clarify and define roles of the community college with respect to coordination among other institutions of secondary and higher education.
>
> To correct misconceptions held by the professional

educator and layman alike in matters relative to the community college.

To present a more accurate description of community college students and teachers.

To present a comprehensive analysis of the community college as an institution that evolved from more simple two-year institutional forms to a multipurpose institution that is distinctively an American innovation.

To review recent developments in secondary and higher education that have a direct bearing on present and future characteristics of the community college in transition.

Chapter 2

HISTORICAL PERSPECTIVE OF THE TWO-YEAR JUNIOR COLLEGE

An understanding of the comprehensive community college is not possible without a knowledge of past events and forces that guided the two-year junior college through periods of evolution and revolution in educational history. The purpose of this chapter is to provide a historical perspective of the junior college concept from which an in-depth analysis of the community college can be better articulated and understood.

Higher Education In Transition: An Overview

The forces that brought about higher education in America were borrowed from the traditions of almost-finished cultures which can be traced to the Middle Ages and earlier. "American colleges were established to perpetuate a society nurtured by a Protestant equalitarian determinism. Colleges generally preceded a culture; where the university came first in Europe, it came last in America" (Lunden, 1939).

The private sector of higher education set a tenor and purpose which all colleges followed into the twentieth century. While Harvard was founded in 1636, state or public higher education was not established until 1790 in South Carolina. Public governance was careful to recognize the importance of education while leaving its practice to be defined elsewhere. In many ways, education was held to be equal in stature and sanctity with religion. For a long time these two aspects of life held a symbiotic relationship which has survived to the present day. Although America was founded out of religious oppression, the Ordinance of 1787 clearly maintained a value construct for education: "Religion, morality and knowledge, being necessary to good government and the happiness of mankind, schools, and the means of education,

Historical Perspective

shall forever be encouraged."

From the very beginning, education was deeply valued and engrained in our society. An inherent faith in schooling led President Eliot of Harvard to say that education is "the religion of America." George Washington, in his <u>Farewell Address</u> of 1796, urged his countrymen to "promote, then, as an object of primary importance, institutions for the general diffusion of knowledge." And in a letter to Dr. B. Rush, John Jay, Chief Justice of the Supreme Court, affirmed, "I consider knowledge to be the soul of a Republic." Thomas Jefferson perceptively sensed the challenge that a free society faces when, in 1816, he warned: "If a nation expects to be ignorant and free in a state of civilization, it expects what never was and never will be."

College became a way of life; an environment in which four years could be spent with pleasure and profit; a popular life style for some. Attending college was an integral part of the rising standards of living and not to attend was to undergo a social deprivation as well as to suffer a professional handicap (Chase, 1938-39). But like other social institutions, colleges underwent certain morphological changes with the passing of time and the variations of environment. As the cultural components and the social configuration of society varied, the character and types of educational institutions also differed. This process of change or evolution was usually slow but continuous. It proved to be incorrect that once the institutional structure of higher education was built, society would have neither the concern nor the need for additional institutions. Lunden (1939, p. 152) was wrong when he concluded, "Structurally, therefore, higher education may be complete."

Change in American education usually occurred in response to the external pressures of society, environment, and technology, rather than from within. Dissatisfaction with elitist higher education and Latin grammar schools gave rise to academies and the public school concept during the eighteenth century. But because of organizational problems, even the academy came to be challenged by growing popular support for the public high school. In time, the junior high school was to evolve as a response to inadequate education for the period between the primary grades and the high school. Later innovations included the junior college on the terminal end of the high school and the middle school on the upper end of the primary grades. New institutions were seldom able to resolve the problems for which they were developed, however. As Briggs (1930) concluded, "We fail to make adequate efforts to ensure that the new institution remedy the deficiencies that brought it into being." The academy and the junior high school alone, of all our educational institutions, came into being with clearly stated goals and practical programs. Their general failure to accomplish the objectives for which they were organized created a dilemma which should not be repeated.

Our faith in democratic education was always great, as is evidenced by the following:

> We believe in democracy, even though we usually do not know clearly what we mean by it. We believe that democracy alone can save civilization, which is on the verge of collapse. To us, democracy is not just a political doctrine but is bound up with our moral aspirations and our religious convictions. The reason why this great national faith has not functioned more effectively is, in large part, that it has not yet been illuminated and directed by education. It is our obligation as educationists to interpret and apply this faith in order to reorganize our educational activities so as to make them effective for the furtherance of democracy (Bode, 1922, p. 96).

Faith in education by American citizens led to its eventual democratization; first at the secondary level, and then at higher levels. And even though people expressed more concern about schools than education, an early critic wrote:

> There is only one sound justification for the provision of free education at public expense, and this is that it may make each individual better able and better disposed to contribute to the betterment of the supporting society (Briggs, 1930, p. 215).

Nevertheless, both secondary and higher education went through various phases in which they were criticized for uncertain and undemocratic policies. At one point, secondary schools became extremely selective institutions in an effort to match the tenor established in colleges (Campbell, 1942). Disenchantment with this policy caused people to look elsewhere for help. Harvey (1908, p. 61) wrote, "We must recognize that the public school system is but one factor in the education of the individual. We must not demand that it shall be the only factor." And even when the high school seemed productive, Koos (1925) showed that most of what was offered in the high school overlapped with the college curriculum.

In 1921, the President of the University of Minnesota revealed a frustration which is not uncommon today:

> State universities since they were first established have been regarded as a part of the public school system. There have been occasions when the relationship was more theoretical than real. Universities have at times attempted to isolate themselves, to set up highly artificial entrance requirements, and to administer their affairs without reference to the other units of public education.... We have consistently maintained that the doors of the schools should be free and equally open to all from the kindergarten to and through the university.... Whenever universities place unnecessary and artifical limitations upon their registration, they will become aristocratic in form.... They will be in danger of ceasing to be the creative agents of democracy and may become the agents of class and station. Both the program of American education and the philosophy of the American people have been opposed to anything [like] this (Coffman, 1921, p. 1).

Certainly the educational structure was meant to reflect the ideals of a free society. How did it manage repeatedly to drift away? More than a century ago Francis Wayland saw that community needs were in some way related to the goals of higher education. Like others, he saw that higher education was supposed "to survey the wants of the various classes of the community ... and adapt courses of instruction, not for the benefit of one class, but for the benefit of all classes" (Wayland, 1850, p. 51). A similar feeling was expressed at the first annual meeting of the National Society for the Promotion of Industrial Education in 1908. The Society called for educational opportunity for all with the following statement:

> The ideal of a public school system that aims to benefit all should be to provide facilities which through adequate organization, equipment, and

administration, will open to all the opportunity to
secure such knowledge and training during the
school age as constitutes the best possible preparation of the individual for that effectiveness, through
which he may make the most of himself, may render the largest service to society, and become
most valuable to the state as a citizen (Harvey,
1908).

Education passed from homogeneity to heterogeneity
as it responded to variations in socioeconomic-political configurations in society. According to the noted British economist John Vaizey (1962), the United States always trusted
its resources to further the education of the masses. He
wrote:

In the U.S.A. ... it was always a principle
of American democracy, and of the reformed religion that was its main impulse, that the people
should be well educated; and this was an impulse
given an enormous boost after the Civil War by
the Land-Grant Colleges. All along, too, American education has had an important job, the aim
of preparing people to earn their livings.... Thus,
in America, democratic impulses and the needs of
the economy created a skilled and educated population through a mass education system; and consequently America has tended to spend more of its
national income on education than other countries.

In the period following the Civil War, high schools were
claimed to be bulwarks of democracy; they were to be the
agencies by which citizens prepared for life (Chase, 1938-39). The unresolved issue of whether high schools prepared
people for life or college was often renewed, as were issues
related to general and specialized education, and to the
dichotomy between teaching and research. Each generation,
in its own manner and style, asked the same questions, often
arriving at conclusions which past generations had frequently
rejected. The importance attached to getting an education
was soon to match the lack of consensus about the manner
in which one should be provided.

During World War I there was renewed interest in
education as a means of maintaining and developing the democratic social order. Certain aspects of this issue were
vigorously stated in ancient and honorable terms, such as

Historical Perspective

"cultural vs. utilitarian," "academic vs. vocation," "basic vs. practical," "scholarship vs. training" (Campbell, 1942). And, as is often the case in periods of war and rising nationalism, secondary and higher education became provincial and subservient to the respective governments. Prussia was the first modern nation to control the school and use it as "an instrument for promoting the interest of the State. Under Napoleon, France sought to turn the schools into instruments of politics, power, and government in an attempt to conserve the accepted social order, nationalism, and the Empire." (Lunden, 1939). In part, this was also true for Fascist Italy, Nazi Germany, Soviet Russia, and Imperialist Japan.

The United States was fortunate not to nationalize secondary and higher education. Diversity of function and purpose has evolved as the pattern of American education. As a result, our system of education is still fractionated, self- or nonregulated, mostly unstructured, independent at all levels, with little or no effective coordination, and accountable to practically no one. In general, American education tends to be severely institutionalized, to the point where concern for the institution dominates concern for the individual. Wrote one critic:

> I am pleading that colleges and universities come to understand themselves, to see clearly their own real function. Upon doing this, they must then interpret themselves to the public, not as places where jangling and raucous people come for myriad and confusing reasons, but as places where those who can think come to think (Ross, 1970).

Of higher education, and with particular reference to the university, Robert Hutchins voices a timeless argument:

> They haven't any clear idea of what they're doing or why. They don't even know what they are.... The people ... are supposed to maintain a very expensive system of higher education without any comprehension of what these institutions are supposed to be about (In The Chronicle, March 9, 1970).

Similarly, Sir Eric Ashby states that the gravest problem facing American higher education is an "alarming disintegration of consensus about purpose." He continues:

> It is not just that the academic community cannot
> agree on technicalities of curricula, certification,
> and governance: it is a fundamental doubt about
> the legitimacy of universities as places insulated
> from society to pursue knowledge disengaged from
> its social implications. There will remain (unless
> some unforeseen factor eliminates it) a streak of
> frustrated aspiration running through the whole system: two-year colleges striving to do para-academic work, four-year colleges itching to set up
> graduate programs, undistinguished universities
> bidding in the market for academic stars ... (In
> The Chronicle, April 26, 1971).

A re-evaluation of the relationship between higher education and society is in order. Institutions of education are not only misunderstood but also oversold. It is doubtful that universities can do much to cure the emotional or psychic ills of students, even though students seem to feel that universities could do such things if only they would (Ross, 1970). Other sectors of higher education are better-suited to familiarize students with life; Ross concludes that "universities are highly artificial constructs, and as such they are great only in that relatively restricted spectrum of life with which they are equipped to deal. Beyond these borders they have few capabilities" (p. 48).

Contemporary education is again at a turning point. Higher education is confronted with some new problems, but mostly old ones in newer form. One of the major factors that appears to be influencing future directions for all post-secondary education is the emerging structure of community and junior colleges. But much still remains to be learned about the idea which underlies different kinds of two-year colleges. In The Contemporary World (1960), the authors conclude:

> There is not one educator among four who has a
> clear understanding of the unique partnership that
> has evolved, (and is evolving) between the junior
> college and other segments of education (Bonner,
> et al., 1960, p. 380).

It becomes apparent that citizens and educators alike must address themselves to this problem.

Discussion Of Terminology

Educational terminology tends to interfere with one's perception of the two-year college. It may be said that some two-year junior colleges perform the unique functions of the community college. And sadly, it may also be said that many so-called "community" colleges do not perform adequately, either in scope or philosophy, to earn the title of community college. Many private two-year institutions, as well as some limited versions of public institutions, have capitalized on the popularity of the community college by adopting its name in title form. Of course, the same can also be said of other educational institutions. Thus, many "universities" are nothing more than fine colleges, and many "colleges" readily admit to being advanced high schools or preparatory schools. Whereas, at one time "there was a meaningful distinction between those institutions known as universities and those called colleges, the title university has been so bastardized that it is no longer a significant indicator of institutional status" (Graham, 1969, p. 6). Unfortunately, nebulous terminology and interchangeable labels continue to impair a clear understanding of both junior and community colleges.

The traditional functions of colleges and universities are firmly entrenched in the minds of most people. However, since the community college is a more recent phenomenon, its purpose and philosophy are too readily interpreted in terms of other institutions. This has created additional confusion in higher education at a time when governance, unrest, and accountability have all but dominated current thought. And while the terms "junior college" and "community college" are carelessly interchanged, they are not synonymous (Getty, 1970).

As early as 1905, some writers called for more realistic descriptions of "high school," "college," and "university":

> If the state legislature, the state department of public instruction, or the American commissioner of education would once and for all define these three items, they would free us from much inextricable educational jumble in our use of [these] terms (Brown, 1905, p. 16).

Of course, the term "higher education" itself has been

changed dramatically from its traditional meaning. Due to the impact of the community and junior college on higher education, it is more appropriate to describe present higher education as postsecondary education. The term "higher" was appropriate when curricula were supposedly designed as "college level" or "collegiate." This is no longer feasible since all but the highest levels of study tend to have various degrees of overlap. In his higher education message to Congress on March 19, 1970, President Nixon used his own definition of "college":

> ... I use the term 'college' to define all postsecondary education--including vocational schools, four-year colleges, junior and community colleges, universities, and graduate schools.

To some degree, two-year institutions have suffered from all-inclusive definitions. The Executive Director for the American Association of Junior Colleges has warned repeatedly, "Until some of the misconceptions about what constitutes higher education are eliminated, the potential of community colleges and technical institutes will not be realized" (Gleazer, 1966b, p. 340).

A spokesman for the California system of community colleges says that higher education

> ... is thought of as an education beyond high school and serving the educational needs of post-high school age men and women without identifying 'collegiate' education with four-year colleges and universities ... (Toews, 1964c, p. 10).

Collegiate education need not be classically associated with the ivy halls of four-year institutions. But while some states recognize collegiate education to begin inclusively with the twelfth grade of high school, others plainly identify junior college education as a part of secondary education.

Descriptive nomenclature that describes the two-year college student is vague also. Speaking against the proliferation of such loose nomenclature, a former president of the American Association of Junior Colleges cites this condition as one of ten critical issues in education. He questions the use of such controversial words as "junior," "terminal," and "transfer." In their place he calls for a new and understandable vocabulary that would eliminate the concept that education so different is inferior (Littlefield, 1961).

Describing the two-year college, its students or programs as "terminal" is considered inappropriate and undesirable (Scannell, 1966). Thus, the more acceptable [and correct] term, "nontransfer," is used as a euphemism. Defining the public two-year college as "secondary," however, often provides some benefit. California, for example, defined public higher education as consisting of all public junior colleges, state colleges, and all campuses of the University of California. In addition, junior colleges in California are legally classified as "secondary schools" in order to be eligible for financial support on the same basis as high schools. Thus, a dual status allows for free public higher education.

Article XIII(A), a constitutional amendment in Oklahoma, defines higher education this way:

> ... [It will] include all education of any kind beyond or in addition to the twelfth grade or its equivalent as that grade is now generally understood and accepted in the public schools in the state of Oklahoma (Dunlap, 1969, p. 32).

But Cross (1968c) argues that even if we were to agree on what constitutes institutions of secondary or higher education, each would necessarily have different tasks. If similar tasks were posed for all institutions of higher education, the junior and community college segment would become a "watered-down version" of the senior colleges.

Another area closely associated with two-year colleges is vocational-technical-occupational-career-type education. A complete lack of consensus is found in differentiating these concepts in both secondary and higher education. To further complicate the problem, newer terms such as semi-, quasi-, sub-, and para-professional education keep appearing. Science Research Associates, Inc., in a study dealing with the assessment of goals of vocational education, summarized the dilemma as follows:

> First, there is the problem of what is meant by the term 'vocational education.' In its broadest sense, it could mean education preparatory to the entering of all occupations, both professional and non-professional, and thus encompass the entire

> educational process. In its narrowest sense, it
> could assume the meaning given to the term today
> in educational literature and refer only to those
> very precise courses of study found in most schools
> that prepare students for direct entry into a finite
> group of skilled occupations ...
>
> The literature provides no help on this problem of
> definition; rather, it reflects the lack of consensus
> on the part of the 'expert' writers ... (Burt, 1967,
> p. viii).

As a field of study, the area of industrial arts usually refers to the use of techniques and devices which, with further study and training, will be useful to a person in industrial employment below the management and policy-making levels. For example, the industrial arts student may learn something about drafting, but his industrial arts training does not make him a draftsman. There is a wide difference between the study of industrial arts and vocational-technical education (Burt, 1967). The latter is designed to gainfully employ individuals as semi-skilled or skilled workers or technicians in recognized occupations. The dilemma here becomes one of recognizing and solving educational problems associated with a multitude of new occupations that are continually created to fit the needs of a changing society.

It is difficult to define and articulate what constitutes high school vocationalism and what constitutes community and junior college vocationalism. Overlapping programs exist in such areas as drafting, mechanics, secretarial science, business, and nursing. To identify one as higher education and another as secondary education is not only difficult but often misleading. Furthermore, some community colleges offer no specific vocational-occupational programs while many junior colleges do. Labels and nomenclature used in this field are ineffective and, indeed, useless as a means of differentiating between secondary and higher education. In Search for Relevance (1969), the authors rightly conclude:

> ... general education and specialized studies, liberal
> arts and professional education, occupational and
> transfer curricula--are false distinctions for today
> and tomorrow, however useful they might have been
> in some other world of the past. They not only
> obscure vital issues but do us the further disser-
> vice of contributing to the dysfunction that

characterizes [higher education] today (Axelrod, et al., 1969).

Apparently, the professional educator has chosen to overcome both industrial and public prejudice by generating new terms to replace unpopular ones. Thus, "paramedical" is replaced by "health related"; "voc-tech" programs are now "occupational" or "career" programs; and "terminal" education is replaced by "continuing education" (Menefee and Cornejo, 1969, p. 5).

Similar discrepancies exist among proprietary junior colleges, technical institutes, regional vocational centers, public and private junior colleges, state junior colleges, university branches, centers and campuses, community colleges, and other such institutions. They vary mostly in function, philosophy, purpose, and service. To identify all such institutions collectively is misleading and incorrect. Furthermore, they are not "two-year" institutions any more than they are one-year, three-year or five-year. Such anachronistic vestiges do not recognize the uniqueness of the community college among other institutions of learning.

Educational literature tends to use the generic "two-year" or "junior" college term for convenience. At times, the community college may be known as "county college," "city college," or plain "college." Legal definitions employ terms such as "unified," "joint," "union," "state," and others. Now, an attempt is being made to recognize the "community" aspect of this newer form and "community-junior" college has become a popular expression. In several ways, this parallels the manner in which the original term "junior college" evolved. At first, the concept was mainly identified as a "junior-college department." Successive terms included "lower division," "six-year high school," "junior-college grade," "grades thirteen and fourteen," "high school college," "university junior-college," "junior division," "junior-college," and finally "junior college."

It is evident that many problems are encountered in defining the junior college in simple, all-inclusive terms. Most definitions use other vague or undefined words to encompass the numerous variables associated with the junior college concept. The Encyclopedia of Educational Research (Harris, ed., 1960) reports that even extensive definitions are not complete. For example, the Dictionary of Education devotes 185 words to a two-sentence definition followed by definitions of seventeen distinct types of junior colleges.

Even the U.S. Office of Education and the American Association of Junior Colleges use different criteria in describing junior colleges. The former includes legally designated community or junior colleges and excludes branches, extension centers, and other divisions of existing institutions. The American Association of Junior Colleges uses more liberal criteria, such as college, community college, extension center (including division and branch), junior college, seminary, technical institute, and teachers college (Bogue and Waterman, 1957). As many as nine additional classifications were also used at various times.

As early as 1926, the use of the phrase "community education" began to reflect community and social implications for junior colleges. For example, the Pasadena (California) Board of Education wrote about "Fitting the Commercial Course of the High School and Junior College to the Needs of the Community" in its <u>Education Research Bulletin</u> (1926), in which an attempt was made to determine what subjects would be relevant for use in the community. And then, Byron S. Hollinshead wrote about "The Community College Program" in 1936. Three years later, Sheldon Hayden (1939) attempted to describe "The Junior College As a Community Institution," but "community college" did not receive popular use until the late 1950's.

Scholars and historians of higher education make little or no reference to the community college, except in a few notable instances. The reader is usually referred to "junior college" or "commuter college" for fragmentary comments. Studies of student cultures, campus unrest, curriculum, and relevance generally ignore the community college. Even the American Association of Junior Colleges fails to give due recognition to the community college as a distinct form of junior college. In the closing address of the A.A.J.C. Conference in March, 1970, Harlan Cleveland suggested that the word "junior" be dropped altogether since the community college concept offers far more than the commonly recognized intermediate educational step. "'Community college' is a good, populist phrase," he said, "or maybe you would prefer to take the semantic bull by the horns and call yourselves the American Association of Relevant Colleges." [The American Association of Junior Colleges has since consented to become the American Association of Community and Junior Colleges.]

Historical Perspective

The dilemma in nomenclature was cited in <u>The Chronicle of Higher Education</u>, March 30, 1970, letter to the editor:

> Your March 9 issue contained two articles reporting on the annual conference of the American Association of Junior Colleges. In one article the terms 'junior and community college,' 'community college,' and 'junior college,' were used. In the second article the terms 'two-year and community colleges,' and 'junior college' were used.
>
> As a representative of a private two-year college, I find the intermingling of these terms is most confusing so I can imagine what it must be to those people who are not familiar with this type of institution.
>
> ... I realize that the A.A.J.C. itself has done little to point out the difference between the two types [public and private] and it becomes even more confusing when Mr. Gleazer, the executive director of A.A.J.C., uses the term 'junior and community colleges.' If by junior he means private, I wish he would say so instead of adding to an already confusing issue.
>
> Director of College Relations
> Green Mountain College, Vt.

Obviously, if one is to develop an understanding and appreciation of the community college, a more critical analysis of the differing functions and purposes of "two-year" educational institutions is in order. The free interchange of "community" and "junior" in describing these institutions is not only vague and misleading, but incorrect. A greater degree of understanding and awareness is needed before making a simplistic differentiation. As the subtleties unfold, so too will the attributes that distinguish "junior" from "community."

Periods Of Development For Early Two-Year Colleges

Developmental factors which led to the existence of the two-year college have evolved slowly during the past century. Eells goes further: "There are those who would trace the beginnings of the junior college movement ... to the Renaissance ... in the sixteenth century" (In Getty, 1970). While early two-year colleges grew out of circumstances and accident, later ones grew out of design and planning. The beginnings of the junior college movement reflect the strength of the private sector of American education as well as the educational diversity that has since become a national trademark.

It remains difficult to synthesize a variety of independent beginnings into a cogent report, but it is interesting to look at some of the earliest two-year colleges. The initial period of development for two-year units started around 1835. These units generally were private academies that offered elementary, secondary and collegiate courses in varying amounts. The private junior college evolved from this movement in the period from 1835 to 1900 (Parker, 1970), which is described by Kelly and Wilbur (1970) as the initial period of private development.

The academy was a particularly versatile institution. In 1871, President Barnard of Columbia University reported that academies "gave instruction in as large a range of subjects as the colleges themselves" (Doran, 1969, p. 3). Students did not find much need to go on to a college after completing a good academy curriculum. The curriculum of early Harvard only required a Latin prerequisite to study such subjects as arithmetic, a little geometry and astronomy, among other religious and humanities-oriented courses. Such men as Andrew Draper, first New York State Commissioner of Education, Leland Stanford, and John D. Rockefeller were to be found among the academy graduates at Albany, Cazenovia Seminary, and Owego Academy, respectively. The comprehensive academy served all curricular functions, including transfer, terminal, and vocational-technical programs with such offerings as bookkeeping, surveying, and navigation, in addition to collegiate level courses--all of this in the early 1800's.

The academy, like other educational institutions, had overlapping functions with the college from the start. New York Regent Ezra L'Hommedieu demanded, as far back as 1787, that both the academy and the college be allowed to grant Bachelor of Arts degrees. As might be expected, this proposal was defeated by a Columbia faction in the Legislature. The strong opposition included Hamilton and Jay, among others, and the academy was officially made subordinate to the college. Still, the academy was recognized as a viable institution and was allowed to become a "college" whenever its curriculum and funds would so warrant. In recognition of their "collegiate" status, academy graduates

Historical Perspective

were authorized from one to three years of advanced placement in college upon examination by the college professors (Doran, 1969).

In his autobiography Secretary of State Seward reveals that he was more than qualified to enter the junior class at Union College because of academic work previously done at Farmers' Hill Academy in Goshen. DeWitt Clinton, among the first students to be admitted to Columbia after the Revolution, was admitted as a junior because of substantive work done at an academy in Kingston. Two of the most influential proponents of the junior college concept were also to receive academy training. Henry Tappan, first President at the University of Michigan, attended Greenville Academy, south of Albany, and secured sophomore standing at Union College on this basis. And William Watts Folwell, first President of the University of Minnesota, entered Hobart as a sophomore after attending Ovid Academy (Doran, 1969).

To a great extent, such academies gained strength in New England and other eastern states. Elsewhere, two-year normal schools were about to develop and two-year Negro schools were already operating in the South. The public sector of junior college education did not even begin to develop until around 1900. As a result of this early growth pattern, private junior colleges appeared mainly in the Midwest, West, and Southwest where they were relatively free of the New England influence. Eastern states were to be last in their efforts to develop the public junior college concept. Indeed, this phase of development was passed over in the eastern states and community colleges started in their own right during the 1960's and after.

In the 1930's, Leonard V. Koos conducted studies for several eastern states, including Pennsylvania, to determine the necessity for public junior colleges. The reaction of Pennsylvania is illustrative of those states that failed to accept the challenge. Even though a bill was introduced to the Pennsylvania Legislature as early as 1937 to initiate public junior colleges, it and twenty-four consecutive annual attempts died quietly. The power politics of education and vested private interests were to play a major role in the anomalous development of the two-year college. Referring to Pennsylvania, the President of Northampton County Area Community College, (Pa.), Richard C. Richardson, concluded:

In a state where higher education has been governed

so long by power politics, it is difficult for a new type of institution to achieve the level of recognition necessary to serve important legislation ... (In Denton, 1970).

Many two-year educational institutions did manage to start early, however. According to Walter Crosby Eells (1931, p. 57), former Executive Director of the American Association of Junior Colleges, "[What] might be called the earliest junior college is to be found at Newton, Maryland, where the first Catholic 'college' in what is now the United States was opened in 1677." Later, Eells (1941) suggests that the oldest junior college is the privately-owned Lasell Junior College in Massachusetts which was established in 1851 as Lasell Female Seminary. Lasell was actually founded forty-five years before President William Rainey Harper of the University of Chicago coined the term "junior college."

From its inception, Lasell offered a complete curriculum which included two years of postsecondary school work that was definitely on the college "level" at that time. Lasell also started with what amounted to a high school department--lower grades that prepared students for the upper school. The lower grades were always subordinate and were dropped in the 1940's. President Wilson of the University of Baltimore examined this situation and concluded:

> The parallelism between the offerings at Williams College (where Edward Lasell was a former professor) and Lasell Seminary is obvious. The parallelism between the offerings at Mt. Holyoke and at Lasell is likewise evident, both institutions attempting to offer the courses which were most essential to the higher education of young women ...
>
> From the above evidence, it is clear that Lasell Seminary was offering in fact, though not in name, two years of junior college work in 1852, and, therefore, presumably in 1851. It has continued to offer two years of post-high school instruction to the present day. Not until 1932, however, was the name changed to Lasell Junior College. The change was then made by action of the Legislature of Massachusetts ...

Historical Perspective

> Three conclusions are inescapable: (1) In 1851, Lasell Female Seminary was offering two years of instruction in advance of high school; (2) In 1851 Lasell Female Seminary was organized as a four-year unit which integrated the last two years of high school and the first two years of college; and (3) By 1874, Lasell Seminary was emphasizing the Terminal Cultural Curriculum (In Stanley, 1965, p. 38).

Another forerunner of the junior college was Packer Collegiate Institute of Brooklyn, New York. Established in 1845 as Brooklyn Female Academy, the school suffered a fire loss and, in 1854, was renamed and chartered with a two-year college program (Kelly and Wilbur, 1970). Other similar proposals included Harper's Academic College concept and University College concept which were to develop in Chicago. Also, the Universities of Georgia and Michigan prepared plans for two-year colleges in the early 1850's (Brubacher and Rudy, 1968).

Ferrier (1937) reports the first private two-year college to be Lewis Institute, which came into existence in Chicago in 1896 and joined with Armour Institute in 1940 to become Illinois Institute of Technology. William Rainey Harper was as influential in starting Lewis Institute as he was in developing Bradley Polytechnic Institute in Peoria in 1897 and Joliet Junior College (Illinois) around 1902. While Joliet Junior College enjoyed a continuous existence, a neighboring "six-year high school junior college" existed only briefly in Goshen, Indiana around 1900. Hillway (1958) traces the early junior college back to several Negro colleges which were two-year units in operation prior to 1896. And Graham (1964) reports that the oldest two-year institution, founded in 1842, was Marion Institute, a member of the Alabama Association of Junior Colleges.

Another institution that serves as a prototype is Vincennes University (Indiana) which, prior to the 1880's, announced in its *Catalog* a broadening of its then preparatory function:

> Our course of study is designed to meet the needs of those who desire a thorough, practical, and liberal education, and who yet do not have the desire or opportunity of spending four years in a collegiate course.... Anyone so desiring it can

enter advanced classes in any college, after thoroughly completing the course (In "Letters," 1966, p. 48).

The Catalog for 1884-1885 stated:

> The certificates of work completed here will enable graduates of our classical course to enter the Junior Class of any State University without examination.

And the 1899 Catalog, issued under President Albert H. Yoder, identified Vincennes University as a junior college:

> The Vincennes University occupies a unique position in the educational field. It is halfway between a commissioned high school and a full-fledged college; it is, in fact, a junior college. Its graduates are admitted to junior standing in all the best universities....

This institution's unique position between the high school and college was to be an attribute of junior colleges to come. In the meantime, the junior college was still an amorphous conglomeration of two-year institutional forms which included the academy, the normal school, and a variety of institutes, seminaries, six-year high schools, junior college departments in high schools, and lower divisions of universities, among others.

The growth period from 1835 to 1900 has been presented as one of diversity and unstructured growth. Private sectors of higher education demonstrated much expansion during this period. Other periods are often suggested which reflect greater public interest and curricular development. For example, Kelly and Wilbur (1969) cite the period from 1901 to 1920 as the initial period of public two-year college development; 1921 to 1947 as the period of expanding occupational programs; and 1948 to the present as the period of the comprehensive community college.

Thornton (1966) characterizes the evolution of the two-year college in three stages which are related to the purpose and function of the institution. Thus, 1850 to 1920 becomes a period of education for transfer; 1920 to 1945, a period of expanding occupational programs; and 1945 to the present, the period in which the junior college began adding community

Historical Perspective

services, thus evolving into a community college.

Some of the better-known, publicly-supported junior colleges started after 1900, and for many people this period represents the real beginning of two-year colleges. For example, the American Council on Education, in An Introduction to American Junior Colleges (1967), lists the oldest publicly-supported junior college still in existence to have been founded at Joliet, Illinois in 1901. Toews (1964a) lists the earliest junior college as having been founded in 1902 when the University of Chicago considered it necessary to separate the general education program in the first two years from the more specialized junior and senior program of the University. Other public two-year colleges started in California (1904-1910), Missouri and Minnesota (1915), Kansas and Oklahoma (1920), and Texas (1921). By 1920, the American Association of Junior Colleges was publicly to announce its goal to make higher education available to an ever-increasing number of people. Soon thereafter, the Association organized five commissions which began to study administration, curriculum, instruction, legislation, and student personnel services.

The great majority of early junior colleges were still privately controlled and supported during these early years. In 1915, about 75 per cent of the junior college enrollment was in the private sector. By 1920, a total of eight thousand students were enrolled in fifty-two junior colleges across twenty-three states, and by 1922 there were sixteen thousand students in 207 junior colleges; seventy of which were public and 137 private. Michigan and Kansas, particularly, experienced rapid junior college growth in 1933, when more than 106,000 students enrolled in almost five hundred junior colleges around the country (Walters, 1934).

By 1940 there were 557 junior colleges with 196,710 students, and in 1950 there were 634 junior colleges with 562,786 students distributed as follows: 456,291 students in 329 public junior colleges and 106,495 students in 305 private junior colleges (Parker, 1970). Kelly and Wilbur (1969) indicate that by 1947 the private two-year colleges reached their maximum growth with 323 junior colleges, but public institutions finally surpassed them with 327 junior colleges in 1952. The Fifty-fifth Yearbook of the National Society for the Study of Education, The Public Junior College (Henry, ed., 1956), notes the declining rate of private junior colleges. For example, during 1956, these institutions represented only 45 per cent of all junior colleges. A trend was emerging which would soon reverse the dominance of private junior colleges.

Institutional growth of the two-year college entered a boom period in the decade of the 1960's, mainly because of the emergence of the community college concept. From approximately 640,500 junior college students in 1960, the enrollment today includes a quarter of the nation's eight million college students in more than eleven hundred two-year institutions. Even this growth is expected to double within a decade. Within the past sixty years, the number of two-year institutions grew to exceed the number of four-year colleges and universities in America, institutions with more than three centuries of development.

The remarkable growth of the two-year institution was due, in great part, to its curricular relevance, accessibility, and adaptability to constantly changing societal needs. This growth provided a stimulus to the public sector of junior colleges while limiting the further expansion of private two-year institutions. Before 1921, the curricular emphasis was placed on transfer programs and many private institutions adopted the elitist attitude of "finishing schools." Between 1921 and World War II, emphasis shifted to vocational-technical programs of a "terminal nature." Naturally, not all junior colleges followed a common path in areas of curricular development. Nevertheless, patterns showing response to local needs and interests were about to develop.

The 1922 Principals' Convention in California revealed that very little had been done with vocational-occupational curricula at secondary and higher education levels. The principals recommended a new postsecondary curriculum that would offer a certificate which would enable a student to transfer to the university; a curriculum for all high school students regardless of grades. Designed for anyone over eighteen years of age, this program was to be vocationally-oriented with emphasis on such areas as homemaking, citizenship, and personal health (Proctor, 1923). During this period, Koos and Whitney analyzed the popular purposes of the junior college and Kemp (1930, p. 189) summarized them as follows:

> 1. The offering of two years of work acceptable to the university;

Historical Perspective

2. The providing of occupational programs of 'junior-college-grade';

3. The completing of education for students not going on;

4. The popularizing of higher education through propinquity of opportunity for higher education at less cost to parents;

5. The offering of work which meets local needs;

6. The continuing of the home influence during immaturity.

According to one junior college principal, it was "along specific vocational courses and cultural courses designed to develop within the students what is sometimes termed 'social intelligence,' and courses in many fields for the adults of the junior college communities, and courses yet to be developed" that the junior college of the future would gain recognition--not for the strictly lower division academic transfer courses (Ferrier, 1937, p. 354).

From his early studies, Koos reported that opinion was likely to remain divided as to whether the differentiation between "diploma" and "certificate" programs or "transfer" and "terminal" students was a commendable practice. Quite often, university admissions' criteria forced junior colleges to resort to ability grouping as a means of filtering out those students unable to meet transfer requirements. In California, the attitude of the State University in ranking high schools on the basis of transfer-student success encouraged principals not to recommend continuing education for the great majority of high school graduates. Very often students were classified into such categories even before entering the junior college.

With a social science core composed of citizenship, sociology, psychology, philosophy and applied economics, the junior college entered a period of changing its programs to culminant and completion-type programs. During this early period, three-quarters of all students who completed a junior college education had not gone on to the university. The two-year institution was seen as a college of technology by many people and some of its career programs in 1929 included the following:

Accountant
Bank teller
Buyer-shipper
Cafe manager
Dairy farmer
Detective
Draftsman
Embalmer
Hotel keeper
Landscape gardener
Large-scale farmer
Librarian
News reporter

Nurse
Nurseryman-orchardist
Optometrist
Physiotherapist
Photographer
Printer
Station agent
Stenographic secretary
Stockraiser
Storekeeper
X-Ray operator
Watchmaker

(Bennett, 1929, p. 77).

World War I is seen by Campbell (1942) as a notable turning point for curricular emphasis in the junior college. The era preceding the war placed greater emphasis upon the natural and physical sciences while the following twenty-five years favored a corresponding increase in the social sciences. Several "popularizing" influences were subsequently demonstrated by many junior colleges. Koos (1924) lists some of these as: provision of opportunity for training for social leadership, improvement of instruction over that available in the universities, and increased attention to the individual needs and interests of students.

Private enterprise still constituted the main resource for creating both junior and senior colleges between World War I and World War II. Democratization of higher education remained dormant and, even though there was a slight increase in enrollment during 1943-1944, the war period caused a reduction in the number of junior colleges from 624 to 586 (Eells, 1944). In the years following Pearl Harbor, King (1944) reported that seventy-seven junior colleges had closed. But since new ones were opening during the same period, the net loss was only about thirty-eight junior colleges.

The democratization of higher education suddenly became a reality after World War II. Koos (1944c) identified the local public junior college as the institution that most democratized education. The birth rate had peaked in 1947 and the stage was set for rapid development of this institutional form which was evolving from the more limited junior college to a multipurpose community college. While the general population had tripled during the past seventy years, school attendance was doubling each decade (Henry, 1956). But few people were anticipating mass education in a technological society. The expanded influence of labor was among the first forces that gave impetus to the public junior college movement. At its 1943 convention in Boston, the American Federation of Labor adopted the following resolutions:

> Resolved, That the American Federation of Labor go on record in favor of the junior college as a means of offering opportunity for higher education to all young people of this nation with limited resources; and be it further
>
> Resolved, That the American Federation of Labor promote suitable activities tending to encourage the establishment of such educational facilities throughout the entire nation.
> (In Johnson, 1944, p. 607).

After World War II, junior college programs began to reflect an involvement with public need and community service on a level never before attained. Programs were especially well suited for veterans and the curricular diversity contributed to the further development of the junior college as an institution with comprehensive programs and many purposes.

The Carnegie Unit

The general period from 1850 to 1900 represents much change and revolution in American higher education. An increase of population brought more and different schools in addition to a growing demand for scientific and technical education, problems of certification, an expansion of the public sector of higher education, and the elective system. Earlier years of undirected growth left trails of confusion in both secondary and higher education. There were no general requirements for admission to college at this time and many institutions that called themselves colleges were still performing at the academy or high school level. Andrew Carnegie was influential in detecting and exposing the dilemma. He provided ten million dollars to establish a teachers' pension system and to resolve the "confusion that existed in American higher education." Carnegie suggested that specific criteria be established to define or differentiate the nature of a college.

In 1892, the National Education Association Committee of Ten was appointed to investigate procedures for bringing about uniformity in college admissions requirements. This group was instrumental in forming the Committee on College Entrance Requirements in 1895 which, in 1899, "published a credit table requiring that each high school student preparing for college take three studies each day for five days a week...." "Unit" meant either one year of study five times a week or two years of study three times a week. Thus, the Carnegie Foundation for the Advancement of Teaching encouraged the acceptance of a standardized unit to help clear the confusion among educational institutions.

After much discussion, the Carnegie Unit was generally accepted and nationally defined in 1909 as follows:

> A unit represents a year's study in any subject in a secondary school, constituting approximately a quarter of a full year's work. This statement is designed to afford a standard measure for the work done in secondary schools. It takes the four-year high school courses as a basis, and assumes that the length of the school year is from thirty-six to forty weeks and that the study is pursued for four or five periods a week; but, under ordinary circumstances, a satisfactory year's work in any subject cannot be accomplished in less than one hundred and twenty sixty-minute hours or their equivalent. Schools organized on any other than a four-year basis can, nevertheless, estimate in terms of this unit (Roush, 1970. Reprinted by permission of Kappa Delta Pi, an Honor Society in Education, copyright owners).

The Unit helped to distinguish between secondary and higher education; high school and college. It also differentiated the American system of secondary schools from the European system. The latter required that students study eight to ten subjects at a time, each requiring seven hours per week and a comprehensive examination to graduate from the lower school to the university (In Roush, 1970).

While many high schools still maintained their junior college or college departments, senior colleges began to close their high school departments but still required

Historical Perspective

students to graduate from a four-year high school to gain admission. To some extent, this weakened the position of the junior college, which was given no consideration when the Unit was devised. Further, the Carnegie Unit indirectly supported the establishment of an educational hierarchy, with each institution being subservient to the next higher one while dominating the one below.

In 1906, the Carnegie Foundation used the recommendations of the Association of Teachers of New York and Vicinity as the criterion for defining a high school. It was proposed that fourteen to fifteen units be the equivalent of high school preparation for college. The Foundation also went on to describe "college" in a manner that disparaged the junior college:

> (1) [It] had at least six professors giving their entire time to college and university work, (2) had a course of four full years in liberal arts and sciences, and (3) required for admission not less than the usual four years of academic or high-school preparation, in addition to the pre-academic or grammar school studies (Roush, 1970, p. 73).

From its inception, the Carnegie Unit was taken literally and quickly led to an accepted rigidity in locked-step education. Henry S. Pritchett, President of M.I.T. and the first President of the Carnegie Foundation, recognized a limited value for the Unit: "These units have now served their main purpose. They were never intended to constitute a rigid form..." (Roush, 1970, p. 74). Yet not until 1971 was Maryland the first to challenge the legitimacy of this system by permitting students with three years of high school to be admitted to a community college or other postsecondary institution.

Reorganization In Higher Education

Seldom have new institutional forms been organized or old ones reorganized according to planned and coordinated efforts. Educational development has virtually remained an ad hoc, piecemeal process with many aspects of chance, fate, and accident. Not until the latter half of the twentieth century were efforts directed to plan, coordinate, and enhance the efficiency of education in the United States. Failure to agree on educational purposes has assured regional and local control in educational matters.

Higher education has traditionally enjoyed a controlling influence over all other kinds of education, both directly and indirectly. Consequently, an artificial hierarchy of educational institutions has continued to emerge. This continuum has been deeply implanted in educational thought and remains difficult to challenge. Not always visible, these conditions have been a subtle factor in the evolution of secondary and higher education. In 1908, Harvey warned:

> No division of our educational system has a right through its demand upon the next lower division, to divert effort away from the accomplishment of important specific purposes for which that lower division exists. The high schools are supported by the people, and for the people; not by the people for the universities. The elementary schools are supported by the people and for the people, and not for the high schools (p. 72).

Conditions no longer warrant hierarchical distinctions among educational institutions. They may have evolved out of necessity, but the need for them no longer exists.

The organization and implementation of the high school concept went through various stages of conflict with higher education. The first public secondary school opened in 1635 and was known as the Boston Latin School. But not until 1821 was the classical approach in this school replaced with a general high school concept in the form of the Boston English High School. The organization of high schools and other postsecondary institutions was generally controlled by curricular programs and needs of four-year colleges. In the early 1900's, public school systems were sporadic and looked like their academy counterparts of the post-Revolutionary War period. Although public schools sent less than 10 per cent of their students on to college, their curricula were already dominated by the collegiate influence.

Many secondary schools continued to group their classes into a system which would ultimately serve four-year colleges, thus allowing the higher institutions to drop their lower division preparatory programs. The high school included such divisions as the first and second primary departments, the intermediate department, grammar and academic departments, and a collegiate department. Each department covered two or three years while the whole school took students from age eight or nine to the eighteenth or twentieth year. The rise of public union schools and other types of mergers gave much importance to the high school as a feeder institution. Even with this type of organization, one needed only to pass an examination in reading, writing, arithmetic, and English grammar to gain admission to high school. It was also common to complete college by age eighteen. But even while this arrangement was being established, it was condemned as a system which "forces or permits a deplorable number to leave school and become, for the most part, either discontented misfits or else hardened, unaspiring, inefficient citizens" (Davis, 1911, p. 272).

About 80 per cent of those who entered the primary grades in 1908 failed to complete eighth grade; 90 per cent failed to enter high school; and 96 per cent failed to graduate from high school. Yet, the curriculum remained oriented to satisfy requirements of four-year colleges. Some writers began to express concern for those students who would not go on to college. One observer wrote:

> The most vital problem before the American people today is to find some means whereby every young man and woman, who is desirous, can find an opportunity to prepare himself or herself to meet the demands of complete citizenship (Perry, 1908, p. 8).

The middle years of grades seven and eight went through a problem of organizational modification not unlike that of two-year colleges. The ages of thirteen and fourteen were recognized as requiring special needs; physical activity was considered more necessary than abstract thought. Aims for elementary and secondary education were uncertain and often undeclared. Subjects formerly in the domain of colleges began to appear in high schools. Likewise, high school subjects began to appear in the elementary school, and the middle years of grades seven and eight belonged to both elementary and secondary education. This gave temporary support to the six-year high school and later brought about the junior high school, comprehensive high school, middle school, and open school as distinct educational institutions.

While organization was important, it proved to be

insufficient in replacing institutional objectives as a major factor in establishing sound educational programs. There was little agreement on the objectives of education. In fact, one searched in vain for any satisfactory statement of general objectives in any form (Briggs, 1930). Those educational objectives that were found suffered from a conspicuous lack of comprehensiveness. Sporadic efforts at articulation and curricular development were unable to synthesize what education was all about. Nevertheless, Americans continued to hold a strong belief in organization and institutionalism as extensions of a democratic philosophy. By 1930, the situation had not changed. According to a critic of that period:

> In the United States we have congeries of schools rather than systems. Junior high schools are too often remote from the elementary; senior high schools have too frequently ignored the programs of the lower grades; and the colleges are notoriously independent of the secondary institutions (Briggs, 1930, p. 213).

Blind faith in educational organization characterized all levels of American education. More than fifty years ago, the President of the University of Minnesota gave this challenge:

> The entire program of American education is on trial. It is being tested and criticized in new and untried ways. Its purposes and aims are worthy of our ardent defense. Its organization is crippled by attempts to preserve traditional distinctions, historical anomalies, and a blind faith in the boundaries of the various administrative units. Shall [we] wait for outside forces and pressure to bring changes ... or will [we] assume some leadership in the matter? That is the challenge of the day! Refuse it and we become the unthinking adherents of faith and tradition; accept it and we become the leaders of a new day, the true exponents of a great profession (Coffman, 1921, p. 5).

Coupled with problems of general education, specialized education, and a rising case for vocationalism in an egalitarian setting, all social institutions were forced to react to new societal pressures and demands. Trade schools were established both in and out of high schools. Some were independent schools, while others were clearly offering work beyond that offered in high schools. Generally, however, vocational schooling remained in the shadow of academic training.

Colleges began to face the same problems which high schools had to struggle with earlier. It soon became apparent that colleges had to become sensitive to changing social and economic needs. Nevertheless, they did little to bridge the gap between themselves and the people (Rudolph, 1962). The Jacksonian era had left a far-reaching, complex influence on the reorganization of higher education, which was seen as the "steering gear" of society and the "bulwark of Democracy." To many, the transition and reorganization that was to follow merely represented the linear process of social change which stipulates that society is passing through a series of unfolding changes which mark the several stages in the history of mankind.

On the practical level, social conditions were calling for a reorganization of higher education which would recognize the importance of two-year colleges. There had been a growing awareness of dislocation, especially during the time covered by the last two years of high school and the first two years of college. According to Chase (1938-1939), "The work of senior high school and the junior college years forms the quadrennium during which it is generally felt our educational efforts are least satisfactory." This led Dean Alexis F. Lange of the University of California to declare that a university should begin "in the middle of the inherited four-year scheme" (Rislov, 1957). Already the junior college resembled the European experience in education: the gymnasium in Germany, the lyceum in France, the "public school" in England, and other similar arrangements in Italy, Holland, and Scandanavia; all were carrying their students into the domain of the sophomore year.

The junior college had encouraged various forms of institutional reorganization. A number of the older four-year colleges had already reorganized into junior colleges (Kemp, 1930), and many of the two-year normal schools became four-year colleges, often with junior college departments. By the 1930's, it was noticed that enrollment in home state universities and colleges was lower due to the attendance of many students at their local junior colleges (Walters, 1931). The call for even stricter reorganization was made by Coffman (1921):

> There is another practical suggestion that I should
> like to make, and that is the freshman and sopho-
> more years disappear from the university, as I
> feel certain they will in the next twenty-five years,
> exactly as the academies did during the last twenty-
> five, there must follow a complete and genuine re-
> organization of the whole public school program
> below the university. Instead of the public schools
> adding the freshman and sophomore years, adding
> them as thirteenth and fourteenth years, they can,
> through an effective reorganization ... of instruc-
> tion ... and administration, accomplish for the
> bright student in twelve years what he is now
> spending fourteen years upon, and do it better ...
> (p. 3).

And finally, the first major hint of what reorganization would actually bring was issued by President Truman's Commission on Higher Education in 1947. The report, <u>Higher Education for American Democracy</u> (1947), says in part:

> The ends of democratic education in the United
> States will not be adequately served until we
> achieve a unification of our educational objectives
> and processes. American education must be so
> organized and conducted that it will provide, at
> appropriate levels, proper combinations of general
> and special education for students of varying abil-
> ities and occupational objectives (Vol. I, p. 62).

It remained for the community college to accept this challenge in a meaningful way while providing the necessary resources to guarantee relative degrees of success. The challenge, however, may yet prove to be too much for any singular institutional form.

An Upward Extension: Secondary Status

While some aspects of early reorganization in higher education left the junior college as an institution of higher education, others clearly identified it as an <u>upward extension of the secondary school</u>. Both situations are correct if viewed in context. In the early 1900's, McLane (1913), Harper (1903), Gray (1915), Angell (1915), Koos (1927), and others wrote about the junior college movement in the high schools. McLane described it as an "upward extension,"

Historical Perspective

while The Educational Review (February, 1915) reported that the "so-called junior college" was popularly being built upon the high school. Koos (1927) argued that a two-year period was insufficient for a separate educational unit, and reported several considerations that favored a firm integration of the junior college with the high school. These included increased efficiency in instruction, economy of time, closely knitted curricula, and less overlapping and duplication of services and efforts.

College work first appeared in some high schools in Michigan and Minnesota well before 1915. And under the leadership of Dean Lange at the University of California, "the extension of high school" had its greatest impact in California, mainly because of the large size and shape of the state, which made it quite difficult for many to attend the universities located at Berkeley and at Palo Alto. Dean Lange favored operating the junior college as a part of secondary education (Krug, 1964), partially because of his conviction that secondary education began too late and ended too soon (Toews, 1964c).

As Koos (1924) ably demonstrated, the conception of the two-year college as the culmination of the American secondary school is not of recent origin. In its first stages it seems to have enjoyed the upward extension both from and within the high school, but without any line of demarcation between the two levels of training. Actually, lines of demarcation were only superficially imposed upon the various levels within the institutional hierarchy to maintain a sense of order and student self-interest. Koos, however, was among the first educators who tried to define reasonable lines of demarcation among the general aims of the secondary school, college, and university. Table 1 presents his study of aims and functions which call for specific values in the secondary school, college, and university.

An analysis of Koos' study reveals that secondary school and college aims have much more in common than do college and university aims. Consequently, a general line of demarcation may be said to exist separating the collective functions of high school and college from those of the university. While there is some degree of overlapping, a line of demarcation falls more naturally at the end of the college period than at its beginning. The relative position of the junior college would necessarily be somewhere within the collective functions of high school and college. Thus, the

TABLE I

COMPARISON OF SECONDARY SCHOOL, COLLEGE, AND UNIVERSITY AIMS, 1924

Aims and Functions Calling For Values In:	Secondary School %	College %	University %
General or Liberal Training	61-80	61-80	21-40
Training for Life's Needs	21-40	21-40	0
Civic-Social Responsibility	81-100	61-80	1-20
Morality and Character	61-80	61-80	0
Religious Training	41-60	21-40	0
Domestic Responsibility	21-40	1-20	0
Training and Leadership	1-20	21-40	21-40
Recreational and Aesthetic Aspects of Life	81-100	1-20	0
Occupational Efficiency	81-100	21-40	61-80
Physical Efficiency	61-80	1-20	0
Intellectual Efficiency	21-40	1-20	1-20
Mental Discipline	1-20	21-40	1-20
Democratic School System	61-80	1-20	0
Recognizing Individual Differences	81-100	1-20	0
Exploration and Guidance	41-60	1-20	1-20
Selection for Higher Education	1-20	1-20	1-20
Preliminary Training	61-80	21-40	0
Recognizing Adolescence	41-60	0	0
Training in Fundamental Processes	21-40	1-20	0
Community or Public Service	1-20	1-20	1-20
Coordinating the Student's Knowledge	1-20	1-20	1-20
Knowledge for Its Own Sake	0	1-20	1-20
Developing Scholarly Interest and Ambition	0	21-40	1-20
Research	0	0	81-100
Instruction	0	0	41-60
Extension	0	0	21-40
Publication	0	0	21-40

(In Koos, 1924, p. 371).

Historical Perspective

functions of the high school, college, and, presumably, the junior college, fall into a category distinguished from the more notable functions of the university.

The German Influence

One of the first notable proponents of the junior college idea was Henry Phillips Tappan. Earlier, he had experienced a lower division schooling at Greenville Academy which allowed him to gain advanced standing while a student at Union College. A staunch supporter of the German-style university, Tappan called for a reorganization of higher education along the European plan. As President of the University of Michigan, he managed to advocate the State's educational system by openly declaring that it was copied from the Prussian, "which was acknowledged to be the most perfect in the world." He saw the American college as little more than the gymnasium, a place for immature students (Tappan, 1851). As a result, he proposed dropping the first two years of university and giving this responsibility to the secondary school, preferably in the form of junior college work. Tappan had little faith in private or collegiate education and indirectly continued to enhance the status of the public junior college.

Another influential leader of this formative period was William Watts Folwell, former President of the University of Minnesota, who, in his 1869 inaugural address, suggested:

> [Relegate to the secondary schools] those studies which now form the body of work for the first two years in our ordinary American colleges. It is clear that such a transposition must by and by be made. How immense the gain ... if a youth could remain at home at the high school or academy, residing in his home, until he had reached a point, say, somewhere near the end of the sophomore year ... then ... emigrate to the university, there to enter upon the work of a man ... (Folwell, 1909, p. 37).

A proponent of the German system of education, Folwell worked out a plan in harmony with his conception of the secondary schools taking a greater burden of the workload from the universities; an idea which gave further support to the junior college concept. Secondary school aspects of the junior college are embraced in the following statement:

> While American experience formed the guide and principle of the arrangement under discussion, that of foreign countries, in which education has been authoritatively organized could not be left out of account. The new secondary department will be found to correspond in location, in object, and in scope, with the gymnasia and real schools of Germany and the lyceums of France and Switzerland. Upon this point I am happy in having the conclusive testimony of President McCosh [of Princeton] who says, 'The course of instruction in the gymnasia and real schools ... embraces not only the branches taught in our high schools, but those taught in the freshman and sophomore classes of our university courses.' My own observation not long before, brought me to the same conclusion ... (Folwell, 1909, p. 103).

Folwell goes on to ask for high schools more generous in scope than ever before and affirms that the "work of the first two years of college is the work of the secondary school, and there it can be done most efficiently and economically." Having experienced such a preparation himself at Ovid Academy, Folwell was enthused to set his ideas into practice at the University of Minnesota, but they proved to be too advanced for that period and subsequently received a "decent burial" from later administrations. Looking back on the "Minnesota Plan," Folwell (1930) later wrote:

> It is now easy to see that the project was a premature romance. It was one to be agitated in reviews, magazines, and newspapers, to be dallied with in educational conventions, timidly proposed to college faculties, referred to committees, reported on and recommitted, and, after some decades, adopted, with misgivings, 'in principle' (p. 119).

Reorganization of school systems was a notable topic for William Rainey Harper, first President of the University of Chicago. In speaking about the "high school of the future" he always supported

> ...the principle that the line of separation at the close of the second college year is much more closely marked, pedagogically, than the line at the close of the present high school period (Harper, 1903, p. 1).

Historical Perspective

Harper estimated that one-fourth of America's colleges were doing academy and high school work around 1900. He was quite familiar with "the practice, [then] in common vogue, of making the first two years of college work only an extension of the work in the secondary school." With some hesitation, he cited a "fear that the college idea would be injured by the rivalry of the new high school college." But, like Folwell, he ultimately saw the junior college freeing the four-year college to regain its collegiate status.

Different Organizational Formats

The early forms of the junior college were many and varied, as were their organizational and curricular patterns. Angell (1915) described the "junior-college movement in high schools" as "junior college high schools" and "junior college schools" in an attempt to differentiate their organizational status. Public schools took on new and different forms in an attempt to fit the junior college idea into their system. Proctor (1923) described the junior college pattern which made use of four grades reorganized on the 6-4-4 plan. This plan was to aid the adolescent and allow the university to return to its rightful domain which included advanced liberal and professional training. The 6-4-4 plan was also designed to bring more students to the junior colleges and, at the same time, reduce their numbers in the lower divisions of universities. Koos (1924) favored six elementary and eight secondary grades arranged in the 6-4-4 pattern, as did others during this period. He suggested that the middle four-year period be referred to as "junior high school" and the latter four-year period be identified as "senior high school" or "junior college."

As an aid in determining the relative status of the two-year college, Bolton (1944) proposed that the 6-4-4 plan be utilized to assist the junior college in making its organizational scheme more apparent, and to effect an earlier and "closer integration of the elementary, secondary, and higher grades." A suggested redistribution of institutional jurisdiction was called for by Angell (1917) who suggested the 6-4-4-2+ organizational plan. The first six years were to include the elementary grades; the next four-year period was to be the "junior high school," followed by a four-year continuation called "college"; the last two years were to be in preparation for professional schools or the doctorates. A line of demarcation was then suggested to associate the junior college more closely with the high school:

The period at which junior-college training is completed under ordinary conditions represents a more strategic line of division than either that at the end of the present high school or that at the end of the present four-year college (Angell, 1917, p. 395).

Even now, a strong argument is made by Gillie (1970) who feels that the 6-4-4 plan currently reflects the trend whereby associate degrees are replacing the high school diploma as the minimum educational certificate. The following points were summarized by Cubberly and Koos (In Kemp, 1930) as favoring the 6-4-4 plan:

1. It eliminates the duplication of one extra unit of grounds, buildings, and equipment required for the operation of the 6-3-3-2 plan.

2. It eliminates one group of administrators and the requisite office force, forming a less expensive situation.

3. It offers one group of secondary courses, and makes it administratively possible to avoid much of the overlapping of high school and college courses.

4. It adds one more year to the exploratory period of the junior high school and thus offers a better selection of courses. It allows an organization of programs leading to specific objectives, thus aiding in the better organization of vocational education.

5. It provides opportunities for orientation and terminal courses in the last four years of the 6-4-4 program.

6. The educational progress of the pupil through the adolescent period is less strenuous. It also eliminates one break in his college course.

7. It gives the administration an opportunity to offer cooperative training and terminal courses to a larger number of students.

8. It allows a student to graduate from junior high school at the age of sixteen years, at

Historical Perspective

> which age full time compulsory
>
> 9. The administration can bring c
>   tional, and pre-professional tr
>   the people and thus encourage
>
> 10. This plan is nearer to progressive educational
>   thoughts and ideals of the day than is the
>   6-3-3-2 plan or any of the other plans thus
>   far tried.

There was some concern that a junior college in the high school would not be worthy of collegiate status. Nevertheless, for more than four decades, about 85 per cent of all public junior colleges were located in high schools (Hutchins, 1936a). At Joliet, William Rainey Harper used his influence to extend the high school courses to include basic college courses. Principal J. Stanley Brown of Joliet Township High School and Junior College reported in 1906 that the first of the graduates from the six-year high school had received his baccalaureate degree on the completion of only two years of additional work. However, he did caution that this two-year addition to secondary schools was not desirable as a general modification for all schools ("Editorial Notes," 1906).

By 1930, the faculty at Joliet High School-Junior College offered a curriculum in junior electrical engineering because of prospective employers located in the area and the availability of necessary equipment and facilities for training (Castle, 1930). Other six-year high school plans had already developed such as the one at Elgin, Illinois, where the principal wrote:

> We must extend the courses of study, not downwards, but upwards to five and six years, while at the same time it should be maintained that the college course should begin where the present course of the strong high school now closes; this would be an extension of the free school two years beyond its present limit (Pierce, 1897, p. 120).

Another variation of extended secondary education is described by the high school principal of Saginaw (Michigan) East Side, who said:

> For the past three years we have offered courses

The Community College

> corresponding to freshman work at the University of Michigan in Latin ... trigonometry and algebra ... paragraph writing, and in English history. We have sent to Ann Arbor eight or ten students who have received sufficient credit for work done in our high school to enable them to complete their college courses in three years.... The work done in our graduate courses has been satisfactory to the University authorities (Warriner, 1897, p. 127).

At Goshen, the well-known "six-year high school" was established with the cooperation of the University of Chicago and Goshen High School (Hedgepeth, 1905). An agreement was established whereby advanced standing was given to successful high school graduates. Here the junior college was completely <u>within</u> the high school. However, teachers, courses, examinations, and visitations were to be under university control, while paid for by the high school.

The six-year high school junior college plan was popular for a while because its six-year period corresponded closely to the period of adolescence, but the dominant motive was economy in education (Zook, 1922). Many of the universities in the Midwest and West gave serious consideration to dropping their lower divisions altogether since junior college departments were performing the same function in high schools. In 1935, the College of the Pacific virtually eliminated its lower division, although others, such as Stanford, retained their lower divisions because of significant financial benefits.

The National Conference Committee on Standards of Colleges and Secondary Schools tried to reconcile the differences between the high school and junior college by adopting the following report on March 10, 1921:

> The junior college is an institution covering the first two years of a standard college course, based upon the completion of four years of high school work. It may be a division of a large university ... it may be a separate institution ... it may be a graduate annex to a local high school organized primarily to gratify local pride or to aggrandize the local school system.... It must ordinarily be a separate institution, with its own building, its own president, and its own faculty.... The method of instruction should be collegiate rather than

secondary, and the atmosphere should be the same.

> The extension of a high school course by the addition of one or two years of more advanced work may meet a genuine local need, but such an annex to a high school is not necessarily worthy of collegiate standing. In general it may be said that such an institution with the high school principal becoming the president of the college, with certain of the high school teachers taking over the work of instruction, and carrying it on with the high school facilities, does not deserve to be called a college and should not be recognized as such (Committee on Standards, 1921).

Apparently, the two-year college concept, while gaining momentum as a desirable innovation, was not to be a general modification for all secondary schools. Nevertheless, the work of the university included secondary school subjects, and a move to do away with the freshman and sophomore classes continued to persist for many years.

In an effort to gain self-identity, the high schools continued to fight the colleges which looked down on them through the established order. By the 1920's, high schools were more than preparatory schools for college. The secondary schools waged and "won" a war for independence against the domination of their curricula by higher institutions (Zook, 1922). This situation was not unlike the struggle undertaken by junior colleges in later years when they too sought self-identity. But clear separations were simply not possible. President Nicholas Murray Butler of Columbia wrote:

> As the public high schools multiply and strengthen, they will tend more and more to give the instruction now offered in the first year or first two years of the college course ... they will become local colleges ... without student residences (In Bolton, 1944, p. 92).

In agreement, Bolton (1944) wrote:

> The first two years of college and university work are confessedly a part of secondary education. The boys and girls are of secondary school age and must be dealt with by secondary school

methods, no matter where they are.

Indeed, a symbiotic relationship was proposed for high schools and junior colleges by Zook (1930):

> Junior college education would be established in the closest possible correlation with the local high schools of every community--the administration, teaching personnel, and physical facilities of the two should be knit together in a close correlation which would do away with the duplication of subject matter and misgivings now existing between [them] ... (p. 560).

The organization of education again became one of the ten most "critical" issues in American education. John E. Corbally (1945) noted the dilemma when he asked, "Will we have a 6-3-3; a 6-6; a 6-4-4, or some other plan? The [Washington State] legislature [had already] legalized the upward extension of the high school to include the 13th and 14th years...." With students now being forced by parents and other home influences to seek education even beyond the junior college (Bush, 1929-30), terminal and vocational aspects of junior college education began to suffer.

By 1923, California had twenty-six junior colleges, but six were in teachers' colleges while twenty retained their connection with high schools (Proctor, 1923). Not until the 1930's did other organizational models appear. California was among the first states to organize junior colleges into district, union, joint union, county, and joint county arrangements. Other arrangements already included junior college courses in high schools; the junior college as part of the high school (the 6-4-4 plan at Pasadena); and the junior college in teachers' colleges at Fresno, San Diego, and San Jose. Despite the various organizational arrangements, the junior college was still clearly identified with secondary education. According to Professor Lange:

> The junior college is by descent and nature a secondary school. Its legal existence as far as California is concerned was ushered in by the Law of 1907 <u>as an extension of the high school.</u> Subsequent legislation ... has fixed its status as an institution devoted to secondary education.
>
> The junior high school, the high school, and the

junior college occupy the domain of secondary education. Their interrelations may well receive various forms of adjustment and their articulations with the elementary school and with the university will doubtless need time for adequate development, but even now a new order exists, that is, a secondary school system ministering over a rapidly extending area to the whole of adolescence. And so the junior college must never be thought of in terms of the adolescent order. In the new order its place is at the top. It is the culmination and fulfillment of the educational design incorporated in the intermediate (that is the junior high) and the high school (In Kemp, 1930, p. 192).

The need for the junior college was always open to question (Koos, 1921a). Nevertheless, some people projected that the states would come to foster this institution in the same manner that they supported universities. Certificates to teach began to be awarded in many southern states upon completion of a junior college program with additional education courses. And Koos (1921b) saw the junior college providing "service" to local communities in addition to encouraging universities to differentiate their activities from the lower schools. Furthermore, the junior college often assured small four-year colleges a definite function in the educational system, even though many of the latter were forced to become junior college finishing schools to survive economically.

The high school influence or secondary nature of the junior college continued well into the 1940's. Koos (1944a) then reported that the junior college was housed in one of five patterns:

1. Entirely separate from high school on a separate site;

2. Entirely separate from high school but on the same or adjoining site;

3. Partly in separate buildings and partly in high school buildings;

4. In a separate wing or floor of high school buildings;

5. Combined and cooperative use with high school years in the same facilities.

About one-third (57) of all junior colleges were in the first category while the other two-thirds had varying degrees of association as noted in the other categories. And, in addition to the four-year junior college concept, Koos (1944b) reveals that others, such as the 7-3-4 and the 5-4-4 plan, were also being used. These and other patterns were indicative of the reorganization brought about by the junior college. As of this period, no singular pattern had proven popular enough to gain regional or national support.

General Education and Vocationalism

The confusion brought about by the reorganization of secondary and higher education caused many people to question the indeterminate purposes of secondary education. Even though the junior college had an extended high school curriculum, the high school itself was still unable to determine whether it was preparing students for college or life (Hutchins, 1936a). The high school took on terminal and vocational programs in addition to the college preparatory type. In self-defense, the junior college did likewise. The unresolved dilemma of offering general or specialized education had already begun. Many people viewed the junior college as the final stage of general education (Smith, 1930; Brubacher and Rudy, 1968) with guidance being the major single function.

General education was seen as serving a terminal function in the junior college and a liberating function in the four-year college. Hutchins suggested that general education start in the eleventh year and continue four years to the end of the sophomore year. Further, he contended that the university should not deal with such "philanthropy" as dispensing general education. The call for general education to be emphasized in the high school and junior college became greater, although there was little agreement on what general education meant or what it related to in terms of a liberal education. Writing in the Fifty-fifth National Yearbook of the National Society for the Study of Education (1956), James Reynolds gave the following popular description of general education for junior colleges:

> General education refers to programs of education specifically designed to afford young people more

effective preparation for the responsibilities which
they share in common as citizens in a free society
and for wholesome and creative participation in a
wide range of life activities (Henry, ed., 1956,
p. 118).

The diversified expansion of clientele for higher education required the junior college to become especially effective in designing college programs to provide a common, unifying, enriching education for all students. Reynolds saw this function to be even more demanding for the junior college than for the four-year college which had more homogeneous groups. But, after studying junior college programs in general education, it was concluded that they were already seriously inadequate in all areas (Reynolds, 1945a). In his dissertation at the University of Chicago, Reynolds (1945b) correctly concluded that the necessity to develop courses which parallel university offerings had discouraged junior colleges from experimenting with additional nonparallel courses. Of the four-year college, and presumably the two-year institution also, Dressel and Mayhew (1954) later concluded that general education classes were not well-planned to make the most economical use of time, of teaching aids, or of student motivation and interest.

Much earlier, the National Society for the Promotion of Industrial Education called for efficiency in learning by separating general education from vocational education (1912). It urged that vocational education be a separate and independent entity. Some felt that the trades should be learned only in the high school (Perry, 1908), others that such occupational programs should begin in high school and reach into the junior college (Kemp, 1930). A revised emphasis was suggested by Higgins (1908) who asked that a trade school be a shop with a school attached rather than a school with a shop attached. The mythical dichotomy between general and specialized learning caused many people to vacillate in their understanding of both secondary and higher education functions. For a long time, the junior college came to be viewed as the agency for meeting the needs of "the non-academically minded high-school graduate" (Snyder, 1930, p. 76).

Vocationalism has made substantial gains in the liberal arts curriculum, especially in the public junior and community college. Similarly, the secondary school has accepted broad responsibilities which are attributes of any comprehensive institution. These proper responsibilities include:

    1. Preparation for adult citizenship in the community, the state, the nation.
    2. Preparation for international understanding and world citizenship.
    3. Ability to think straight in social and economic problems in a democracy.
    4. Willingness and ability to adjust one's thinking to the demands of the day.
    5. Willingness to be subject to authority as well as to use one's own initiative and freedom.
    6. Preparation for home and family living ...
    7. Participation in studying community resources and in meeting community problems.
    8. Preparation for vocational work and occupational success.
    9. Preparation for further study in college for those who wish it.
    10. Provision of work experiences ... well-regulated school-work cooperative problems.
    11. Guidance ... emotional, social, moral, and other personal problems.
    12. Placement of graduates in suitable occupations ...
    13. Follow-up and supervision on the job until successful adjustment is achieved (<u>Our Schools</u>, 1944, p. 26).

An analysis of current reports and documents in the career education fields suggests that the junior college must aid the high school if occupational education is to be made available on a large scale. Skaggs (1966) predicts that most occupational education of the future will have to be taught on postsecondary levels. Apparently, the quantitative and qualitative efforts of the high school are insufficient for present and future needs in this area. Even now it is recognized that separate vocational high schools are more effective than their comprehensive high school counterparts (Kaufman, <u>et al.</u>, 1968).

The factors that distinguish between vocational curricula in secondary schools and junior colleges are basically unreliable. Many educators believe that the high school industrial arts curriculum can also prepare students for entry-level jobs as semiskilled workers since most high schools offer programs ranging from the beginning level to intermediate and advanced levels at grade twelve. Such vocational education is also offered as a postsecondary school program, "often cited as grades 13 and 14" in technical high schools, area vocational schools, technical institutes, junior and community colleges (Burt, 1967). Since other schools such as specialized and comprehensive high schools also provide comparable vocational or career education at both the high school and post-high school levels, areas of distinction are indeed vague.

Emerson (1965) predicted that occupational education would become an integral part of the entire educational picture rather than a separate branch. He saw it becoming fully accepted on a par with other college programs due to the involvement and influence of the emerging community college. Whether vocational, technical, occupational, and career programs should be offered at the secondary or postsecondary level is a question that deserves further study. For the present, however, occupational programs should be given preference at the postsecondary level under the following conditions:

1. If the occupational curriculum is generally classified as semiprofessional.
2. If the geographical area required to recruit sufficient qualified students for a program of optimum size is substantially greater than the area ordinarily encompassed by the high school district.
3. If the maturity demanded by employers for entrance into the occupation is beyond that of the average high school graduate.
4. If the prestige of a post-high school institution is needed to attract the type of student required for the program.
5. If on-the-job learning time required for development of full occupational competency is substantially less for a graduate of a post-high school program than for a high school graduate in the same field.
6. If the level and type of curriculum requires high school graduation, including the completion of specified courses, as a minimum foundation for undertaking the occupational study.
7. If the cost of initial installation of equipment, and its upkeep and maintenance, is beyond the fiscal ability of the high school district.

8. If the state proposes to meet the needs of students from widely scattered communities whose small high schools have little or no provision for occupational education.

9. If the state desires to meet the needs of people who want to work after high school graduation with no specific occupational training, and who later want to enter full-time training to prepare for better jobs.

10. If there is need for a wide range of evening courses in the community which require advanced technical equipment beyond that normally possible in high school occupational training programs.

11. If a suitable post-secondary educational institution is available--such as a junior college--to which may be added appropriate occupational education curriculums (Emerson, 1965, p. 5. Reprinted from the March 1965 issue of Technical Education News by permission of McGraw-Hill Book Company).

Such criteria reflect a popular view of "occupational education in the future community college" and suggest that certain degrees of overlap and duplication of instructional program may indeed be necessary. Similar programs have been placed at the secondary level in one instance and at the community junior college level in another. The integrity and success of each plan apparently rests on local and regional acceptance.

Vocational education has long been funded at the Federal level, although it has only been since 1917 that funds have been provided regularly for this type of learning at the secondary level. Indeed, the land-grant colleges were conceived to promote the liberal and practical education of the industrial classes, but their limited success has actually encouraged the growth of the junior college to meet unfulfilled promises. It took the Smith-Hughes Act of 1917 to provide funds for training "of less than college grade" which, according to Koos (1944d), fell within the province of terminal education at the junior college level. With only indirect aid and minimal coordination, the junior college was left to resolve issues relating to general and specialized education at its own level while at the same time articulating its programs with secondary and higher education. With little coordination these issues remain unresolved.

Historical Perspective

Universal Higher Education

The post-war period in the 1940's brought about new demands on all of our educational systems. A new spirit of democracy blended with a growing technological society to make education a public business. Schools had the potential to modify the social order. Under our political structure, it was the right of each individual to have a voice in the making of social policies, as well as in the determination of political affairs. Organized, established, and maintained to serve state purposes, public schools had local control that brought them closer to the home than any other institution. But could the high school handle the needs of all citizens in a democratic society? A government publication asked:

> Do you agree with this point of view--that every child, regardless of racial or social status, should have opportunity in the secondary school for education suited to his adolescent requirements? (Our Schools, 1944, p. 25).

An answer was suggested by President Truman's Commission on Higher Education (1947, p. 37) which arrived at the following conclusion: "The time has come to make education through the 14th grade available in the same way that high school is now available."

Universal education was to become a reality in the extended high school or junior college. Hardly anyone saw that this would extend beyond the high school and junior college and into higher education itself. Some expected a mere decline in high school enrollment to provide the stimulus for growth in the junior college ("Population Trends," 1940). Others saw equal opportunity for universal education as an "automatic upward extension of high school to the 13th and 14th grade" in a two-year college that was destined to remain such because its faculty, "without Ph.D.'s, fears for its status and security if their institution upgrades itself, and partly because of a genuine commitment to general education for the many" (Sanford, 1962, p. 86).

Social conditions combined with the democratic spirit to establish a real need for universal higher education. The institution most suited to this task proved to be the public junior college which was about to receive its greatest thrust for growth and development. The Educational Policies Commission (1964) prescribed the national goal of Universal

Opportunity for Education Beyond High School as follows: "The Nation's goal of universal opportunity must be expanded to include at least two further years of education, open to any high school graduate." To guarantee success in this endeavor, the Commission advocated that such universal education be tuition free. The spirit had caught on and, in the same year, the Democratic Party Platform stated, "Regardless of family financial status ... education should be open to every boy or girl in America up to the highest level which he or she is able to master" (Johnson, ed., 1967, p. 10).

The need to accept the challenge was met with mixed reaction. Historian Henry Steele Commager foresaw that much change would be needed if we were to meet the challenge:

> The extension of schooling to the age of twenty is consistent with the American tradition and with American faith in the sovereign effect of education in our kind of society.... If we are to expand universal education by two years, let us be sure that we make no little plans. Let us not permit the potentialities of this forward leap to go by default (In Johnson, ed., 1967, p. 16).

In a greater sense, former United Nations Ambassador Arthur N. Goldberg advocated "that public education ought to be expanded broadly at all levels," but, "in particular ... that fourteen years of compulsory education for all would be desirable" (In Johnson, ed., 1967, p. 9). Thus came the challenge which was to give rise to a broadening of the junior college function.

A Collegiate Status

Having reviewed the nature of those junior colleges that developed as institutions attached to the high schools, it is appropriate to take note of others which came into existence because of various movements within the structure of the university itself. It can be shown that the collegiate phase of development was independent and afforded an opportunity to gain status as an institution of "higher" education.

The first twenty years of junior college development gave rise to three basic institutional types:

Historical Perspective

1. <u>Private</u>: Church or religious groups; about one <u>hundred</u>, which represented 75 per cent of the total.

2. <u>Public</u>: A part of secondary school systems; often known as junior and senior years as opposed to the previous high school years in grades eleven and twelve known as the freshman and sophomore years. Most of these units were housed within high schools with varying degrees of separation of teacher-administration, student body, and social life. Exceptions were to be found in Kansas City, Missouri and Grand Rapids, Michigan where the junior college was some distance from the high schools.

3. <u>State institutions</u>: By 1924, there were at least six universities (University of California, Chicago, Washington, Minnesota, Leland Stanford Junior University, and the University of Nebraska) that reorganized by creating two-year colleges. Three called it a 'lower division,' two called it a 'junior college,' and one named it a 'junior division' (Koos, 1925, p. 8).

Accommodations were first made within institutions of higher education to include lower divisions concerned primarily with general education and the liberal arts. There was also a recognized cleavage within such universities to provide many three-year programs. This combined arts-professional curriculum included arts-engineering, arts-medicine, arts-law, and so forth. Various arrangements provided for a fourth year to be taken in a professional or technical school, either at the university or elsewhere in a transfer program. Such plans encouraged both two- and three-year pre-professional curricula in business, law, agriculture, medicine, nursing, dentistry, journalism, forestry, and theology. These curricula were general in nature and offered without announced affiliation to other programs. More than 190 departments existed bearing professional names and offering varied courses ranging from agriculture and commerce to secretarial training and law. Some departments offered only a few courses of an applied sort while others included more extensive offerings. Hence, the universities had made some accommodations to the desires and needs of those who wanted nonoccupational collegiate education less than four years in length (Koos, 1925).

Many students were able to complete a liberal training period in two or three years and then transfer to a professional school within the university. Professional studies were more and more becoming a part of the upper end of the four-year collegiate period. This liberalization movement and its shift to vocationally-oriented curricula were factors that stressed the necessity of organizing "lower" colleges. This, in turn, tended to intensify the already established line of cleavage which provided more substance to the collegiate status of junior colleges appended to universities.

In the 1880's, the University of Michigan undertook to establish, within its own confines, a distinction between university work and college work. In a similar move, President James of the University of Illinois suggested a reorganization of the university structure along the lines of junior colleges. These plans for restructuring the university came at a time when junior colleges already existed within high schools, normal schools, four-year colleges, and junior college departments within the universities themselves. But while universities were granting advanced credit for work done in the "fifth and sixth year" of high school, in no case was there any indication of support for "definite relations with junior colleges based on high school foundations" (Angell, 1915, p. 291). The junior college was about to experience a collegiate status as an unintended effect of university reorganization.

Bifurcation

The bisectionalization of the university structure became inevitable when the first American earned a German Ph.D. in 1817. The German influence was to be seen in all aspects of "American" education. Such influences included the kindergarten, normal school, engineering school, graduate and professional schools, lecture system, the blackboard, seminars, the elective system, the semester plan, and the Ph.D. degree. Men such as Ticknor, Tappan, Folwell, Harper, Eliot, White, and others "Prussianized" American education in its founding years. While two hundred scholars had returned from Germany by 1850, some ten thousand were to make the trip by 1914.

The bisection movement began to have its influence on American education in the middle of the nineteenth century. Many educators came to believe that there was a distinction in function and structure between the first two years

Historical Perspective

of college and the last two years, including graduate-professional schools. Operating in what educational scholars refer to as the Anti-Thesis or Revolution Period (1850-1900), the bisection movement developed the junior college into a truncated version of the four-year college. In an era of expansion, changing goals, and counterrevolution, the lower division junior college was seen as a practical means of freeing the university to develop along higher paths.

In planning for the University of Chicago, President William Rainey Harper clearly indicated his belief that most small four-year colleges should either "die" or become junior colleges offering freshman and sophomore work only. The growing state and land-grant universities encouraged the bisectionalism. According to one observer:

> The idea of a college offering only a two year course has been welcomed on these western prairies ... here a state university has effected an arrangement whereby nearly a score of colleges-- ill-equipped and ill-endowed--have been transformed into junior colleges, whose students attend the state university for their junior and senior year (McConaughy, 1919, p. 607).

The efforts of Michigan and Minnesota saw large state universities undertake to separate the university from lower division preparatory work. It is Harper, however, who is most often given credit for coining the expression "junior college" which, according to Krug (1964), effectively did away with the connotation that the two years beyond the twelfth grade were a part of the secondary school movement.

Angell (1917) explains that the junior college of the University of Chicago was instituted in the belief that a rather sharp break could be made between secondary and university studies; the former representing closely supervised routine forms of work, and the latter emphasizing "free, specialized, professional, and research work." However, the curricula of all junior colleges were reported to be comparable regardless of whether they were built upon high school foundations, independent foundations, or differentiated parts of the modern university.

For the most part, Harper's attempt to divide the upper and lower parts of the university into senior and junior divisions was unsuccessful. Chicago's <u>Official Bulletin No. 1</u>

(1891) called for

> ... two equal parts -- the first to be known as the junior college or academic college, where the spirit would be collegiate and preparatory, and the second to be known as the senior college or the university college, where the spirit would be advanced and scholarly; a university where a system of major and minor studies permitted a student to pursue one subject in depth while devoting less time to another (p. 7).

It remained for Robert Hutchins to bring a form of the 6-4-4 plan of organization to Chicago, with a break in upper and lower curricula as well as in faculty. Eleventh graders were admitted to Chicago as freshmen while Hutchins tried to organize a "new" four-year baccalaureate institution out of the last two years of high school and the first two years of college. The idea received little support from colleagues and other educators. Even junior colleges failed to support this idea which may have been much too daring for the time.

The bisection movement was strong in the midwestern states and relatively unknown in the elitist colleges of the eastern seaboard. The lower division of Louisiana State University offered a general education program which, in effect, provided a basis for selecting students who were interested and capable of proceeding to advanced education. Louisiana's lower division also offered supplementary help and guidance at the "junior college level" (McNutt, 1939). Unfortunately, tests in this lower division were issued by a testing bureau, with final grades being issued by departmental chairmen using statistical curves.

Early enrollment reports referred to Stanford University as Leland Stanford Junior University and not until 1925 was the institution referred to as Stanford University at its own request. In 1922, and for some years thereafter, reference was made to the Junior College Department, Southern Branch, at Los Angeles when enrollments were cited for the University of California. Established in 1919, it took until 1928 for the institution to call itself the University of California at Los Angeles (Parker, 1970). Even in 1941, it seemed that "madness" had accounted for the "projection of a community college at Rutherford, New Jersey" (Rudolph, 1962, p. 487); the college later being known as Fairleigh Dickinson University.

Historical Perspective

The University of California established University Junior Colleges to aid high school graduates who were unable to meet university entrance requirements ("Educational Events," 1935). Vice President Touton of the University of Southern California and Director of the University Junior College described the rationale as follows:

> ... The success of the first year's operation of the plan shows that many high school graduates previously denied admission to the college should be given an opportunity to study college subjects under controlled college conditions, in a campus environment characterized by encouragement, motivation, and use of effective study methods before final judgment can be reached as to promise of achievement on the college level ("Educational Events," 1935, p. 328).

To a great extent, the junior college function was developed by university influences to aid the preparatory or transfer curriculum. This phase of development saw the junior college become a feeder institution for advanced learning. It also became a filtering or "weeding-out" institution. Other variations of this theme developed, as in the case of Bucknell University, itself a college which had sponsored a remote junior division in Wilkes-Barre. Serving as a feeder type junior college since 1933, this latter institution became Wilkes College in 1947.

Institutional Characteristics

Understanding the idea of the junior college in transition has proven to be difficult because of the variety of institutional forms and patterns that have developed during the past century. Some of the characteristics that tend to give it a secondary status have been discussed, as have others which give it a collegiate status. However, no consistent set of characteristics apply to the junior college movement viewed in its entirety. Although the public community college is quickly becoming the largest and most important segment of higher education, educational research has generally failed to identify aspects that vary greatly between different kinds of colleges in different regional settings. Institutional studies that merely describe quantitative factors such as the number of books or Ph.D.'s in an institution are proving to be of little value in determining value characteristics. Researchers must consider comprehensive regional and institutional factors that characterize two-year colleges if a clearer understanding of these institutions is to come about.

Several methods of describing institutional characteristics have been tried with various success. Pace and Stern (1958) developed the College Characteristic Index (C.C.I.) which can be used in modified form to analyze the two-year college. A true-false inventory, the C.C.I. measures thirty features of the environmental "press" of the college. Astin and Holland (1961) developed the Environmental Assessment Technique (E.A.T.) which assesses eight characteristics of the student body in relation to the college environment. These characteristics include Size, Average Intelligence, and six personal orientations--Realistic, Intellectual, Social, Conventional, Enterprising, and Artistic. Still another way to assess the college environment is to study a set of potential stimuli or observable characteristics that are capable of producing sensory change in the students.

Among recent reports, the general work of the American College Testing Program (1969a) suggests some patterns which describe the junior college on a regional basis. Regions have been defined which are descriptive of certain patterns and tendencies and include Mideast, New England, Great Lakes, Plains, Southeast, Southwest and Rocky Mountains, and Far West states.

1. Age (Conventionalism): Describes colleges that vary in age, the number of full and part time faculty and students, few working students, many from out of state, and a sense of traditional exclusiveness;

2. Transfer Emphasis (Social Orientation): With heavy loadings on teacher training, and a high percentage of teachers with the master's degree, teacher education programs, liberal arts, and spending more money for each student's education;

3. Cultural Affluence (Private Control): Seen in library facilities, foreign and out-of-state students, usually private or well-financed colleges;

4. Technological Specialization: With many males, few secretarial-education programs, nonliberal arts, and public;

5. <u>Business Orientation</u>: With many Ph.D.'s, bright students, management-business oriented, also associated with high cost;

6. <u>Size</u>: Relatively heavy loadings on enrollment, library facilities, variety of curriculums, urban, open door, comprehensive, and impersonal.

The Cultural Affluence or Private Control factor tends to be lower for junior colleges in the Great Lakes states and in the Far West. In part, this is due to the strength of state universities and public education in general. Junior colleges in these regions have usually sought their own identity rather than imitate senior institutions. The major trend in the Technological Specialization category is for junior colleges in New England and the Southeast to be lower than others. The American College Testing Program sees this as partially due to an emphasis of agriculture over industry in the South, and to a de-emphasis of vocational training. Other reasons for a low rating in Technological Specialization in these regions derive from the social conditions that prevail and different conceptions of what the junior college is supposed to be.

As might be expected, junior colleges in the Southeast, Southwest and Rockies, and Plains states are high on the Age or Conventionalism factor while junior colleges in the Far West are low. New England's two-year colleges are only average in this factor due to the long tradition of four-year colleges in that region. The Southern Negro Colleges are quite old, but no longer within the junior college category. They are most unlikely to be innovative because of socio-political conditions (A.C.T., 1969a, p. 37).

On Transfer Emphasis, two-year colleges in New England and the Mideast are extremely low, with few significant differences among other regions. In part, this results from domination by a few private, prestigious four-year colleges and universities. And while most regions favor teacher education in junior colleges, New England generally restricts it to four-year colleges. (A.C.T., 1969a).

A major trend on the Business Orientation characteristic is for junior colleges in New England, the Mideast, and the Great Lakes to be much higher than other regions. This characteristic implies "high cost" as a more suitable term and is in keeping with the patterns already established in four-year colleges.

The factor of Size shows the Far West to be high because California has heavy enrollments in junior colleges, while the Mideast and New England regions score much lower. The Age factor shows the Far West to be low while the Southeast, Southwest and Rockies, and Plains states score high. The older Mideast section scores low, which fits the latent historical development of the junior college in that region. (A. C. T. , 1969a).

In comparing the junior college with the senior college, the A. C. T. Program (1969a) found that studied factors were not congruent except for the Size factor. Was the junior college unique then? Diplomatically, "yes," but that remains yet to be affirmed. It may be that all educational institutions are evolving toward a common median position. New trends may include accelerated faculty and administration migration, increased Federal spending for higher education, and the development of a more national, rather than regional, social environment. Regional differences may continue to converge and make institutional differentiation a thing of the past. (A. C. T. , 1969a).

As the A. C. T. profile points out, research on community and junior college institutional characteristics is useful on a regional basis. Investigations of this type will ultimately help to differentiate between public and private forms of community-junior colleges within the broader context of the generic two-year college.

The Degree Structure

A major factor that appeared to give the junior college a collegiate status was the granting of the associate's degree. Although typically a junior college degree, it is often awarded by other colleges and universities to represent two years of college-level work.

The history of the associate's degree can be traced to European origin. In England, the University of Durham granted the Associate in Physical Science to mark a two-year course of study in 1865. In 1873, the degree was granted in the form of Associate in Science, and in 1877 as Associate in Engineering and Associate in Coal Mining. By 1927, Eells (1963) reported that thirteen types of associate degrees, including the Associate in Theology and

Associate in Music, were in use in British universities.

Although the University of Chicago began to award the Associate in Arts degree to its junior college students in 1900, not all educators were in agreement as to what the degree meant. In the <u>President's Reports,</u> William Rainey Harper envisioned the following:

> Upon the recommendation of the Faculty of the Junior Colleges and of the Senate, and upon approval of the University Congregation, the Trustees have voted to confer the title or degree of Associate upon those students who finish the work of the Junior Colleges.... The proposed policy has already excited some interest. It is hoped that the new plan may receive the careful consideration of other institutions interested in the same problem (In Eells, 1963, p. 94).

A statement of standards was then issued in 1915 by the Association of Colleges and Secondary Schools of the Southern States prohibiting the granting of degrees by accredited junior colleges. Part of this dilemma came about because many junior college graduates in the South were still becoming teachers soon after graduation. Certificates and diplomas, like those issued in certain secondary and normal schools, were thought to be more appropriate rewards.

The practice of granting associate degrees caught on, however, as did the practice of granting hundreds of other degrees in the university. Nicholas Murray Butler of Columbia University supported Harper's move. He wrote, "By establishing an academic designation to be conferred at the close of a two-years' college course, the University of Chicago has taken a step of national importance" (Butler, 1900, p. 411). And in 1899, the U.S. Commissioner of Education reacted favorably and quoted Harper's statement of the benefits that he expected to follow from the use of the new degree:

> It is believed that the results will be five-fold: (1) Many students will find it convenient to give up college work at the end of the sophomore year; (2) Many students who would not otherwise do so well will undertake at least two years of college work; (3) The professional schools will be able to raise their standards for admission and in any

> case many who desire a professional education will take the first two years of college work; (4) Many academies and high schools will be encouraged to develop higher work; (5) Many colleges which have not the means to do the work of the junior and senior years will be satisfied under this arrangement to do the lower work (In Eells, 1963, p. 96).

Yet, the associate's degree did not gain immediate popularity. In 1956, it was reported that "recognition of the associate's degree has gained wide favor in educational circles. It is now authorized in all states ... with the exception of Virginia, and granted by junior colleges and many senior colleges.... The granting of the associate's degree places the official stamp of approval on junior college education as definite collegiate accomplishment" (Colvert, 1956, Chapter II).

While the University of Chicago discontinued the use of the associate's degree in 1918, it had already spread to other schools. It was re-established at the University of Chicago in 1931 and continued until 1942. Even high school graduates could qualify for it by successfully passing seven comprehensive examinations. Lewis Institute and other two-year institutions quickly offered such variations of the associate's degree as Associate in Arts, Associate in Domestic Economy, Associate in Letters, and Associate in Science. Eells (1963) reported the first associate's degree issued by a junior college still in existence to have been presented at Stephens College, Missouri. This particular institution became a junior college in 1911 and awarded the Associate in Arts to eight women in 1912. Meanwhile, the first public junior college to award the degree was the Junior College of Kansas City, Missouri, which conferred the Associate in Arts degree on one man and seven women in 1916. (Eells, 1963).

For almost twenty-five years, Harvard and a group of associated Massachusetts institutions awarded the Associate in Arts degree as the equivalent to a bachelor's degree upon completion of a four-year extension-study program. In 1910, the Overseers of Harvard University voted:

> To confer the degree Associate in Arts upon nonresident students who have attended the class exercises, completed the other work, and passed the examinations in the University Extension Courses (including summer courses) equal in number and

standard to the courses required of a resident for the degree of Bachelor of Arts (In Eells, 1963, p. 98).

In 1918, about seventeen junior colleges (23 per cent) reported the practice of awarding associate degrees. By 1942, 244 junior colleges (40 per cent) had joined this effort, and by 1960, 444 two-year institutions (75 per cent), including those not designated as junior colleges, reported use of the associate's degree. In 1960, 156 four-year institutions (including 27 universities, 82 liberal arts colleges, 20 teachers colleges, and 27 other institutions) were offering the associate's degree. More than 137 varieties of associate's degrees were being used, the most popular being Associate in Arts, followed by others which included Associate in Science, Associate in Applied Science, Associate in Business Administration, Associate in Education, Associate in Engineering, Associate in Secretarial Science, Associate in Commerce, Associate in Business, and Associate in General Studies. (Eells, 1963).

Business and industry have since come to recognize the associate's degree as the first collegiate degree of a series that identifies the holder as having completed the equivalent of two years of college. Additionally, this implies that the recipient has completed a general-liberal arts curriculum or a vocational-technical-occupational program, the latter type most likely of a semiprofessional or paraprofessional nature leading to a career opportunity. Even the Navy has set up an Associate Degree Completion Program as a career incentive to retain enlisted men in critical ratings whether ashore or at sea.

While the degree structure has enhanced the two-year college as a collegiate institution, it has also added another form of currency to the already crowded academic marketplace. While many of the new community colleges find multi-degrees to be a selling point, others have discontinued all but the Associate in Arts and Associate in Science.

With regard to degrees and how they are earned, William Birenbaum cautions the community college as follows:

> [It] must stop saying that its ultimate records--degrees--will be apportioned according to the system's rigid view of time by the credit hours.

> Instead, it must regard the infinite variety of human styles, commitments and talents, and deliver its rewards in terms of the humans it serves....
> The variable should be the person, not the scheme (In Doran, 1969, p. 9).

Having obtained the power to award the associate's degree, the junior and community college must now give it substance and meaning. Hopefully, it will be more than the high school diploma of the future.

The Conflict of Dual Status

The unresolved nature of the present two-year college is not apparent to most educators. Its relative status in secondary and higher education is merely viewed by some to be a futile exercise in logic. Others, however, see its dual status as a nebulous condition which has not been resolved satisfactorily. The United States Office of Education recognizes this problem by asking:

> <u>Are Public 2-Year Colleges Secondary or Higher Education?</u> This question is repeatedly asked, sometimes by people who enjoy academic exercises and sometimes by people who really believe the question is a fundamental one. If the question is reworded to say, 'Is a 2-year college a high school or a university?', the answer is simply, 'Neither.' ... [Some] 2-year colleges do include some work that is high school level in nature, as many universities did until recently and as a few still do ... much study is needed to present a clear[er] picture of the image or the several images of 2-year colleges (Morrison and Martorana, 1962, p. 33).

It is often safe, but confusing, to take a middle-of-the-road position. For example, Kelsey (1968) sees the junior college as being "higher" than high school but "lesser" than the four-year institution.

The dual status of community and junior college is noted by the Executive Director of the American Association of Junior Colleges who asks pointedly, 'Is the public junior college more a part of secondary education or higher education?" In speaking of this "new social invention," Gleazer goes on to say:

> The community college has its most productive development not when it is conceived of as the first two years of the baccalaureate degree program, nor when seen as grades thirteen and fourteen, but as an institution in its own right--a new kind of college--standing between the high school and university--offering broad programs of experiences of value in and of themselves, neither post-high school as such or pre-college as such (In Friedman, 1966, p. 417).

This position identifies the community college as an institution that serves both secondary and higher education while still retaining its own unique identity. There were several advantages to the junior college-high school idea that called for a close union. Angell (1917) cites the advantage of stimulation and outlook. However, he notes that a separation of identity has its advantages too. These include a greater *esprit de corps*, better instructors, and a more conducive "college tone."

Thus, the junior college was seen as an in-between institution that served as a "shock absorber" (Wilbur, 1926), offering "relief" to the universities (Magruder, 1921). It was more than "just advanced high school work" (Gray, 1915) that gave life to the "people's vocational college" (Okerlund, 1929). In the early period of indecision about identity, an astute observer warned, "Let us be on our guard against any suggested interpretation of the junior college as half secondary and half senior college or university" (Kemp, 1930, p. 193). It was the spirit of the institution that was to determine its identity, and the spirit of the schools was determined by the spirit of the nation. After all,

> Secondary education is secondary only in the sense that it comes after primary and before what is called higher education. This formula runs around in a circle and gets us nowhere. If there is to be continuity in the education of the American youth, each of the stages of schooling must be planned and executed in its vital relation to the whole (California High School Teachers' Association, 1924, p. 15).

There has always been a lack of agreement among scholars as to the nature and character of a social institution. Even today, the public is still confused about the relative status of the junior college. A noted sociologist studied such attitudes and concluded:

> The people will confuse junior college and junior high school. They hardly know what they are talking about sometimes. The newspaper consistently includes news of the junior college with the high school. I mean news from the junior college goes on a page with all the school news, from the grade schools up. Just a little paragraph about a rhythm band in one of the grade schools and a little paragraph next to it about the junior college (Friedman, 1966, p. 419).

For many, the junior college role seems to be a novelty. Referring to the American people, Gleazer correctly says:

> [They] have yet to figure out fully this junior college, which insists that it is not a high school (though it offers many programs similar to those in high schools), claims to be higher education (while teaching printing, welding, and data-processing), but is in many respects obviously unlike what the public have for many years conceived higher education to be (In Garrison, 1967b, p. 30).

Most junior colleges were ambivalent and had acquired a dual status which was most difficult to understand in conventional terms. The earlier efforts of Tappan, Harper, Folwell, and White to establish "intermediate colleges" had not been popular everywhere. In fact, the New York Regents found the idea "repugnant." In 1878 when the Regents academic examinations were initiated, they were specifically planned for the twelfth grade level and financial aid was refused for any subject offered beyond this level in academies, high schools, and, presumably, junior colleges. And when Harper introduced the term "junior college" in 1896, "the State Board of Regents again reacted sharply and decisively the same year by issuing a definition of the single type of organization which could legally advertise itself as a 'college' in New York State." A "college" was to have "a course of four full years of college grade in liberal arts and sciences, and must require for admission four years of academic or high school preparation ..." (Doran, 1969, p. 4). Thus, the

Historical Perspective

junior college was not to achieve any relative significance within the jurisdictional boundaries of the Regents for many years.

It is sad that such a shortsighted view caused the then largest state to be among the more cautious and wary advocates of two-year colleges. Of course, part of this dilemma is due to the overlap of secondary and collegiate functions. Even the overlap between the various efforts and projects initiated by junior colleges is considerable (Popham, 1970). To some extent, the dual function of the junior college is seen diluting post-high school education in an effort to please everybody. Devall (1968, p. 168) sarcastically concludes that most educational problems could be better handled by other organizations than "this bugaboo in American education." He labels the two-year college an "organization of the past" and suggests the following alternatives to replace it:

> Proprietary schools--To offer specific vocational education; this is just as good, more efficient, flexible, and reduces the tax burden because they are not publicly supported.
>
> Training on the job--The most efficient and quickest training method; corporations fill their own needs, taxpayers are relieved.
>
> Universal National Service--Between the ages of eighteen and twenty-four, men and women would spend two years in the service of their country. The armed forces already have the most extensive educational facilities in this society.
>
> A nation-campus--Take education to the people by expanding the continuing education function of the universities; this does not have to be on a 'campus' per se.
>
> Extension programs--Extend the facilities of state universities; offer better liberal arts programs and provide easier transfer procedures (p. 172).

This proposal was not popular for many reasons, chiefly because these current options are not new nor as simplistically effective as one might expect.

In rebuttal to Devall's dissenting view of the two-year college, a spokesman for a community college with more than 25,000 students said that such comments reflect a startling lack of knowledge (Masiko, 1968). It is easy to be misinformed about the function and purpose of the two-year college, even unknowingly. Blocker and others (1965) note that much of the current confusion concerning the dual status of the two-year college is due to a lack of knowledge on the part of college professors. As an illustration, they cite a statement by a former university professor which reads in part:

> By way of summary, to establish an inferior institution whose faculty will be composed of high school teachers, because no first-class scholar will teach in a junior college when he can secure employment in a first class college or university, and whose courses of study will not prepare anyone to enter the University or fit him for life ...
>
> Businessmen will not employ incompetent people. What is needed is for parents to send their boys and girls who have failed in high schools back to school to make up their deficiencies (In Blocker and Campbell, 1963, p. 11).

Thus, the junior colleges were often seen as "institutions of inferior instruction" (Anderson, 1964) that provide a "natural and dignified stopping place for those who here reach their natural limits" (Doran, 1969, p. 4). But the problem of dual status relates to much broader issues. Dean W. Blair Stewart (1959) of Oberlin College justly directs his criticism to the entire educational hierarchy, including the liberal arts college:

> Most of the four-year liberal arts colleges in this United States are merely glorified secondary schools. Attitudes and procedures that are appropriate to the secondary school pervade the entire educational process (p. 325).

Criticisms of this type have always been aimed at the overlapping functions in secondary and higher education. Much of what is taught in the high school is indeed repeated in the liberal arts colleges as well as the junior colleges. B. E. Blanchard, Coordinator of the Graduate Programs at DePaul University's School of Education, conducted a study

Historical Perspective

which reveals that courses were being duplicated considerably in high schools and colleges of liberal arts. With more than 400 faculty members from 269 colleges and 665 teachers from 520 high schools participating, it was felt by the high school teachers that 30 per cent of all subjects taught in the first two years of college repeat what is taught in the last two years of high school. High school and college teachers generally agreed on the amount of repetition in English and the social sciences. High school teachers said that 35 per cent of high school English is repeated in college, while the college teachers put the total overlap at 24 per cent. For the social sciences, a 29 per cent overlap was seen by high school faculty and 24 per cent by college faculty. It was felt that the overlap was due to the fact that colleges had not kept up with changes and improvements in secondary education. This "tends to suggest poor coordination and articulation between colleges of liberal arts and secondary schools," said Blanchard (In The Chronicle, May 3, 1971, p. 5). While the overlap for all subjects as seen by the high school teachers was 30 per cent, the college teachers saw a total overlap of 23 per cent.

Part of the problem is due to the common or traditional type of curriculum that is more concerned with the organization of knowledge on paper than with a concern for how students learn (Sanford, 1962). Knowledge tends to be departmentalized and packaged into artifical layers. In turn, this supports existing institutional arrangements which continue to weed out certain kinds of students. There always were too many institutions attempting higher types of professional training and nowhere enough giving attention to the intermediate needs between high school and college. According to Castle (1930, p. 78), "The most fertile field in the entire range of education in the public schools apparently has been overlooked."

The dual status of the community and junior college has not been resolved for numerous and complex reasons. Many of the original ties still remain for those institutions that "evolved as upward extensions of high schools" (Cohen, 1966). These roots are still evidenced in jurisdiction by local boards, legislated tax-supported bases, and coordination efforts by state Departments of Education, credential-granting agencies and regional accreditation associations. It is the carry-over from secondary influences that has caused many observers to refuse to accept the two-year college as a part of higher education (Morrisett, 1967). Others, however, regularly call for the junior college to be free and separate from the control and supervision of higher education (Price, 1959).

Dotson (1963) correctly charges that gains made by the two-year college are often without regard for and at the expense of teachers and students in the elementary and secondary grades. Some educators even see the two-year college in competition with the high school for state and local revenue. But Medsker (1958) views the overall high school-college interrelationship as a subbaccalaureate function of the two-year college and suggests that it supplements the secondary school while offering little competition.

While the junior college is a good place to make up school deficiencies (Medsker, 1958), it is also viewed as an institution that fulfills certain aspects of adult education that were formerly a secondary education function. Vail (1945, p. 50) aptly describes this characteristic as "a downward extension of various aspects within elementary and secondary schools accompanying an upward extension or post-school for adults." Whether this function is exercised within a junior college or high school with grades thirteen and fourteen is still seen to be of little consequence. However, by 1967, Harper's Magazine (February, 1967), among others, was concerned with the "Junior College Dilemma" which had persisted because the adult and continuing education function had been tossed about indiscriminately. Senior colleges and high schools were seen as being aloof and unprepared to face the problem while junior colleges vacillated with their ambivalent positions. The university was cautioned against overemphasizing its service function lest it become a conglomerate of trivialities (Brubacher, 1970). As a result, adult and continuing education continued to suffer.

By 1944, the junior college increasingly reflected the fact that it was primarily a "terminal" unit. While 80 per cent of the students entered transfer programs, less than 25 per cent needed them (Johnson, 1944). Support for additional four-year junior colleges was growing at the time that President Franklin Roosevelt addressed the A.A.J.C. Convention in Cincinnati. In support of the two-year college and its broadening function, he said:

> The junior college has now become a robust youngster in the family of American educational institutions. My particular interest at present centers in

> the part that the junior college may play in providing suitable education for many of the returning soldiers and sailors.
>
> These men and women will wish, in many cases, terminal courses which combine technical or other vocational preparation with courses which assure a basic understanding of the issues confronted by them as American and world citizens. It seems possible, therefore, that the junior college may furnish the answer to a good many of these needs (In "Events," 1944, p. 150).

James Conant's challenge to the American high school also applied to the expanding role of the junior college. In <u>The American High School Today</u> (1959), he pointedly asked:

> Can a school at one and the same time provide a good education for <u>all</u> the people as future citizens of a democracy, provide elective programs for the majority to develop useful skills, and educate adequately those with a talent for handling advanced academic subjects...? The answer to this question would seem to be of considerable importance for the future of American education. If the answer were clearly in the negative, then a radical change in the structure of American public secondary education would be in order.... On the other hand, if the answer is in the affirmative, then no radical change in the basic pattern [is] required (p. 15).

Clearly, the task was too majestic for the provincial high school and junior college. Attempts to meet the challenge would bring about the comprehensive high school and comprehensive community college.

The fact that many students were unfairly denied admission to higher education provided stimulus to the junior college movement. An early study made in Pennsylvania by the Carnegie Foundation revealed that as many promising high school graduates stay out of colleges as unworthy ones get in (Chase, 1938-1939). For many principals and deans, the junior college offered only a partial remedy. Its early advantages included economy, small classes, personal attention, extended home influence, adaptation of teaching methods to adolescents, extension of educational opportunity, and the

ability to develop qualities of leadership (Proctor, 1923).
By 1960, the President's Commission on National Goals was to recommend that two-year colleges be placed within commuting distance of all high school graduates, except those in sparsely settled regions.

Even though some educators saw the junior college as a high school extension, the growth and development of the institution took on the force of a movement (Clark, 1960b; Medsker, 1960). The diversity among institutional forms did little to stop its physical or dual status growth. In addition to the academic transfer programs, the expanded role of junior colleges enhanced a renewed career education function which is described by James E. Allen, U.S. Commissioner of Education:

> Federal funding will improve in the area of career education. By career education, the Administration means post-secondary education that gives students opportunities to advance in their careers rather than training that would lock them into particular jobs for the rest of their lives. Career education would include both academic courses that would prepare students for further education and vocational training that would qualify them for specific jobs (In The Chronicle, November 24, 1969, p. 2).

The public junior college had bridged the gap between high school and college and was about to try to bring respectability to career and occupational programs within the rigid context of higher education. Something had to change.

After serving a "parallel function" since its inception (Young, 1962), the junior college, like any "new" educational idea, seemed to need the traditional fifty-year lag to be incorporated into our education system (Deyo, 1963). Defensive attitudes slowly began to wane. It was declared by junior college proponents that the junior college is not "junior" to any other institution and, therefore, it should be accepted as an institution in its own right, with independent roles and functions based on a structural, philosophical concept which, while making it a part of higher education, also distinguishes it from all other institutions.

Provisions established for administration, support, and legal control were often seen as being detrimental to the junior college and raising confusion because of its dual

Historical Perspective

status. Consequently, efforts were made to break all ties with secondary education in order to affirm a stronger, more prestigious position within higher education.

By seeking a firmer identity, the junior college seriously tried to remove itself from "local" control as vested in local public school systems. The dual functioning board of education-board of trustees is rapidly becoming an outmoded form of control and the public junior college is making strides to sever this tie, thus enhancing its higher education status. The Maryland Association of Junior Colleges suggests the following:

> To function effectively in the academic community, the community colleges must be more closely allied with higher education than with elementary-secondary education (In P. Johnson, 1968, p. 3).

To effect this position, the Maryland Conference of the American Association of University Professors added:

> The consensus ... that the present practice of having one county board responsible for all public schools and all public junior and community colleges was now, or would eventually prove, not in the best interest of higher education ("Conference Activities," 1968).

According to Fretwell (1968), community colleges are closely related to comprehensive high schools in terms of their desire to serve a broad spectrum of educational needs and interests; nevertheless, "they are full-fledged members of higher education." With such being the case, it is ironic that the great majority of writers and researchers in higher education have continued to neglect the community and junior college as a serious force in American higher education. Even Sanford's book on The American College (1962), a psychological and social interpretation of higher learning, fails to give the junior college as much coverage as it does to house masters at Harvard. The majority of references in works of this type generally "patronize and dismiss the junior college" as another two years of high school (A.C.T., 1969a, p. 9). Indeed, one has to search hard to find references to the community college among the generic clutter of junior, commuter, and two-year college references throughout the current literature. The dual status of this institution has not been adequately resolved. Rather, the community and junior college have been left with the unearned stigma of being an educational paradox.

Legislative, Legal, and Judicial Influences

The dual status of the junior college was, in part, nurtured by a lack of insight and comprehensiveness in the enabling legislation that brought the institution into being. Some legislative actions made the junior college a legal extension of the high school while others made it a legal part of higher education. States formulated a variety of sketchy plans that often provided for junior, community, or extension-type colleges without much regard to their interrelation with other existing institutions. Most current legislation will have to be modified and clarified if these institutions are to have a positive impact on postsecondary education.

Typical of the point being made here is the following astute observation:

> One of the great difficulties in the establishment and support of junior colleges has been the question of whether they are a part of the public school system or a part of higher education institutions. Each state should settle that decisively and either classify them as public schools or as higher educational institutions. If they are public schools [then] they should be financed ... in precisely the same way as elementary and secondary schools. If they belong with the higher educational institutions, their maintenance [should be comparable to state universities] (Bolton, 1944, p. 91).

Lack of identity became a fundamental issue for the public junior college. To a great extent, the recurring issues of identity and status were exacerbated by the enabling legislation that created the two-year college. Each state handled the matter in its own time and manner, which brought further frustration to those who thought they saw the diversified activity as a "movement."

California and Other States.
The social, political, and economic conditions varied greatly among the states and it is enlightening to trace the diversity in the manner in which junior colleges were established. The lack of consensus on status, purpose, funding, and educational philosophy left the two-year college as a problematic institution

for many years. Still, some common qualities begin to surface. Such states as California, Florida, New York, Pennsylvania, Ohio, New Jersey, Illinois, and others are selected to be broadly representative of geographic as well as statutory and philosophical differences that exist among two-year junior colleges.

California was among the pacesetters when, in 1907, the Legislature authorized the addition of two years of postgraduate education to the existing secondary high schools. This set the pattern for high schools to offer freshman and sophomore courses comparable to those in the four-year institutions. Under this authorization, Fresno High School offered postgraduate classes in 1910, thus becoming California's first and the nation's second oldest public junior college in continuous operation. By 1917, statutes authorized the establishment of "junior college" departments within the high schools with the obligation to offer postgraduate classes. At that time there were eighteen high schools involved with such programs (Toews, 1964a). In 1915, the Attorney General of California had ruled that school districts were ineligible to receive State aid for "post-high school" courses. This caused the Commissioner of Secondary Schools, Will C. Wood, to suggest in 1916 that junior colleges receive financial support based upon average daily attendance as in the high schools, thus opening the way for State aid.

A special committee appointed by the 1919 Legislature recommended a reorganization of the entire educational system in the State in an effort to better coordinate the various factions. It proposed that university education should begin at the junior year within a group of professional schools of which the university was composed; all the normal schools (which were two-year colleges) were to be converted into senior colleges with junior college departments. Additionally, it proposed a 6-3-3-2 organizational pattern in which the junior college would be organized and maintained by independent junior college districts.

The 1921 Legislature quickly authorized independent junior college districts. And by 1926, there were thirty-one junior colleges: sixteen were departments in high schools, six were attached to State colleges, and the remaining nine were in independent junior college districts (Toews, 1964c).

By 1935, the junior college in California had expanded

its role to include programs for transfer, vocational-technical, and general education needs in local communities. And in 1940, the junior college was still a legal but integral part of the public school system in which youth were entitled to "be educated at public expense." In "Fees, Charges, and Deposits in California Public Schools" (California Schools, May 1940), it is noted that even laboratory fees and school supplies were to be furnished free to all students from the kindergarten through the junior college. But not until 1963 was financial assistance allocated for construction and capital expenses from State funds.

Early legislation and school codes defined the mission and status of the junior college in a manner that was to carry over to the present. According to the California School Code,

> ... each junior college shall provide for the education of pupils in the thirteenth and fourteenth grades and for the education of such adults and minors as may properly be admitted but who are not classifiable by grade ... the courses of study for two-year junior colleges shall be designed to fit the needs of pupils in the thirteenth and fourteenth grade ... (Bolton, 1944, p. 92).

Originally, the California School Code established the junior college as an integral part of the high school system and admitted graduates of any high school and "such other candidates over eighteen years of age as may be recommended for admission by the principal of the junior college" (Harbeson, 1932, p. 3). It was not until after 1948 that the California junior college was identified as an institution of higher education; in that year the Strayer Study recommended that the junior college be defined as a unique institution in higher education. A Bureau of Junior College Education was established, first as a part of the Division of Instruction, but later as a part of the Division of Higher Education. While the former association reflected a concern with secondary education, the latter was clearly with higher education.

Not until twelve years later did California publish a Master Plan for Higher Education (1960) in which the junior college was clearly designated as a segment of higher education. The Master Plan also cited the exclusive function of the junior college to be that of providing vocational-technical

Historical Perspective

programs in higher education. Still, a dual characteristic remained. It is best described by Toews (1964c):

> The past is characterized by a legal and functional association with secondary education; the future indicates a legal and functional association with higher education ...
>
> The identification of junior colleges legally as well as functionally with higher education is a trend of concern ... the community college [should] serve the educational needs of the majority of students who will not, cannot, or should not undertake a post-high school program of four or more years (p. 8).

Many requests from junior college educators to the Superintendent of Public Instruction, asking for a junior college division within the Department of Education, went unheeded. As a result, the Legislature recently created the Board of Governors of the California Community Colleges. This Board has since relieved the State Board of Education with respect to financing and controlling junior colleges. In effect, this legislation represented a desire on the part of legislators and educators alike for a break from secondary status.

The need for a chief spokesman caused the California Junior College Association to plead for a "higher" status. The Association's position stated that:

> Since the chief executive officer will serve as a state spokesman for the junior colleges in their relationships with other state agencies, his position should be comparable to the chancellorship of the state colleges, the presidency of the university, and the directorship of the Coordinating Council for Higher Education (In Lombardi, 1968, p. 28).

Legal tactics definitely proved to be important in the struggle to shed the dual status of junior colleges in California. For example, "community" was used in the title of the Board of Governors of the California Community Colleges because "junior" clearly implied unequal status connotations. The term "board of governors" was clearly differentiated from the "board of trustees" and "board of regents" to prevent further confusion of identity. Nevertheless, some junior colleges wished to remain directly under the State Board of Education because it was so involved with the problems of elementary and secondary education that little time was left to interfere with matters related to junior colleges. This minimum control by the State was seen as desirable since it would inevitably lead to a separate board for junior colleges anyway.

By 1968, there was still much concern about the "issue of secondary versus higher education status for the junior colleges" in California. With eighty-two junior colleges in the State, eight called "city college" and sixty-three simply called "college," not one made use of the term "community" in its name. At this same time, the California Junior College Association offered a legal opinion which stated that "the junior colleges are included with high schools in the classification of secondary schools under the governing provisions of the constitution and statutory law" (Lombardi, 1968, p. 29). The junior colleges thus enjoy the best of two worlds. They are allowed to be collegiate institutions while maintaining eligibility for an equitable share of Federal funds allotted to the secondary schools, particularly in the area of vocational-technical training. The Board of Education is still the responsible State agency in such matters, acting upon the advice and recommendations of the community college board.

Legislation was enacted to prohibit the State and high schools from establishing new junior colleges. Furthermore, it permits new junior colleges to be governed by boards independent of high school or unified districts. This was a necessary step in developing a higher education status for the junior college. The State's position on higher education is clearly embodied in the Donahue Higher Education Act. In part, it reads:

> Public higher education consists of (1) all public junior colleges heretofore and hereafter established pursuant to law; (2) all state colleges ... and (3) each campus, branch, and function of the University of California ... (Education Code, Section 22500).

But another section makes it quite clear that:

> The public junior colleges are secondary schools

and shall continue to be a part of the public school system of this State (Section 22650).

The Education Code in California then standardizes the functions of the junior colleges as follows:

> Public junior colleges shall offer instruction through but not beyond the 14th grade level, which instruction may include, but shall not be limited to, programs in one or more of the following categories: (1) standard collegiate courses for transfer to higher institutions; (2) vocational and technical fields leading to employment; and (3) general or liberal arts courses. Studies in these fields may lead to the associate in arts or associate in science degree (Section 22651).

Legally, all offerings of the public junior colleges in California are to be considered higher education and therefore "collegiate." This now leaves several myths to be dispelled:

> Myth 1--Only those courses which are recognized by universities for transfer purposes are college-level.
>
> Myth 2--There is some sort of absolute standard for college courses which is determined by the nature of subject taught, and which can be readily determined and applied regardless of the students being taught.
>
> Myth 3--Education for immediate employment is somehow less collegiate than education for work which requires transfer to another institution (In Tyler, 1965, p. 7).

A broadened concept of "standards" and "college-level" has emerged as a result of the growing number of junior colleges. In a seminar paper, Tillery expresses his interpretation of these concepts as follows:

> "Standards": The only meaningful definition of "standards" in education is determined by the quality of teaching and the resources for learning. Badly taught courses have low standards whether they are at the freshman or graduate levels.

> Excellently taught courses have high standards whether they are concerned with remedial English or quantum physics ...
>
> "College-level": Those courses which concern themselves with the educational needs of young and mature adults as they prepare for advanced study, skilled work, or as they seek greater freedom and refinement of mind, are of college-level. In California such courses are to be determined by the characteristics of students who are to be educated in the various segments of a differentiated system of higher education (In Tyler, 1965, p. 7).

Thus, the California system of higher education places its public two-year colleges in a flexible but dual status as public schools of higher education. Only traditional thinking compels us to seek an "either-or" situation when, in fact, it is "both-and." Legislative influences have strongly supported both secondary and higher education qualities of public junior colleges. The secondary nature will probably remain in such areas as budgets, teacher credentials, multi-financing units, apportionment, attendance reports, equalization aid, articulation procedures and unionization.

Florida has experienced three phases of development since 1927 when its first junior college was established at St. Petersburg. Originally private, St. Petersburg Junior College became public in 1947, while the first public junior college in Florida was opened at Palm Beach in 1933. The Omnibus School Bill in 1947 permitted State and local funds to be used for the support of community-junior colleges as well as grades one through twelve (Christian and Wattenbarger, 1967). Establishing and maintaining junior colleges was kept as a local responsibility primarily vested in boards of education. Two additional junior colleges were established between 1947 and 1957, and the Council for the Study of Higher Education recommended the establishment of a Community College Council to develop long-range plans.

The Florida State Legislature created a Junior College Board in 1961 to coordinate statewide growth of these institutions with the help of the Division of Community Junior Colleges in the State Department of Education. Recognizing the value of the comprehensive community college concept, Florida is continually increasing its operating funds for vocational and technical courses in occupational programs. By

Historical Perspective

1968, the junior colleges were operated by local districts with each having a board independent of the high school board. Also, upper division or senior colleges are now being established to offer junior-senior and graduate level opportunities as a complement to the junior colleges. This type of legislative influence has furthered the separation from secondary school affiliations while providing a more distinct identity to the junior college movement.

New York cautiously entered the junior college movement in 1948, although it had earlier sponsored two-year technical colleges. Legislation now requires a "comprehensive community college" that asserts itself with functions that are different from both the high school and senior college. Legislation makes provisions for "community and junior" college students and, in 1964, a statewide plan recommended the abolition of legal provisions authorizing establishment of "four-year community" colleges. Like Pennsylvania, New York relied heavily on its private colleges for many years before a pressing social need brought about the necessity for community colleges.

Pennsylvania traditionally faces opposition in its attempt to establish public junior colleges. As one citizen concluded:

> Pennsylvania, like many Eastern states, has traditionally held that only the economically and academically able are entitled to higher education. In such belief it continues to live in the past, refuses to recognize its obligations in this modern society to educate all of its people, and continues to experience a tragic loss of human resources (In Yarrington, ed., 1969, p. 150).

Not unlike New York's predicament between upstate and downstate, Pennsylvania has long had its east-west counterpart between Philadelphia and Pittsburgh. The political scene has always used education as a selling point when, in fact, it was a political football. Operating in a deficit condition for many years, Pennsylvania has caused its State-supported educational institutions to rely on privately borrowed operating funds. Organizational and funding procedures have allowed single school districts to bring community college programs to a halt. Because of vested interests in the quasipublic State university and its system of eighteen campus centers, the community college has had to fight for its very existence. Only local need and persistence have permitted some thirteen community colleges to get past the planning stage.

Ohio's first attempt to provide for community colleges in 1959 was vetoed by the governor because of "inadequate provisions" for their financial support. A similar bill was introduced to the Legislature in 1961 but was also defeated. A companion bill calling for the establishment of technical institutes fared better. As the bill was presented, a strategic motion to amend was made which would change the words "technical institute" to "community college." Within one hour, the community college law had been enacted over the violent protests of those who opposed it. In 1963, a rewritten bill was passed with clarification of financial support and authorization to offer technical-occupational subjects. The law recognizes the community college in Ohio as a part of higher education. (Yarrington, 1969).

By 1970, Ohio had four community colleges among its ten technical institutes, twenty university centers, and four two-year centers associated with urban universities. Enthusiasts of the community college movement have constantly urged that a State system of community colleges be created. They have also included proposals which would abandon all State university branches, or at least convert them into community colleges. The unresolved question is whether a community college is preferable as an educational agency to a university branch (Ohio Board of Regents, 1966). As in Pennsylvania, both types can coexist, but it remains for their similarities and differences to be articulated in order to develop a semblance of harmony, coordination, and efficiency.

New Jersey sponsored the County College Act of 1963 to establish its community colleges. It did so despite the opposing efforts of eastern seaboard tradition to maintain the status quo. Venerable institutions of higher learning had firmly molded the public image of what constitutes higher education. Nevertheless, the Legislature planned for county colleges that would provide transfer and "technical institute type programs" upon local initiative. The fact that New Jersey led the nation in the proportion of its high school graduates "exported" to out-of-state colleges helped to establish a real need for community colleges. (Yarrington, 1969).

The Higher Education Act of 1966 created the

Historical Perspective

Department of Higher Education in New Jersey. This was an attempt to upgrade the image of all postsecondary education. Among the dual status problems that remained for the community college to resolve was the fact that occupational education is regulated and funded by the Division of Vocational Education within the State Department of Education. It might be beneficial if the State would rewrite the plan to allow these colleges to receive their share of vocational funds without being subjected to the controls of the Division of Vocational Education in the same manner that high schools are. In addition, technical institutes and other post-secondary occupational programs in the State should come under the control of the Department of Higher Education rather than the State Department of Education.

Junior colleges in the state of Washington have passed through nearly every phase of development that characterizes the evolution of the national movement. First conceived as extended secondary education, the junior college was usually attached to a high school. Later it was started as an independent two-year college without tax support. Not until 1961 was this institution finally designated as a "community college." In effect, this reflected growth and transition in programs, comprehensiveness, and purpose. The Legislature controls the growth of the college with its fiscal authority while still promoting local operation by school districts. The controlling influence is clearly stated in the Legislative Act of 1961:

> A community college shall be an institution established with the approval of the State Board of Education and maintained and operated by a school district, offering two years post-high school curricula of general education or vocational education, or both (In Yarrington, ed., 1969, p. 97).

A later stage of evolution declared that the community college was to provide educational opportunities for all citizens of the State. To this end, coordination and planning of vocational-technical education proved to be most difficult. A Coordinating Council was implemented to express the feelings of the State Board of Education, the State Board for Community Colleges, and representatives from labor, industry, and business. As in other regions, the two-year college in Washington passed through various stages of development which culminated with the comprehensive community college being the characteristic educational institution.

Illinois presents a case study of the junior college in transition. Having had the prototype at Joliet in 1902, it took sixty-three years of rambling efforts before the junior college really caught on. Until 1931, the junior college grew despite a lack of specific legal sanction. Legislation was then enacted to allow Chicago to "manage and provide for the maintenance of not more than one junior college, consisting of or offering not more than two years of college work ... as a part of the public school system of the city." By 1937, legislation permitted the establishment of additional junior colleges throughout Illinois. In order to achieve financial support from the State, the 1951 Legislature sanctioned the junior college as a part of the public school system. Junior college districts with separate boards of control were permitted in 1959. (Yarrington, 1969).

In 1963, the Board of Higher Education was developed to coordinate what had already "happened." Shortly thereafter, the 1965 Junior College Bill authorized a new Junior College Board to act on behalf of all two-year colleges. Immediately, the junior college was designated as a part of higher education in contrast to its former secondary status. The law permitted those junior colleges operated by high schools to continue, but with State aid for operation costs only. Clearly, a differentiated status was recommended for the independent and "comprehensive junior colleges" as they were legally defined. (Yarrington, 1969).

After World War II, the community college concept began to develop in Illinois as elsewhere. Expanded curricula, public service, evening classes, guidance, adult and continuing education services slowly began to enlarge the nature of the junior college. Recognizing the "comprehensive junior college" as a formidable educational institution, the Illinois Association of Community and Junior Colleges emerged as a strong voice in State affairs. The transition will undoubtedly continue as high school districts slowly divest themselves of junior colleges and the State recognizes the community college as their successor. (Yarrington, 1969).

Until 1965, Texas allowed its junior colleges to grow without plan or pattern. Then the Legislature approved a master plan which placed these colleges under the same control as four-year colleges. Subsequent legislation proposed a Community Junior College Division which recognized the junior college as one of three component groups in higher education; each with specific roles, specialized governance,

Historical Perspective

and interlocking coordination. The public junior college has gone through a typical pattern of transition: from obscure beginnings to fill a higher education need with no State aid, through recognition without aid, then to State aid through public schools, and finally to inclusion in a master plan for a State system of coordination in higher education.

Michigan was among the early advocates of the junior college concept with Grand Rapids Junior College dating back to 1914. However, only in the last decade did the idea of the junior college receive adequate statewide attention. A series of studies, commissions, and reports were then employed to inform the public about the community college. In a concerted effort, community college administrators grouped together to aid in this task. Their purposes were as follows:

> 1. To recommend to the state legislature the amounts needed for operation and capital outlay after reviewing on a statewide basis the financial requirements of all public community colleges.
> 2. To improve the administration of community colleges by exchange of information.
> 3. To inform the public about the purposes and functions of community colleges by distribution of brochures and special reports (In Yarrington, 1969, p. 107).

The Michigan Legislature provides for the establishment of "public community and junior colleges" as a response to growing local needs. The impact of legislation significantly redefines the nature of the two-year college in the broader context of the comprehensive community college. Act 237 of the Public Acts of 1964 gives the community college permission to offer both collegiate and noncollegiate programs, while at the same time removing the previous two-year limitations on the length of courses offered. These and other provisions extend the role of the community college both upward and downward into the domains of other institutions on the educational continuum. The breadth and depth of programs are to be comprehensive, limited only by the needs of individuals and the society of which they are a part. (Yarrington, 1969).

Oklahoma presents an unusual case study because only two new public junior colleges have been established since 1919. Higher education institutions are plentiful and include five municipal-type community junior colleges, eighteen State-supported institutions with five junior colleges, and twelve private-church colleges and universities. Most of the present State junior colleges were initially established as preparatory schools for the university. When the need for preparatory institutions subsided, the system of existing secondary schools became State junior colleges and four-year colleges. With broad intentions to coordinate all of higher education, Oklahoma has both State and local versions of junior colleges, with emphasis on the collegiate functions of general and preprofessional education. (Yarrington, 1969).

The need for postsecondary educational opportunity is generally recognized by most states. However, the historical development of the junior college reveals an evolution with certain characteristics that have either prevented, curtailed, or stifled the establishment of the comprehensive community college. According to a spokesman for the Pennsylvania Department of Education, "Nobody scorns the community college more than snob educators at big universities" (Denton, 1970, p. 22). Wattenbarger cites similar conflicts with four-year colleges and their presidents, institutional jealousy, empire building, poor or, in a number of instances, no leadership at state levels (In Yarrington, ed., 1969). Other problems include power politics, a false dichotomy between academic and vocational education, and archaic patterns of state funding and educational organization. The greatest problem that has contributed to the irregular development of the community college is a lack of correct information on the idea or essence of this institution. Misinformation is evident at all levels, including top government, throughout education, and even among the people for whom the institution holds greatest potential--the taxpayer-citizens.

Legislative intent is best reconciled in comprehensive master plans which are recent phenomena in most states. The emergence of the community college forces many states to re-examine their "systems" of education with the idea of bringing some coordination and articulation to the various stratified levels. The status quo of false institutional hierarchy is now being challenged, as is the whole idea of "higher" and "lower" education. Continued pressures inevitably bring about state provisions for community colleges, even if ex post facto. We are in need of legislative revision that specifies, rather than implies, the various forms of two-year colleges. It is time to recognize and provide for

Historical Perspective

the support and maintenance of specific functions in higher education. Referring to the Vocational Education Act and Nurse Training Act, Mallan (1966) wrote:

> ... [the two-year college movement is] trying to insert its interests and concerns into legislation which is already proposed to support other branches of the field of higher education (p. 52).

While the Federal influence is best seen in the Higher Education and Vocational Education Acts, inevitability of a national Community College Act will surely come to focus attention on the community college as a distinct response to current educational problems.

The number of states with no laws providing for community or junior colleges is decreasing. While all fifty states have some form of public two-year college, the states of California, Florida, Illinois, Michigan, New York, Texas, and Washington account for over one-third of all such institutions. Various stages of development exist in other states with no pattern of legislative intent yet being clearly identified. It must be concluded that state legislation and master planning are potentially among the strongest, but least productive forces in all but a few notable cases. While several states have junior colleges that evolved over the past seven or eight decades, most states have only recently taken an active part in community college development. Even when several historical stages are by-passed in the newer institutions, the same degree of caution and phlegmatic development prevails in their philosophical growth. Once created, legislative shortcomings remain difficult to correct.

Judicial involvement constitutes a more recent phenomenon than legislative action in junior college development. One of the earliest cases that permitted the use of public funds for the junior college was reported by The School Review in 1930 in the case of Zimmerman v. Board of Education of Buncombe County (154 S. E. 397). The Supreme Court of North Carolina reversed the decision of a lower court which had adjudged the defendant perpetually enjoined from maintaining and operating a junior college. Furthermore, the decision upheld the use of public school funds from a city school district to pay for junior college expenses.

In a Kalamazoo-type junior college case, a plaintiff contended that the Chicago Board of Education had exceeded its authority by maintaining three junior colleges when the law had permitted "not more than one." The right of the public to establish and maintain public junior colleges was affirmed by Cook County Court when it ruled in favor of the defense. The head of the junior colleges was the City Superintendent of Schools and the college deans were directly responsible to him. A single curriculum and a unified examination service for all three colleges was used. Significantly, the Court decided the case on the point that a junior college program of this nature was part of a complete program of secondary education.

The dual status of the junior college is clearly visible in other legal-judicial incidents. Kentucky, for example, is typical of several states in which the court held that the junior college was not part of the "common school" system and that taxes were not to be levied for its support. Louisiana, on the other hand, is representative of those states in which the court emphatically concluded that the junior college was merely a "superior high school" and, consequently, public taxes could be used for its support. In some cases, the matter has swung both ways. For example, a lower court in North Carolina held that a junior college was not part of the public school system, but this decision was later reversed by the State Supreme Court. And in a legal precedent, Illinois was among the first states to permit community college districts to be organized with taxing power. Although often inequitable, this may be considered the primary means of keeping these institutions under local control and responsive to local needs.

It becomes apparent that judicial and legislative influences have often encouraged a dual status for the junior college because of the uncertainty associated with institutional purposes. While Kansas and California legally defined the junior college as an extension of the high school, Utah and Georgia defined it as an integral part of higher education. California is the only state to mention junior college education specifically in its Constitution (Article IX, Section 14); recognition in other states varies from vaguely implied inferences to highly structured school codes and public laws. Many two-year colleges retain their dual status while being identified as a part of the tripartite structure of higher education along with state colleges and universities.

The whole area of judicial-legislative involvement is just beginning to make an impact on junior college education

Historical Perspective

in both public and private sectors. A recent example of major importance is the Supreme Court ruling in the Marjorie Webster case, in which a private junior college contended that it had the right to be examined for regional accreditation. To deny this right was asserted to be a violation of Federal antitrust laws by "unreasonably" restraining the private college's trade. The Supreme Court, however, refused to review an Appeals Court decision that denied Marjorie Webster Junior College's contention. In effect, this strengthened the position of the public junior college which has always enjoyed the right to be examined for accreditation.

Court involvement in junior college matters and increased legislative activity under state and Federal sponsorship are areas that deserve further analysis and study because of their decisive influence on the future of community college development.

On Becoming A Four-Year Institution

As might be anticipated, the junior college often finds safety and convenience in closely following the established patterns set by four-year colleges. The attitude that brought about public acceptance of the role of the junior college as an adolescent or incomplete college has also caused many two-year institutions to seek four-year status. It is not unusual for junior college faculty and administrators to express a desire for four-year status at their institution. Thus, Detroit Junior College eventually became Wayne State University. And when Nassau Community College opened in New York, the local press immediately expressed concern for it to grow up and become a "real" four-year college. In Texas, Hardin Junior College grew from high school to junior college status, then continued on to become Midwestern University in 1961. Earlier, South Park Junior College (Texas) became Lamar College of Technology in 1951. Hardly a junior or community college exists for which someone has not seriously contemplated a change to four-year status. This possibility will always remain as an alternative growth pattern for the two-year college.

Maintaining too close a relationship with other institutions is a danger cited by Jacobsen (1968) for the two-year college. It is easy to forget that the junior college has unique objectives that cannot be realized if it is treated as a stepchild of the secondary school or an affixed appendage of the four-year college. Due to uncertain goals and provisions established for its administration, funding, and control, the junior college is viewed as an institution that is forced to prove itself to its senior partners without duplicating or becoming a four-year institution. James Harlow, Dean of the College of Education at the University of Oklahoma, has suggested that the junior college stop trying to pattern itself after senior colleges because it would quickly lose its distinctiveness among higher education institutions ("News Backgrounds," 1966).

Some state-operated two-year colleges become four-year colleges merely to accommodate inadequacies within the state educational structure. For example, Governor James A. Rhodes has recently proposed that seven two-year colleges in Ohio be expanded into four-year degree-granting institutions by 1973 to relieve pressure on the State university system. This proposal is being fought by supporters of the university system who fear that funds would be diverted from their appropriations.

Many junior colleges are pressured into becoming four-year colleges because of unforeseen forces (Burns, 1962). Others, such as private and religious junior colleges, do so as an alternative to closing their doors for good. Very few public two-year colleges actually make the transformation into four-year colleges by design. One incomplete study from 1940 to 1960 revealed that only eight per cent of all junior colleges had become senior institutions, and most of these were private (Morrison, 1966). Similar studies have shown that when junior colleges do change into senior institutions, they lose their comprehensiveness. Brumbaugh (1966) revealed that seventy-two junior colleges had become senior colleges between 1953 and 1964; only eleven were public, while twenty-three were independent, and thirty-eight were church related. He cites the following to explain why junior colleges change into four-year institutions:

> 1. The junior college is in a period of transition from identification with the public school system to an independent status. Complete identification with higher education is thought to be accomplished by becoming a senior college.
>
> 2. Increasing numbers of faculty members in junior colleges are being recruited from senior colleges and graduate schools. They are less oriented and committed to the distinctive role of the junior

college than those who have been identified with the public schools. Consequently, they tend to support and sometimes promote change to four-year institutions.

3. Private junior colleges are forced to become four-year institutions in self-defense, especially when in the geographic vicinity of public two-year colleges.

4. Political influences within legislative circles sometimes promote the upward extension of junior colleges for the purpose of transferring major sources of support from the local community to the state, thereby increasing public benefit to their constituents.

5. Legislators see more prestige in four-year colleges.

As reported in one publication, "Some community colleges may offer four full years of college work, but most ... will probably stop [in] the fourteenth grade ... " ("Education Adjusted to Needs," 1947, p. 67). When a junior college acquires senior college status, its perspective becomes narrower and emphasis shifts to the academic program as being of primary importance. There is also a neglect of broader types of educational services which are incompatible with the traditional purposes of a senior college.

Changing a two-year college into a four-year institution is not necessarily progress and, indeed, may constitute a disservice. The American Association of Junior Colleges suggests that neither public nor private junior colleges should become four-year colleges unless there are cogent reasons. Gleazer (1968b) even praises some junior colleges for not modeling themselves after other higher education institutions. In Illinois, the State university supports the creation of a system of public junior colleges as long as they "adhere to the general policy of vocational and subprofessional courses, and not attempt to become liberal arts colleges offering a four-year course of studies ... " ("Events," School and Society, 1945, p. 117).

The Strayer Study (1948) assured the unique status of public junior colleges in California by legislating that they do not become four-year institutions. Most states include similar restrictions in their enabling legislation, but do so more for the protection of liberal arts colleges and universities than of junior colleges. The demand for the transition of some junior colleges into colleges with four-year courses was always a vigorous issue with the public and legislature alike (Ferrier, 1937). Not educating the public is still seen as a detrimental factor in establishing a clearer purpose for two-year colleges to remain as such (Jacobsen, 1968).

The proposal to transform two-year colleges into four-year colleges has been around as long as junior colleges themselves. So too have been counterproposals to retain the two-year stature of these institutions. But seldom are such proposals argued in terms of purpose, function, or institutional relevance. Rather, the issue usually relates to vested rights, artificial separation of learning at institutional levels, the pre-eminence of the university, or political expediency. It remains for a clear statement to acknowledge that the goals of junior colleges are real and distinct; that they cannot be achieved by emulating four-year institutions. As a consequence, there are those who would have junior colleges "become evolutionary and revolutionary" institutions and break free from under the shadow of four-year colleges (Sorrells, 1968).

Recommendations to prevent two-year colleges from becoming four-year institutions are becoming more emphatic. From earlier reports conducted by the Commission of Seven for the Study of Higher Education in California (under the Carnegie Foundation) to the recent higher education series sponsored by the Carnegie Commission, a clear trend calls for junior colleges to express their uniqueness within the current organizational structure. The 1957 Report of the President's Committee on Education Beyond the High School reads, in part: "Community colleges are not designed ... to relieve enrollment pressure on senior institutions. They have a role and integrity of their own" (In Morrison, 1966, p. 443). The New York Regents clearly asserted that:

> Two-year and four-year colleges in a planned, coordinated, and complete system of public higher education provide essential and complementary but distinctive services in post-high school education. Therefore, existing two-year colleges should not be converted to four-year baccalaureate college status as an approach to the expansion of college programs

Historical Perspective

in any region of the state (In Brumbaugh, 1966).

But the University Commission on Admissions of the City University of New York (1969) concluded that the most flexible and hopeful way to change some of the current two-year colleges to four-year institutions was to maintain the flexibility and comprehensiveness of the community college. Thus, the rationale that pervades arguments to change junior colleges to senior colleges continues to indicate a misunderstanding of the two-year college concept.

Even though junior colleges are in transition, most are not evolving into four-year colleges. But unless the professional and layman acquire a better understanding of the distinct roles that two-year colleges play, the future direction that the community college takes will remain conjectural and speculative.

An Evolving Institutional Form

The junior college has changed in a drastic, but often imperceptible manner which cannot be summarized in any singular fashion. Moreover, the community college has emerged as the popular form of public junior college and has absorbed tasks and functions that go far beyond those commonly accepted by traditional junior and senior colleges. Doyle identifies this expanded junior college form as that segment of higher education best equipped to cope with "the highest education revolution and the exploding demands of the next decade" (In Newsletter, 1968).

The potentiality of open admissions and equal access has challenged the ideology of the two-year college. Instructional accountability, funding, local control, and public service also tend to make the new form of junior college much different from its predecessor.

Most community colleges are less than ten years old. Some states and the years in which they sponsored community colleges are: Missouri (1961), Maryland (1961), Oregon (1961), Washington (1961), New Jersey (1962), Hawaii (1963), Pennsylvania (1963), Illinois (1965), Montana (1965), Iowa (1965), Connecticut (1965), Virginia (1966), and Colorado (1967). Attempts to develop early two-year colleges at the state level received little support and Koos' feasibility studies for junior colleges generally went unheeded in Illinois (1944),

Maryland (1947), Pennsylvania (1948), and Oregon (1950).

Educators continue to resist change due to what Eurich (1970b) interprets as comfort, laziness, motivation, and tradition. Comfort allows educators to follow the same procedures year after year, while laziness allows them to follow the methods of their predecessors. There is also an inevitable lag between need and sensitivity while traditional images prevail. But it is a startling lack of motivation that lessens our interest in educational efficiency and a blind faith in tradition that makes the customs of academe notoriously conservative. Nevertheless, the sources of differentiation in American life are changing and legacies of a vanishing past are slowly disappearing (Jencks and Riesman, 1968b).

The new institutional form is not without its good and bad consequences. The emerging community college poses a serious threat to the status quo. Jacques Barzun once hinted that the liberal arts college could go out of existence if secondary schools and graduate-professional schools divided this responsibility between them. In a similar fashion, some people feel that the community college is reaching too far into other domains. But higher education and the university in particular have long been oversold for undergraduate education. The university image is quite marketable among the general public. According to Ross (1970), "The public has bought the university, lock, stock, and barrel, but all too generally for confused or simply wrong reasons." Similarly, Wireman (1970) concludes that colleges have promised too much and delivered too little in higher education. It was highly uneventful then, when President Nixon (1970) proclaimed to Congress, "A traditional four-year college program is not suited to everyone."

Education in the United States has generally accepted social promotion from kindergarten through the twelfth grade. Remedial programs have proven to be incongruous to university faculties who generally support the principle of compensatory admission without programs designed to avoid compensatory graduation (Hodgkinson, 1970a). Any open door college necessarily becomes revolutionary in this kind of academic environment. The success of a free form community college leaves many implications for senior institutions. For example, Parker (1970) suggests that more students will soon appear at the upper levels and even more problems will be encountered with curricular correlation, advanced standing, admissions, and general articulation.

A vital system of education is like a social agent with a dual function which enables the individual to approach self-realization while enabling society to identify those who are qualified for each of its significant services. (Comm., 1952). The community college is given a goal which challenges it to be many things to many people. The nation is searching for a new kind of education not unlike that which is contemplated by the comprehensive community college.

New York's 1964 Master Plan formally recognizes the complex tasks that the new college must accept:

> The two-year colleges are the very foundation of the University. More and more, it is they who are opening the door to higher education, revealing to the youth of the State the scope of the total University and the educational opportunities it offers them.... In many respects the demands upon the two-year colleges are far more complex than those faced by other units. These colleges must respond to the widest range of talent and offer a broad spectrum of programs, including the liberal arts and technical and vocational subjects. The two-year colleges must enable a young adult to measure against the needs of society his ability and willingness to work. They must permit him to adjust his educational and vocational goals in the light of his developing talents. These colleges must serve society by preparing the kinds of technicians our economy demands. An increasingly important task of the two-year college is that of continuing education to keep current the skills and knowledge of technical workers. An even more difficult task is that of retraining older workers displaced by technological change. To achieve their objectives, the two-year colleges require an expert counseling service, a wide range of curricular offerings, a detailed knowledge of the needs of the economy, and the finest instruction ... (In Doran, 1969, p. 5).

Under pressure from current social needs and trends, the emerging community college will be challenged to provide universal postsecondary educational opportunity as a national objective. Thus, the charge is given to accomplish what has not been done before. After such a long period of growth and transition, it is ironic that considerable doubt still exists as to whether or not the evolving two-year college is now able or willing to make the necessary changes to fulfill current commitments. If, in fact, the community college has promised more than it can deliver, it too will be challenged, forced to change, and probably replaced with new experimental efforts. Wrote Theodore Parker:

> All man's conscious activity is at first an experiment--an undertaking of which the result is not known until after the trial. All experiment is liable to mistake. There are many ways of doing things, but only one way of doing it is best; and it is not likely that every individual of the human race will hit the right way the first time of trying. What succeeds we keep and it becomes the habit of mankind ... (In Mosier, 1952, p. 35).

Chapter 3

THE COMMUNITY COLLEGE

Robert Hutchins' 1936 prediction has come to pass. The community college is "the characteristic educational institution of the United States just as the public high school has been up to now." The community college represents the most advanced stage in the evolution of the junior college during the past century. With many attributes that differentiate it from the traditional junior college, the community college is formulating characteristics of its own which go beyond semantic arguments.

But despite what appears to be a tale of success and glory, the community college is being challenged to prove its worth and defend its existence. The philosophical tenets and goals that formed the basis for a strong foundation are beginning to weaken. It may be that in one short decade of life, the community college has already "peaked" and its further development and growth will be much less spectacular. The purpose of this chapter is to explore the community college, its uniqueness, and vitality as the pinnacle of postsecondary educational opportunity for a mass technological society.

A Break With Tradition

Almost every aspect that gave rise to the community college is antithetical to traditional higher education theory. What it does, whom it serves, and how it sets out to accomplish its goals are constantly challenged. Nevertheless, the traditional forces that oppose its existence are the same forces that nurture its growth and development. "It is commonly assumed," said Sir Eric Ashby, "that America has to choose between one or another of two patterns of higher education: mass or elite. I would deny this assumption. It is America's prime educational challenge to devise a coexistence of both patterns" (In The Chronicle, April 26,

1971, p. 6).

The nation's educational system, as a whole, has long been grossly imbalanced because of excessive attention concentrated on the 20 per cent of students who go through college (Chase, 1963). The elementary schools are greatly underestimated in their potential impact on society and remain highly invisible. Secondary education has evolved into a sophisticated situation for some, but serves a custodial function for others. Many high school dropouts actually have high ability and differ from those who persist in such areas as personality, willingness to conform, interests, education skills, and family orientation toward schooling (French, 1966). Actually, the high school dropout problem is not basically a problem of the high school. It has become abundantly clear that the damage may have been done to the individual even before he has entered first grade. Still, a high percentage of students are flunked during that first critical year of schooling. There are those who choose not to pursue issues like this even though a realistic view would show the typical dropout's problems to be those of weak self-image, weak communication skills, and the inability to get along pleasurably with others (Cervantes, 1966).

A clearer understanding of the purpose of the high school necessarily alters views of what the elementary school is, and of what the college and university ought to be (Birenbaum, 1968). Yet, all curricula from pre-elementary to postgraduate studies continue to be influenced by university requirements that ultimately provide for an extremely small percentage of all high school graduates. Graduate schools and various positions in them are extremely prestigious in academic society and are, therefore, unfortunately emulated by state colleges and two-year colleges (Yeo, 1970). All schools below the level of graduate institutions continue to serve a selection and filtering function for higher learning. P. A. Sorokin, in his treatise on <u>Social Mobility</u>, confirms that the school is a social institution which serves as a channel of mobility, selecting and distributing people according to their talents. His penetrating conclusion bears repeating:

> The essential social function of the school is not to find out whether a pupil has learned a definite part of a textbook or not; but through all its examinations and moral supervision to discover, in the first place, which of the pupils are talented

and which are not; what ability every pupil has and in what degree; and which of them are socially and morally fit; in the second place, to eliminate those who do not have the desirable mental and moral qualities; in the third place, through an elimination of the failures to close the doors for their social promotion, at least, within certain definite social fields, and to promote those who happen to be the bright students in the direction of those social positions which correspond to their general and specific abilities. Whether successful or not, these purposes are some of the most important functions of the school. From this standpoint, the school is primarily a testing, selecting, and distributing agency. In its total, the whole school system, with its handicaps, quizzes, examinations, supervision of the students, and their grading, ranking, evaluating, eliminating, and promoting, is a very complicated 'sieve' which sifts 'the good' from 'the bad,' future citizens, 'the able' from 'the dull,' 'those fitted for the high positions' from those 'unfitted.' This explains what is meant by the testing, selective, and distributive functions of school machinery (In Lunden, 1939, p. 24).

The elitist position in education has come to be seriously challenged for the first time. It seemed wrong to have more than three million illiterates in our adult population and more than half of our unemployed youth classified as functionally illiterate ("The Right to Read," 1969). The decline and fall of nations has been traced in many ways to a majority of the people having minimal education (Shores, 1970). Someone simply had to care for those who did not go on to a traditional college education.

Career and vocational-technical-occupational education have yet to gain stature and respectability due to distortions and wide ranges of values. The Chairman of the National Advisory Council on Vocational Education sharply articulates the current problem as one of national attitude:

At the very heart of our problem is a national attitude that says vocational education is designed for somebody else's children. This attitude is shared by businessmen, labor leaders, administrators, teachers, parents, students. We are all guilty. We have promoted the idea that the only good education is an education capped by four years of college. This idea, transmitted by our values, our aspirations, and our silent support, is snobbish, undemocratic and a revelation of why schools fail so many students (Calkins, 1970, p. 339).

Education has traditionally demonstrated other paradoxes which weakened the cause of higher education. Beeler and Eberle (1971) somewhat facetiously list the following generalizations:

1. Academic standards and scholastic excellence are worshipped, although neither has ever been defined satisfactorily. In general, that professor who fails the most students thus has high standards, and therefore is the best teacher.

2. By a fantastic stretch of the concept of academic freedom, it can be argued that the college professor should be free to do as poor a job of teaching as he chooses ...

3. Colleges are considered hotbeds of radicalism with regard to economics, politics, and social problems. Internally, they are the most conservative, often reactionary, of social agencies ...

4. Education has been one of the prime stimuli for technology in our society, but has proved to be one of the areas with a strong resistance to the use of technology for its own purposes ...

5. To gain a superior faculty, a university has to decrease concern for undergraduate teaching ...

6. Intellectuality is the prime characteristic of the college campus; intellectual honesty is not ...

7. College teaching is perhaps the one occupation which presumes to identify itself as a profession, yet provides no specific professional preparation ...

8. The graduate school is organizationally subordinate to the college; the college is dominated educationally by the graduate school ...

9. Some people believe society profits most from

an individual's pursuit of higher education, but they expect him to carry a heavy proportion of the cost of study. Some people believe the individual profits most from his pursuit of higher education, but they expect society to pay a heavy proportion of the cost of his education ...

10. Liberal arts colleges have been professionalized increasingly during the first half of the 20th century. Professional colleges have made more strenuous efforts to liberalize their courses of study ...

11. Centers of higher education which are designed to free mankind from ignorance, and the results thereof, seldom, if ever, have any significant salutary impact on the problems, the people, and the progress of the geographical areas in which they are located.

These and other inconsistencies relate to subtle tasks that are included among those placed before the community college. Quantitatively, the growth of higher education has been impressive; qualitatively, it stands on the verge of impotency. According to Wireman (1970), "unprecedented growth, impreciseness of purpose, neglect of the student, ambitious but largely unsubstantiated claims, and a lack of philosophic cohesiveness have all combined to leave higher education in a growing state of confusion."

The democratization of higher education is expected to produce about fourteen hundred community colleges with more than four million students by 1975 (Menefee and Cornejo, 1969, p. 21). But, according to Logan Wilson (1968), "higher education has become too important to the welfare and state of being of various regions and areas, as well as to the entire nation, for its development to be entirely in local or private hands." He sees the community college providing relatively low-cost higher education on a massive scale. Others still view this type of college as being a high school extension, lacking in many of the opportunities to be found in senior colleges. Even in 1980, Joseph Cosand (1968) forewarns, "academic snobs [will] tend to view them as a last resort--the public community colleges for dullards, a handful of fancy junior colleges as finishing schools renamed."

On a number of occasions, H. E. W. Secretary Robert Finch and Commissioner of Education James Allen indicated their belief that the future of American education is bound up nationally with the continuing evolution of the community college (In Johnson, 1970, p. 29). With overall college enrollment expected to increase 50 per cent during the next fifteen years, according to census figures, only an egalitarian spirit in higher education could now cope with the anticipated 11.5 million college students in 1985. In the American College Testing Program's monograph, The Two-Year College and Its Students (1969a, p. vii), the following projection is made:

> Among institutions of higher education, the two-year colleges are the most likely ones for many Americans to accomplish this education. Founded on a spirit of egalitarianism these 'open door' institutions generally emphasize a broad curriculum which includes many fields geared to specific occupational requirements.

Lyle Spencer (1969, p. 33) gives a similar response, but from a publisher's point of view:

> The junior college seems to me to offer our best chance to stimulate genuinely fresh investigations, and then do something about the answers. Free of rigid traditions which tie most schools and colleges to their administrative and instructional arrangements, junior colleges can tinker with all sorts of new ideas and put them to work in the classroom.

Meanwhile, a dangerous situation is growing for the many private institutions that are caught in the wake of widespread public education. Pifer (1970) concludes that they "will do best financially by turning their backs on the hard-pressed middle classes and concentrating their admissions policies on the children of affluent families which can best afford the rising tuition." But in so doing, these institutions will ultimately "pay the price of becoming estranged from the mainstream of the populace," thus increasing their growing insecurity. Pluralism in American education may be weakened by fiscal inequity unless new means are explored to restore the growing imbalance which favors public education.

The College

Funding, Control, and Opportunity

While public funds are not inexhaustible, they do manage to provide strong support to community colleges. In his March 1970 message to Congress on higher education, President Nixon foresaw the value of these institutions in other than monetary terms:

> Two-year community colleges and technical institutes hold great promise for giving the kind of education which leads to good jobs and also for filling national shortages in critical skilled occupations. A dollar spent on community colleges is probably spent as effectively as anywhere in the educational world.
>
> The colleges, moreover, have helped many communities forge a new identity. They serve as a meeting ground for young and old, black and white, rich and poor, farmer and technician. They avoid the isolation, alienation, and lack of reality that many young people find in multiversities or campuses far away from their community.

Linking opportunity with the community college, President Nixon concluded:

> A young person graduating from high school in one of the states that lacks an extensive public junior college system--more commonly and appropriately known as community colleges--today has little opportunity to avail himself of this immensely valuable but economical type of post-secondary education.

Providing postsecondary educational opportunity at a reasonable cost for most Americans is an authentic break with tradition. But even when tuition is as low as two hundred dollars per year, only slightly more than one-fourth of American families are adequately able to meet the cost (Collins, 1969a). The general three-way split, with the state, local subdivision, and students each paying one-third, is rapidly giving way to a reduced portion for students. For example, in Maryland the formula for support provides 50 per cent from the State, 28 per cent from the local subdivision, and only 22 per cent from students.

As might be expected, community responsibility and local control change drastically when states operate or maintain public two-year colleges. As states increase their share of funding, local boards of control stand to lose a large share of their authority (Wheatly, 1971). But even though studies show that community college growth and development are limited in the State-controlled colleges of Georgia and Wisconsin, community colleges in Massachusetts, Virginia, Kentucky, and Minnesota recently went to State control.

Aside from legislative regulation, detailed petty controls accompany state dominance (Read, 1969, p. 20). Furthermore, state fiscal control brings obvious changes in curricular comprehensiveness and definable differences in qualitative standards that relate to faculty, staff, program, and administrative effectiveness. Rising costs and increasing state control are factors that must be weighed carefully if the community college is to retain its regional, local, and individual characteristics. Community college presidents are beginning to raise objections to proposed changes in state laws that would increase a state's share of college costs. As one college president concluded:

> None of us are anxious to see student tuition increased, but tuition hikes may be more acceptable than increased state control. I'm old enough to understand that increases in funding also mean increased state control (In Day, 1970).

California found that a junior college could be constructed in 1958 at a cost of $3,200 per student, compared to a four-year college at $4,280 per student, and the university at $7,400 per student (Browne, 1966). Illinois budgets a cost of $3,000 per student to build and maintain its community college system according to the 1964 <u>Master Plan</u>. Patterns of financial support are changing constantly as can be seen from data (provided by Read 1969, p. 15) on the following page.

The need for additional revenue will eventually force the Federal government to play an important role in supporting community college development. The Higher Education Facilities Act of 1963 was the first legislative Act that singled out the community college as a recipient for 22 per cent of the construction funds then available. This percentage was subsequently increased, as was some aid from other

The College

State	Operating Expenses (In per cent)	Capital Outlay (In per cent)
California	State 22.4 Local 77.6	Local 100
New York	State 33.3 Local 33.3 Tuition 33.3	State 50 Local 50
Florida	State 66.3 Local 13.6 Tuition 20.1	State 100
Illinois	State 45.0 Local 45.0 Tuition 10.0	Local 100

(In Read, 1969, p. 15).

sources, including the Allied Health Professions Act, Vocational Education Act, National Defense Education Act, Higher Education Act, and the Education Professions Development Act. These Acts generally provide grants and loans for classrooms, libraries, laboratories, and other facilities in community colleges and technical institutes in addition to other undergraduate and graduate institutions. Other proposals would even have the G.I. Bill cover up to 98.8 per cent of the cost of education for veterans (The Chronicle, November 3, 1969, p. 2). Furthermore, this aid would encourage veterans to complete their elementary and secondary education in addition to taking college preparatory or vocational courses in a high school, college, or community college.

Preston Valien, Deputy Associate Commissioner for Higher Education in the U.S. Office of Education, indicated that while the community college enrolls a third of the nation's college students, it receives "less than 10 per cent of the funds that all Federal agencies allot to all institutions of higher education for non-science activities" (The Chronicle, March 16, 1970, p. 7). In fiscal year 1969, for example, the Office of Education estimated that about $130 million of its $1.2 billion higher education budget, excluding funds for research and development, went to the community college (The Chronicle, November 24, 1969, p. 2).

In a sense, the community college is caught in a vaguely defined area between programs supporting secondary education and those supporting higher education. Community college administrators generally develop inadequate proposals for Federal support because of insufficient staff time and competence. Furthermore, staffs that operate the Federal programs have not yet broken away from traditional patterns of operation and have generally been insensitive to the emergence of the community college.

Apparently, community college staffs that seek Federal grants will have to develop expertise or run the chance of forfeiting additional funds. The bureaucracy in the Office of Education has grown far too unwieldy to change its format to a more reasonable mode of operation. Meanwhile, the community college stands firm in its attempt to seek larger institutional grants from the Federal government. A larger share of categorical support is being sought under existing programs which are admittedly stacked and administered in favor of four-year institutions. Attempts to secure unrestricted student grants are also seen as favorable techniques to aid the community college. With such grants made available, high-tuition institutions would tend to price themselves out of the academic market. Accordingly, in testimony before the House Special Subcommittee on Education (February, 1970), Kermit C. Morrissey, former President of the Community College of Allegheny County (Pittsburgh) and Chairman of the A.A.J.C. Commission on Legislation, proposed that the Federal Government provide institutions with one hundred dollar grants for each "full-time-equivalent student at every level of higher education."

With college enrollments estimated to increase until the late 1970's or early 1980's, the U.S. Office of Education foresees a leveling-off period in the early 1980's. Therefore, the financial problem will get worse long before pressures are relieved. One of the problems that confronts the community college is the traditional bureaucratic categorization of school and colleges based on year-levels (Sievert, 1971). Experimental programs still tend to have difficulty receiving adequate financial aid unless they conform to preconceived notions of specified levels within secondary and higher education.

Albert A. Canfield, Director of the Washington State System of Community Colleges and Chairman of the National Council of State Directors of Community-Junior Colleges, made the following charge to a Congressional Subcommittee in winter, 1970:

> As improbable as it seems, there is no advocate for the community colleges in the [U.S.] Office of Education. Improbable as it must seem, despite the record of the community colleges, there is no bureau, no division, no branch--only a recent and modest staff in a special office within the Bureau of Higher Education ...
>
> Impossible as it must be, the community colleges participate in only six of the twenty-four institutional support programs administered by the Office of Education (In The Chronicle, March 16, 1970, p. 7).

With funding being a critical issue (Ferrari and Berte, 1969) at the same time that free universal postsecondary education is being promoted, increased Federal aid is inevitable. The Department of Health, Education, and Welfare, in its recommendation Toward a Long-Range Plan for Federal Financial Support for Higher Education (1969), concluded that equality of opportunity in postsecondary education must be strengthened, as must graduate education and research. The report to President Johnson also admits failure to resolve the issue of free higher education since there are those who still maintain that the student should always pay a part of his education expense. The long-range plan is a response to the President's request in 1968 to "shape a long-term strategy of Federal aid to higher education, a comprehensive set of goals, and a precise plan of action." Accordingly, the following objectives were established for all programs of Federal aid to higher education:

1. To increase the number and level of educated people;
2. To equalize opportunity;
3. To strengthen, encourage, and expand existing resources.

In order to accomplish this, the U.S. Office of Education promises to obtain a larger share of funds for the two-year college from such program sources as Manpower Development and Training, Vocational Education, Allied Health Professions, Student Aid, Teacher Training, and the Model Cities Program of the Department of Housing and Urban Development. In general, proponents of the community college favor systems of financing that veer toward the free public education model, with student aid in the form of grants that are administered outside the institution. On the other hand, the community college is now becoming an inexpensive alternative to the higher tuition four-year state and private colleges. As a consequence, it may be legitimate to ask certain students to pay a share in proportion to their individual ability.

The first sign of national recognition for the community college came when Senator Harrison A. Williams, Jr. of New Jersey, the new Chairman of the Senate Education Subcommittee, co-sponsored the Comprehensive Community College Act of 1969 with twenty-seven other senators. He realized that thirteen major cities were without a community college and twenty-five others had only one. Williams, like others, was surprised to learn that even with one-third of all college students, the community college only received four per cent of N. D. E. A. Student Loan funds, six per cent of Educational Opportunity Loans, and 15 per cent of College Work-Study funds. Out of forty-five community college applications vying for a share of $6.9 million under the Education Professions Development Act, only two proposals were accepted and brought $74,000 in aid. Williams placed the blame with the U. S. Office of Education for being insensitive to the special needs of the community college.

While the Williams Bill failed to gain acceptance, it did establish the basis of an inevitable plan. The Bill's provisions would have given each state as much as $200,000 to devise a statewide network of two-year colleges during a year of planning. After the first year, it would have authorized an appropriation of $6 million over a three-year period, with distribution among the states based upon population of age eighteen and older. These funds were not to be in addition to other current funds; rather, they were to replace and expand such efforts. To qualify, a community college would have had to admit every applicant of eighteen years or older, with or without diploma, and would have had to be tuition-free or else provide substantial student aid. A special bureau for community college education was also planned to direct the program.

Growth And Uniqueness: An Emerging Philosophy

The community college increasingly accepts aims and goals which extend its educational service far beyond that of the conventional junior college. This broad range of service helps to distinguish the community college from all other educational institutions while uncovering its basic philosophy.

The community college has evolved from the junior college despite the timid and apologetic defense that is generally offered in its behalf. Still, a variety of problems arise from the lack of well-defined views held by educators in issues related to different kinds of colleges (Donzaleigh, 1969). Misconceptions that lead one to believe that the modern community college is a "halfway house" with overemphasized academic programs and on its way to becoming a four-year college are senseless (Cosand, 1968). So too are misconceptions currently held by high school teachers and counselors as a result of uninformed opinion. Too often, "consultants from university schools of education do not fully understand the mission of the community college, and their advice proves of little value" (Menefee, 1968-69). The community college is no longer an experiment. But most of the thinking about the future of higher education is still timid, according to James Allen (1969a), who warns that local control will soon be challenged unless the quality of education is improved.

The relative success of the contemporary community college is born, in great part, out of limitations of four-year schools (Elliott, 1969). The university is overtaxed in its efforts to provide nontraditional services, and this brings about the need for more and different kinds of institutions. Opening new community colleges has proven to be more realistic than changing old universities. Identified by Jencks and Riesman (1968a) as the "Anti-University College," the community college is in a position to exploit its antithetical nature. According to Cross (1969), the community college practices what students in the prestige universities are demanding: "the democratization of higher education which includes responsiveness to community needs, an open entrance policy, the abolition of the concept of 'failure,' and emphasis on the quality of teaching rather than research." As Wireman (1970) aptly concludes:

> The confusion of process with purpose has left trustees and regents frustrated and often hostile, students bitter, faculty confused, administrators fractured, and the taxpayer disillusioned and even on the verge of revolt (p. 4).

The American society itself has become obsessed with

credentials. This is mainly brought about by institutions of higher learning. The community college, in trying to emulate senior colleges, has only worsened the problem. Birenbaum (1970) suggests that the burden of proof must now shift from those trying to get in to those who would keep them out. Institutions of higher education are "out of touch" with the new knowledge and new society. He calls for change as follows:

> Colleges have become places where young people are being prepared for one version of life, while removing them from life during the preparation. It is essential that institutional forms be changed in order to be more compatible with society in a higher standard of civilization.

In establishing its goals, the community college has too quickly adapted to the mistrials of other institutions. The strength of any new educational form cannot thrive on the cast-off ideas of older institutions. Senior colleges are faltering "because the lecture, the textbook, and the syllabus are not proper tools for achieving such goals. These devices ... contribute to conformity, and they level the college experience to a common denominator" (Clayton, 1970, p. 14). Unique approaches should encourage self-discovery, imagination, creativity, and efforts that are otherwise self-directing.

Traditionally, four-year colleges experience a substantial student attrition which is caused by failure to comply with academic and collegiate standards. As a result, upper division classes are substantially smaller than lower division classes. Where such discrepancies are very great, the senior colleges are performing, in an expensive and inadequate fashion, the role of a community college (Browne, 1966, p. 17). Undergraduate education, especially the first two years, is inadequately prepared to accommodate the present students from secondary schools (Birenbaum, 1968). Philosophically, the community college is just beginning to address itself to this problem.

A Task Force initiated by the Department of Health, Education, and Welfare recently concluded that new ways must be provided for students to acquire an education. Under the direction of Frank Newman of Stanford University, the Task Force produced a report which was highly critical of the overall system of education. Certain recommendations have direct implications for the future development of the community college. Both President Nixon and Elliot Richardson, Secretary of Health, Education, and Welfare, endorse the Newman Report (1971) which states:

> The system, with its massive inertia, resists fundamental change, rarely eliminates outmoded programs, ignores the differing needs of students, seldom questions its educational goals, and almost never advocates new and different types of institutions.

The Task Force, which was supported by the Ford Foundation, also cites a basic problem regarding future trends:

> We have seen disturbing trends toward uniformity in our institutions, growing bureaucracy, overemphasis on academic credentials, isolation of students and faculty from the world--a growing rigidity and uniformity of structure that makes higher education reflect less and less the interests of society (In The Evening Sun [Baltimore], March 9, 1971, p. 1).

Somewhere in our educational thinking something has gone wrong, concludes the Newman Report. A major impediment to sound reasoning is the set of assumptions on which educational policy is based. Thus, in order to provide greater access to higher education, there is too great a tendency to expand present systems, on the assumption that if some is good, more of the same is better. While institutional diversity is a strength, most institutions, both public and private, are becoming more and more alike. Real diversity requires changes in altogether new forms.

Educational thinking leads us to believe that the most pressing issues are intrinsically related to higher education when, in fact, they are more broadly related to social problems in contemporary society. The tendency for all colleges to operate in the "academic mode" dampens the spirit to innovate and leads to large, centralized, multi-campus units which are hopelessly eroded with the concomitant bureaucracy. With the community college growing at a rapid rate to absorb the increasing number of students who want to enter college, the Newman Report cautioned, "community colleges should not be organizations that absorb the left-over problems from higher education, but must develop their own distinctive missions" (In The Chronicle, March 15, 1971, p. 4).

It is highly probable that the community college movement, with few exceptions, has failed to acquire the attributes of a new educational enterprise. These attributes include a multipurpose function of high order with educational formats other than, or in addition to, indoor-seated-verbal-lecture-reading-type learning styles. Much is know about how people learn, but little has been developed into a new working model. The community college must discover for itself what a campus is. It must continually redefine the roles of teacher and student and accept experience as a legitimate part of any educational process for students and teachers. Also, as with any flexible arrangement, a series of attainable alternatives must be made available at various levels along the educational continuum. With funding methods constantly changing and approaching a model that would provide larger resources directly to students, the community college may find itself forced to defend its services in a competitive marketplace. Surely, many educational institutions would price themselves out of a competitive market for other than fiscal reasons.

While trying to protect the standards of education, regional, professional, and specialized accrediting agencies have indirectly caused most new educational patterns to grow in the image established by conventional colleges and universities. Moreover, faculty guilds, subject-matter specialization, departments, and firmly established academic practices such as tenure, have all impeded genuine innovation and fresh thinking. Energetic and creative individuals must be attracted to careers in higher education if real change is to occur. (Newman Report, 1971).

In seeking to establish its unique function in higher education, the community college must aim to break certain traditional habits by sanctioning better ones. For example, the archaic assumption that certain subjects are "college level" and certain ages "college age" should be dispelled. Admissions standards that support a lockstep entry plan are notorious for also supporting the artificial institutional hierarchy that tends to preserve the status quo for non-academic purposes. New learning and life styles legitimize "dropping in" and "dropping out" of college and make the concept of finality in education a poor one. Individuals should be able to choose various levels of entry and departure other than those most convenient to the institution and those who administer it.

The concepts of agrarian calendars and time-based learning are anachronistic. It would be easier to replace them rather than attempt to modify them. The quantum theory of learning overlooks the fact that not all learning occurs in countable units. Terms, semesters, courses, credits, and other divisive techniques tend to sustain a contrived atmosphere. Neither the fiscal year nor the calendar year has as much national effect as the academic year. People who "learn" on weekends, nights, or summers are treated in the periphery of academe. Much of the learning that takes place on a part-time or evening basis is superficially relegated to a second-class status. The insistence upon replicating traditional, on-campus learning experiences continues to hinder any attempt to provide for nontraditional students. Parallel options are needed to provide higher education to different people at different times, still without sacrificing legitimate and definable standards.

Knoell (1971, p. 13) suggests some realistic alternative enrollment-attendance patterns for the community college:

> 1. Delayed college attendance with a guarantee of admission and financial aid, as needed, if the period between high school and college is spent in a program of supervised work experience or service, with counseling and remediation related to the planned college attendance.
>
> 2. Concurrent course enrollment and supervised work experience, the latter for both credit and pay, with students spending two or three days each week off campus.
>
> 3. Alternate terms devoted to study and work experience, with the latter at an ever-increasing level of skill and closely allied to the student's occupational major, with permanent job placement at the end of the final term before the degree is granted.
>
> 4. An 'upside-down' sequence of courses, in which occupationally related courses are taught before general education, composition, and others usually

required in the freshman year.

5. One-plus-two year program for 'undecided' students in need of both remediation and extensive career counseling, the first year to be primarily exploratory and developmental.

6. Planned leave of absence between the freshman and sophomore years to obtain intensive work experience in one or more jobs arranged by the college.

7. Concurrent enrollment in the community college and the transfer institution during the last term before transfer; if possible, or during a summer term, if the transfer institution is not within commuting distance.

8. One or more courses to be taken at neighborhood centers, via open-circuit television, by correspondence, or as independent study.

9. Enrollment in one or two courses full-time for periods of three or six weeks, followed by a break for off-campus activity, after which full-time work in one or two new courses is undertaken.

10. Courses taken to adults out on their jobs with released time given by the employer for their participation.

New methods in education can be expected to appear heretical. Those people with the motivation and ability to direct their own learning generally succeed in spite of any educational system, and even half of those who are compelled to leave eventually return. Unless significant changes occur in their social, financial, developmental, and academic outlook, some people never return.

Divergent views are still to be found about the often-repeated goal for universal education. The popular view is democratically stated as follows:

> The goal of universal education beyond the high school is no more utopian than the goal of full citizenship for all Americans.... If a person is adjudged incapable of growing toward a free mind

today, he has been adjudged incapable of the dignity of full citizenship in a free society. This is a judgment which no American conscious of his ideals and traditions can rightly make (Educational Policies Commission, 1964).

In that context, Arthur Cohen suggests that to bar the ignorant is as undemocratic as it would be to refuse admission to the poor. Postsecondary educational opportunity is a societal right and the philosophy of the community college has been founded upon this premise. Even if we differentiate between natural and contrived hurdles, the community college is still seen as offering more of the same in higher education. We should ask, "Why?"

Those who oppose the community college concept often advocate the investment of an inordinate amount of national resources to further educate the academically-oriented student in order to preserve and promote scientific and technological progress. The opposite view, however, argues that the lowest performing members of society present the greatest loss of resources and, in the long run, the biggest threat to the general welfare of society. Astin (1971) suggests that improving the competence of these lowest performers might ultimately have enormous societal benefits by alleviating poverty, crime, welfare, and other such social problems.

If the community college is to accept the challenge to provide a new educational pattern, it will have to make provisions that adjust to a wider range of people, including women who choose both family and education, workers with jobs and families, the urban ghetto resident with insufficient finances, people in need of retraining, retired persons, the handicapped, disadvantaged, and others alienated from existing programs and institutions. Then, the attitude of employers about academic degrees must be corrected. According to the Newman Report:

> The college degree plays too large a role in American life. Much can and should be done to reduce its influence with employers.... Almost all employers view a bachelor's degree as some sort of minimum credential indicating ability to think or do ...
>
> ... Many are in college simply for the lack of

something else to do ... (In The Chronicle, March 15, 1971, p. 6).

The attempt to provide more and better educational opportunities must not inadvertently produce a paranoia which distorts social thinking and makes degree mills out of overenthused educational institutions. The new plans must provide meaningful alternatives of other than degree status. Only educators can reverse the fallacious attitude which has traditionally stigmatized vocational-technical education, first in the high school and now in the community college. Never has such an injustice been so broadly sanctioned for so long. It is time to reverse the subtle but substantive connotations of inferiority attached to work of less than degree level. The community college is openly challenged to correct this iniquity. Other educational institutions have already failed. To accomplish this task, the community college will not only have to change societal attitudes, but also subversive influences within the community college and the college community.

The philosophy of any educational institution is primarily expressed through the actions and attitudes of its faculty. In general, higher education faculty take a liberal verbal stance on social conditions. A broad survey recently revealed that faculty members tend to see education as a right, not a privilege. However, individual faculty members also say that the right does not apply at their college (Scully, 1970). Attending their college becomes a privilege. Faculty may rightfully be concerned about protecting the gains they have acquired after a long struggle, but this protective attitude generally precludes student involvement in matters relating to hiring, salary, promotion, curriculum, and the like (Blackburn, 1970).

The overflow of Ph.D. recipients has tempted many community colleges to add well-credentialed professionals to their staffs. It is safe to assume, however, that this will not be a popular trend with those institutions that have adequately defined and accepted their role among other institutions of higher education. According to the Newman Report, many students are not academically oriented, but the professors who teach them are increasingly the products of a single, narrow form of graduate education (In The Chronicle, March 15, 1971, p. 7). The new faculty tend to lack broad experience, being more oriented toward scholarship, not teaching; toward departments and disciplines, not choices

The College

students face; toward theory and explanation, not real life problem solving. New ventures in education simply cannot succeed if placed in the hands of traditional or stereotyped personnel.

A plan that encourages teacher mobility between teaching and outside experience may increase both teaching and learning efficiency and should be given serious consideration. Individuals with broad backgrounds may alleviate the Newman Report's contention that "the chief obstacle to enriching the nonacademic experience among faculty will be the resistance of the current generation of faculty members." Whether or not the community college provides the different approaches described here remains to be seen. So far, the results have varied greatly.

Twentieth Century Land-Grant Institution

In a real way, the community college stands as the new twentieth century land-grant college. The original land-grant institutions of 1862 were not quite able to "promote the liberal and practical education of the industrial classes in the several pursuits and professions of life." It has long been an academic view that university responsibility lies more with research than with resident teaching. But while the research function grows stronger, Ralph Tyler reports that only half of the original land-grant institutions offer programs with adult needs in mind (In Allen, 1963). John Gardner reflected on this situation in No Easy Victories (1968) and concluded:

> The greatest American educational invention of the nineteenth century was the land-grant college. The greatest American educational invention of the twentieth century is the two-year community college.

Hodgkinson (1970a, p. 237) concludes that urban universities have worsened the urban crisis at the same time that they have attempted to provide relief. And, as Clark Kerr has often indicated, a new institution similar to the land-grant college was inevitable. The land-grant idea is adaptable to local needs in any nation and it seems only practical that the community college acquire this task rather than the "urban-grant universities" foreseen by Kerr (In Perkins, 1970). According to Philip H. Coombs, former Assistant Secretary of State, "Just as the idea of freedom is not the monopoly of any one nation, so the land-grant college idea of practical services cannot and should not be the monopoly of any one type of institution ..." (In Allen, 1963, p. 3). Thus, the idea of public and community service is identified as a need which could be fulfilled by the community college.

James Allen (1969b) describes the newness of the community college as an asset in permitting educational activities that would otherwise be stifled by tradition. But still, the idea of the community college is so new that it is easily confused, as is evident in the following statement by an English Professor and University Dean at Wayne State University:

> Both the public at large and the students themselves hold inappropriate views as to why the young should attend college, though there is virtual unanimity in the opinion that they should, in fact, attend. Perhaps I should say 'why young people should seek a college degree,' for I propose not to refer to the two-year extensions of high school which are called community colleges ...
>
> Their purposes and their problems seem to me very different from those of the degree-granting institutions ... (Ross, 1970, p. 46).

Like Jacques Barzun, there are those who feel that new institutions will ultimately replace four-year colleges in the future. Alvin Eurich, formerly of the Fund for the Advancement of Education in the Ford Foundation, thinks that only community colleges and universities will remain in the future. Eventually, the baccalaureate could become the terminal degree for community colleges despite the current prejudice which limits them to the Associate in Arts degree (Paschal, 1968). By 1980, Mayhew (1968) suggests that community colleges will teach courses commonly taught in the upper division baccalaureate programs, with liberal arts colleges being forced to specialize in master's level programs. And while some call for closer liaison with the secondary schools (Turner, 1970), others have already shown that up to three out of four community college students were taking courses already offered in the high schools (Moore, 1970). California even encourages 15 per cent of its eleventh and twelfth graders to attend community colleges for specialized programs.

The College

It remains for the community college to make a significant impact on current educational problems. In a frail attempt to change education, professional educators are slowly losing control to external forces which are described by the Director of the Ford Foundation Education Program as follows:

> In recent educational history there are clear warnings that when the problems of education are not solved within the system they are appealed to the public arena. When this happens, the decision is ultimately in favor of the majority. In other words, 'if the educators will not change education, the politicians will' (In Johnson, ed., 1967, p. 15).

The community college has the potential to be strongest where the university is weakest (O'Connell, 1965). In the midst of an educational revolution, the community college must seek "to eliminate all restrictions upon educational opportunity whether based on class, economic status, race, or on a quota system imposed by professionals" (Bowles, 1969, p. 11). This new dimension remains as a task for the community college to fulfill based on the past efforts of established four-year institutions (Shores, 1970). The uniqueness of the community college will be ascertained by the depth to which it perseveres to relate education to the equality of man. The U.S. Commissioner of Education wrote about such goals as follows:

> The purpose of our institutions of higher education must, of course, be identified with the larger purpose of man himself. If civilization is to be defined as 'a state of social culture characterized by relative progress in the arts, science and state craft,' man can congratulate himself on his progress. But if we are to accept a more fundamental definition, one that speaks for the universal life force embodied in the soul of man, one that distinguishes civilization from barbarism and requires manifestations of greater enlightenment and humanity--and if we are to accept such a definition as a reasonable statement of human purpose--then mankind is, relatively speaking, still but on the threshold (Allen, 1969a, p. 2).

The implications of equality, freedom, and democracy relate to the significant and decisive tasks that the ideal community college accepts. The tasks are relevant to individual and societal goals. But relevancy needs a referent: let it be the postsecondary needs and desires of the population (Doran, 1969). This is the kind of relevancy that earlier provoked Harlan Cleveland to ask the American Association of Junior Colleges to become the "American Association of Relevant Colleges." The urgency of the task to democratize higher education provides momentous thrust to the rapid development of the community college. But it will take more than buildings or a theory of educational reorganization to provide a viable response. America has long had many tax-supported institutions to encourage and develop equal opportunity, but it remains necessary to invent mechanisms to circumvent or counteract their tendency to be rigid (Rislov, 1957).

The text of President Nixon's March, 1970 message to Congress on higher education reveals what most educators reluctantly sense:

> Something is wrong with our higher education policy when--on the threshold of a decade in which enrollments will increase almost 50 per cent--not nearly enough attention is focused on the two-year community colleges so important to the careers of so many young people ...
>
> No qualified student who wants to go to college should be barred by lack of money ... I propose that we achieve [equal opportunity] now (In The Chronicle, March 23, 1970, p. 1).

Much remains to be done if equal opportunity is to become a reality. In the event that the community college fails to provide the mechanism to accomplish this goal, it will be transformed or replaced by other social arrangements.

The vitality of the community college as a land-grant institution can be viewed as a response to changing needs of society. Cross (1969) lists two prominent social forces distinctive to the community college as: "(1) The demand of an increasing egalitarian society for the democratization of higher education; and (2) The need of a technological society for a better educated citizenry." Thus, the community college is asked to provide universal postsecondary education in a manner that fits the individual needs of students within the larger framework of a free society. As a college designed

The College

to "fit" its students, the community college remains unopposed in higher education.

Universal postsecondary education has become a national objective in the United States. For the first time, the need for complex and skilled services has surpassed the need for goods. And, to a degree, considerable public agreement exists on these goals for higher education (Bowen, 1970). The goals include: universal access to as much relevant higher education as students can handle; the existence of a great variety of institutions and programs; freedom from financial constraints in selecting educational institutions; academic freedom; and efficiency and equity in allocating the costs of higher education. In addition to the major problem of financing higher education, Ferrari and Berte (1969) identify related critical tasks for the community college: achieving a balance between occupational and transfer curriculums; doing research on how best to serve society, community, and individual; improving the quality of teachers; and establishing a "proper" role.

In 1960, the President's Commission on National Goals affirmed the need for two-year colleges to be established within close proximity of all high school graduates. At least seven states (California, Florida, Illinois, New York, New Jersey, Michigan, and Pennsylvania), with 41 per cent of the national population, have accepted the challenge to place community colleges within commuting distance of more than 90 per cent of their people. But even with more than 200 per cent growth in the past decade, universal postsecondary education remains among many unfinished goals.

Within a decade almost 80 per cent of the younger generation is expected to take some kind of postsecondary education (Perkins, 1970). Even now, Michigan's enrollment pattern is illustrative of a national trend which places half of all first-time college students in community colleges. The State University of New York enrollment in two-year colleges is more than 60 per cent (Doran, 1969), while California enrolls about 90 per cent of its entering freshmen in community colleges (Edelman, 1968-69). With only five per cent of Virginia's college students in two-year colleges, the emergence of the community college in that State is expected to increase participation greatly (Virginia State Council, 1967). As with New Jersey, Virginia exports an excessive number of its postsecondary students and the community college is seen as the only vehicle to reverse this trend. In Florida, growth of the college-age population and the demand for professional manpower is so great "that the original concept of the state college has already been abandoned and new degree-granting institutions have been given university status" (Brumbaugh, 1966).

A decrease in the number of colleges initiated by state legislators was accompanied with an increase in the number of those started under local control. The number of state agencies responsible for coordinating community colleges also continues to increase (Hickman and Lieske, 1969). Control of these colleges is changing from school district and county to multi-county and multi-district arrangements. The percentage of state-operated two-year colleges and university branches continues to decrease while the percentage of state two-year technical schools increases. But until student enrollment trends stop accelerating, existing institutions will grow even larger. In this expansion period, the community college will remain as an alternative to the four-year college, but often for the wrong reasons. With growing enrollments in the community college, students will find a paradox between supporting open admissions and attending overcrowded classes. On the other hand, with institutional growth and enrollment predicted to level off, few people are prepared to adjust accordingly. With these and other changes underway, the community college should be forced to establish its educational aims in more meaningful terms than those that appear in college catalogs.

On the fiftieth anniversary of the American Association of Junior Colleges, the Association expressed broad aims for the community college. Among them, it was suggested that the community college must become available to everyone in its community. This necessarily calls for a diversity of programs, most of which do not lead to degrees or formal certification. By being comprehensive, the community college is challenged to cater to a variety of student needs from vocational training to transfer programs, and from adult to mid-career refresher programs. Other areas that are increasingly becoming community college-oriented include community service, "outreach" programs, day care centers, and inter-cultural educational experiences. The community college is expected to provide curricular experimentation while evaluating the traditionally held concepts of "student" and "teacher." As part of its mission, this college must be willing to find, indeed, <u>make</u> its own identity rather than rely on standards and definitions that are quaint and outmoded. According to Gleazer:

> A community college that exists by imitation will have no magnetism ... [It] has emerged out of social needs and aspirations. These are the sources of its identity. And its greatest worth will be achieved by confidently taking hold of its special assignment as an institution in its own right within a complete program of educational services throughout the nation (In The Chronicle, February 26, 1968, p. 8).

In response to the question, "Who needs the community college?", Stuart Marsee (1968) provides the best answer--"Who doesn't?" Part of the community college philosophy is simple. According to Louis Shores (1970, p. 35), "Anybody can educate the high quality student. Let's see you salvage the dropout. We challenge you to take any high school graduate, discover his talents, and develop him to the utmost in the interest of society." The unique promise of the community college is that it opens its doors to students who would otherwise find them shut. In fact, it opens its doors to nonstudents. This is the essence of the twentieth century land-grant college. This is the idea of the community college.

Opportunities for Minorities and Disadvantaged Persons

As U.S. Commissioner of Education, James E. Allen identified certain tasks for the community college. He said that it should be the prime instrument for providing educational opportunity for minority groups in the cities, as well as Indians, Mexican-Americans, and rural whites (In The Chronicle, November 24, 1969, p. 2). This college was to provide opportunities for all veterans, including work-study programs for the person whose age and family responsibilities make him hesitate to undertake formal study under other circumstances. Such need is plainly visible. In a recent U.S. Armed Forces program called Project 100,000, 68.2 per cent of the young men fell below grade seven in reading and academic ability. In 1960, the nation as a whole had 8.3 per cent functional illiterates in its adult population, and only 7.6 per cent of the adults had graduated from college (Thornton, 1966). Responding to this situation, the Carnegie Corporation funded a program to extend and expand the services provided by the community college for military personnel prior to and after separation from the services. Generally, such programs aim to increase the employability or "educationability" of the disadvantaged individual.

There is an overwhelming need to provide educational services to the marginal or disadvantaged student by use of remedial or developmental studies. In this area, many community colleges proclaim success, although Moore bitterly refutes such claims in Against the Odds (1970). All educational institutions should be serving this clientele (Otto, 1969), but few actually do. Sherman Grant (1968) found serious inadequacies in current community college programs for the disadvantaged, and noted that testing programs are designed for middle-class cultures. There is widespread feeling that standardized aptitude and achievement tests cannot escape cultural bias. They tend to favor certain segments of the population while hindering others.

Programs for disadvantaged persons are not working well and efforts must be redirected so that student needs receive precedence over college protocol. Recruitment of minority students in their own neighborhoods is badly needed, as is further recruitment of minority personnel. Remedial training must be planned from the student's point of view. There is nothing remedial about learning grammar of arithmetic for the first time, even if the learner is older than most others with comparable learning capacity. Gleazer (1970) cites a fundamental attribute of the community college that bears repeating:

> I am increasingly impatient with people who ask whether a student is 'college material.' We are not building a college with the student. The question we ought to ask is whether the college is ... student material. It is the student we are building, and it is the function of the college to facilitate that process. We have him as he is, rather than as we wish he were ... we are still calling for much more change in the student than we are in the faculty.... Can we come up with ... [the attitude to] put us into the business of tapping pools of human talent not yet touched? (p. 51).

The community college must accept the student at his level of entry and advance him as far as his abilities permit. Whether these studies repeat high school work or not is of no importance if they accomplish this task. Credit should

The College

be given and degrees or certificates for general studies awarded upon the completion of basic courses. Minimal levels of student performance should be identified and established for program completion. But high school prerequisites and fixed time standards remain detrimental to the success of any program for the disadvantaged and should be challenged. Maintaining academic standards is not as important an issue as maintaining human standards.

Community college programs that provide for disadvantaged people necessarily transcend the traditional roles of teachers and students. The roles become interchangeable; formal, seated, indoor, verbalized learning with chalk and blackboard changes drastically. How can traditionalists ever cope with this? They cannot and should not. Nevertheless, the public is seeking accountability for educating marginal students. The problem requires the community college to correlate the academic world with the domain of vocational-practical reality; i.e., student need and societal need. Remedial courses by themselves will simply not work.

In Colorado and elsewhere, community college presidents have been asked to de-emphasize the transfer program and ultimately seek a new clientele. Admission policies try to reach the poor and culturally deprived, and colleges remain flexible by providing the necessary services to support nontraditional programs. To a great extent, the college president can best effect major change for such programs by promoting less institutionalized climates even though they encourage a growing potential for temporal conflict.

Testing and admission programs are often abused as filtering devices, though their purpose is basically to help the educator to understand an individual and to help the student understand himself. On several occasions, the College Entrance Examination Board recognized the charge that its tests reflected "a bias against 'disadvantaged' groups that results in their relatively depressed scholastic attainment" (Jacobson, 1970, p. 1). In fact, there is a growing feeling that most college testing admissions programs are useful only in selective colleges and not for the universal population of students and adults "in the context of mass postsecondary education." The report of a commission that evaluated the effectiveness of current testing programs concluded:

The most pervasive tests of the College Board--its

> S. A. T. and the achievement tests--are clearly not
> so appropriate as they might be to support access
> for the great majority of American youth to a
> system of mass postsecondary education.
>
> These tests support ... selective admissions con-
> ducted on an academic criterion among the more
> apt scholastically of American students. They
> support less well the distribution of those students
> to curriculums and courses after the dust of com-
> petition for admission has settled (Jacobson, 1970,
> p. 4).

Tests will have to be modified to take into consideration such variables as ranges in potentials of human talent, adult adaptation to higher education, nonverbal skills, value orientations, and qualifications or classifications of job entry at the postsecondary level. Guidance, counseling, admissions, and placement practices are all in dire need of development and redirection if the community college is seriously to attack the problems associated with disadvantaged students.

Higher education has traditionally been blind to chicanos, blacks, orientals, Indians, and poor people in general. And while the situation is changing slowly, the community college has openly dedicated itself to correcting the imbalance, much to the dismay of many people. A statement by Malcolm X El Shabazz, as quoted in the course bulletin of Malcolm X College (Chicago), is worth noting:

> Education is an important element in the struggle
> for human rights. It is the means to help our
> children and people rediscover their identity and
> self-respect. Education is our passport to the
> future, for tomorrow belongs to those who prepare
> for it today.

The aspirations of minorities can be seen in the names of community colleges such as Malcolm X, Eugenio Marcia de Hostos, Arapahoe, Massahoit, Cochise, Quinnipiac, Black Hawk, Seminole, Sioux Empire, Navajo, King, and Kennedy. Representing the diverse needs and interests of many people, other community colleges are named after Jefferson Davis, George Wallace, Lurleen Wallace, Carl Sandburg, William Rainey Harper, Thomas Jefferson, and John Tyler. But a deeper commitment is necessary. In testimony to Congress in February, 1970, Kermit Morrissey gave fair warning to the Special Subcommittee on Education of the House:

> We must not make the mistake of misreading that undercurrent of comment today which says the community college is another establishment conspiracy to again put the minorities in the back of the bus. The less advantaged are pouring in on the community colleges as much for the promise they see in us, the evidence of a changing commitment, the hopes of an equality still only dreamed of, as for the immediate reality and advantage offered. The long-ignored and neglected publics are in effect giving the establishment another chance. It's a chance the Nation and the community college simply cannot afford to muff.

Blacks. The Special Advisory Commission on Civil Disorders, chaired by Otto Kerner, concluded that our nation is moving toward "two societies, one black, one white--separate and unequal." Despite the advances that blacks have made, black students today make up less than six per cent of the overall college population whereas blacks comprise more than twice that proportion of the national population. According to Harry Bard, President of the Community College of Baltimore, more than 32 per cent of all black college students are enrolled in community colleges throughout the nation. Thus, the community college is trying to rectify a racial imbalance as part of its mission.

Malcolm X College is by all measures an example of what a traditional college could never be (Semas, 1971). A black community college, it strives to educate the uneducable and retains legal counsel to help students accomplish their goals. With a president who dropped out of high school (later being arrested and jailed for the possession of untaxed liquor, then earning a Ph.D.), Malcolm X College set out to become one of Chicago's most notable city colleges. Choosing the college because he wanted "the worst one in the country," President Charles Hurst found his most serious problem to be the faculty. As might be expected, some teachers never cared for blacks or community colleges, held two jobs, and were interested primarily in their own security. However, after paying several teachers to stay away, and exposing others to the community if they refused to teach, counsel, and get involved in the community, President Hurst finally established an attitude and philosophy that works.

Programs provide "college credit in escrow." Under this plan, faculty members go into high schools to teach college courses for which students receive credit when they graduate. Prisoners take courses by mail, both in and out of state. A "street academy" provides help to high school dropouts in the fifteen-to-nineteen-year-old bracket who are too young to take high school equivalency diplomas. A "weekend college" is designed for people who cannot attend classes during the week. But unlike most piecemeal programs, this one is complete and allows the student to earn a degree. In too few colleges is the spirit or idea of the community college expressed as well.

In the closing address of the 1970 A.A.J.C. Convention, Harlan Cleveland related the problems of racial equality to open admissions as follows:

> Racial equality means, first of all, equality of educational opportunity--and, beyond equality, the chance to recover from educational handicaps produced by poverty and racial discrimination ...
>
> Open admissions are going to be a fact of life for those of us who manage public systems of higher education. And even the private institutions feeling the heat and wanting to do their part, will loosen up their admissions, stop thinking of remedial teaching as beneath their dignity, lengthen or shorten, where necessary, the time for achievement of degrees, and increase the amount of relevant work-related education they offer ...
>
> [American educators must] stop fighting the open admissions problem, and start shaping the curriculum to the students clamoring at the gate--rather than, in accordance with tradition, shaping the students to the curriculum (In <u>The Chronicle,</u> March 16, 1970).

After defeating the A.A.J.C. Nominating Committee's choice as an at-large member of the Board of Directors, Charles Hurst (Malcolm X College) tried to use his position to effect three minority-caucus recommendations:

> 1. That 'racism in education and its elimination' be the theme of the 1971 convention;

2. That the Association's Board of Directors be enlarged by three members thereby permitting 'selection of a black person, a brown person, a red person, and a yellow person, and a student, with presidents excluded from eligibility';

3. That the black presidents of the Association's member colleges form an advisory council 'for the purpose of cross-fertilizing the institutional thinking of the organization' (In The Chronicle, March 16, 1970, p. 2).

The call for more and better learning opportunity for minorities was to be answered by some community colleges, but certainly not all. President Hurst's comments dramatically reveal a societal problem that still needs attention:

> Public education as it has existed over the years has systematically discriminated against minority people in most vicious ways--limiting their vision of human existence, narrowing their choice of what they will become, and depriving them of the very pursuit of life, liberty, and happiness which are supposedly sacred to the American society ...
>
> Most minority-group students are being inadequately trained to participate in a society where they do not have equal rights and cannot expect equal treatment by the arms of justice ... [they] are not being prepared to cope adequately with an employment opportunity structure that is distorted and constricted in a way that depresses motivation and discourages effort ...

Referring to the inadequacy of the educational structure, Hurst added:

> Excessively large numbers of minority-group persons are being under-educated or mis-educated in environments hostile to them.

And about racism being extended by inadequate remedial education, he charged that:

> Remedial courses for minority students have become one of the most efficient means of extending

the aims of racism; such courses are under any circumstances demeaning and, when carelessly conceived, psychologically destructive (In The Chronicle, March 16, 1970, p. 2).

Thus, it was not unexpected that the black delegates to the 1971 A.A.J.C. annual meeting called for the creation of a formal black affiliate organization to be made up of administrators, trustees, and students of member institutions. The A.A.J.C. was being asked to reflect upon the manifestations of racism and some possible solutions. In a similar but profound manner, student associations from Illinois and Michigan vociferously protested the exclusion of all students from the Association's decision-making process. In essence, the American Association of Junior Colleges was being asked to modify its philosophical outlook and to bring its actions more in line with stated goals. Not until March, 1972 did the Association indicate that changes were to be made in its manner of operation and representation. Of particular significance is the change in the Association's name: The American Association of Community and Junior Colleges. The change is significant insofar as it represents a formal recognition and differentiation between community and junior colleges. It is also significant that the change was brought about by mounting pressures from within the Association's own disgruntled membership.

Referring to educational programs for blacks, the Southern Regional Education Board concluded that traditionalists may be detrimental to such programs. The roles and values of individuals associated with these programs must be reassessed and the "non-believers" kept from programs in which they do not believe:

> Stronger measures may have to be taken with those individuals who are so oriented that they cannot accept the college's philosophy and direction and who become a detriment to the program's success (S.R.E.B., 1970, p. 10).

Universities that formerly closed their doors to the poor, the blacks, and the confused, have made rapid changes to correct their image. According to Denton (1970, p. 22), in a frantic rush to show they are racially just, "big universities are recruiting the promising black students from community colleges ... after the blacks have proven themselves." It will remain for the blacks themselves to determine the potentialities of the community college and other educational institutions. Experience and time will reveal the effectiveness of any institution's commitment to black America.

Revised Perceptions of Community

The community college professes to relate earnestly to its local community. For many, however, the community is the place where the college happens to be and every college, in essence, becomes a community college. The usual picture of community is "that piece of geography out there filled with taxpayers--or, more generously, with tax-paying citizens" (Collins, 1969b, p. 2). The full impact of the "community" dimension in community college programs is yet to be realized. Transposing the classroom function from one side of the academic wall to the other will not suffice. Rather, dissolving the real and theoretical walls that tend to separate academe from reality is the first step in making the community the classroom.

Identifying the needs of a community is a difficult task that requires more than a casual survey. Even when such needs are ascertained, plans to fund and provide adequate programs often make worthy goals unattainable. A community is its people. It is necessarily greater than the sum of its parts and reflects a continuum of social and economic conditions from rural to urban environments. The community is best seen in terms that describe its people, such as working class, disadvantaged, youthful, ghetto, unemployed, marginal, vocational, welfare, and poor. While not inclusive, this list does suggest ways for a college to perceive its community role.

Community services and involvement necessarily include nontraditional academic areas. With tuition at one dollar per credit, one community college offered the following kinds of educational service during a typical semester: investments and securities training, small business management, personal income tax, real estate license training, consumer protection, and estate planning in wills, trusts, and taxes. Also offered were principles of insurance, women's legal rights, comparative religion, retirement planning, Ukrainian embroidery, small boat study, parliamentary procedure, and community services in health, welfare, and recreation. Other services included training in interior decorating, fiction writing, knitting, golf, photography, landscaping, aviation ground training, slide rule, effective communications, Pennsylvania German customs, geological rock hounding, mass media communications, F.C.C. Commercial License preparation, and a study of drugs in the community.

In addition to providing standard academic courses and a range of vocational programs, the concept of community involves counseling and general consultative services which enable people to pursue problems related to environmental conditions, substandard housing, poverty, unemployment, discrimination, congestion, inadequate transportation, and other issues of concern. Societal rejuvenation extends the concept of community from district, to state, to national boundaries. Indeed, a world community collegium exists in which the majority of people are in pursuit of a better life; to the degree that this goal is achieved, the less chance there will be of sustaining the status quo.

To a great extent, boards of control reflect the power structure of the college's community. Board members are highly representative of selective portions of society (Ebbsen, 1969). A recent study by the Educational Testing Service shows the usual "public junior college" trustee to be white, Protestant, age fifty, earning in excess of $25,000 per year, and most likely a businessman who hears the voice of the people at Rotary luncheons (Collins, 1969b). It also shows the board of trustees to be "more conservative and more repressive of students than any other trustees, except those affiliated with fundamentalist church colleges." Collins suggests that we dispel the myth that the board is "a body of public-spirited, selfless, objective, apolitical citizens." Indeed, he sees the entire educational scene as being politicized.

No college is created or fostered by equal efforts from all people in a geographical area. And it is slowly being realized that it takes more than public tax support to enhance, stimulate, and provide the means by which any community college can best exemplify itself. Several primary groups exist within present communities which, if recognized, can lead to concepts of community and governance. These groups necessarily have different strengths, voice and weight factors, and degrees of input and output with reference to their ability to affect the status of the community college. (Collins, 1969b).

While the legality of recognizing such primary groups

The College

often presents a problem, their existence should be considered in the realistic, as opposed to ceremonial, function of the board. These groups include minorities, students, faculty, women, citizens, evening students, the college president, alumni, and representatives of business and commerce.

The idea of "community" will be better established when boards of control are determined on other than political considerations. Those directly concerned and affected by the everyday affairs of the community college are best suited to determine its program capabilities and range of service. Utilizing primary groups as suggested will reduce the "we-they" dichotomy and end the paternalism of "giving faculty and students a minor role in directing that which is central to their everyday lives." A representative board, chosen in a participatory manner, could ultimately form a colleague relationship with the community and college. The alternative is more of what we now have. (Collins, 1969b).

In his own plan, Collins (1969b) suggests that students have become a formidable power bloc that must be recognized in the community constituency. Even more fractious than the faculty, student groups want greater representation in governance and policy making. The faculty, once organized and tenured, represent a difficult constituency for any president to lead. Acting in the role of mediators, community college presidents often find themselves with no real student or faculty constituency. In a similar way, some community colleges find themselves without a genuine community.

The New Excellence

Two-year college standards of quality and excellence have long been assessed in terms that relate to the number of courses and programs that "fit" senior colleges. Another popular index of achievement is the growing number of students who "make it" by transferring to senior colleges. Still another measure of quality is how well the graduates of junior and community colleges do after arriving at the senior institutions (O'Connell, 1965). Noting the anomaly, U.S. Commissioner of Education Harold Howe said:

> There is a tendency among community colleges to see as the basic measurement of excellence the movement of a very high proportion of their

> graduates into four-year institutions. It seems to me that we need to help the community colleges to develop a concept of excellence in other sorts of services and to take pride in them (In Menefee and Cornejo, 1969, p. 40).

The unique functions of the community college remain to be brought to fruition. While institutional diversity permits the community college to gain acceptance as a part of American education, it also helps to conceal the true identity of this institution. Concerning this diversity, John Gardner (1958, p. 11) said, "Such diversity is the only possible answer to the fact of individual differences in ability and in aspirations--it is the only means of achieving quality within a framework of quantity."

Each institutional form in American education offers its own quality of institutional excellence. This quality helps to describe or differentiate various types of educational institutions. Relating institutional excellence to the community college, Gardner perceptively adds:

> The traditionalist might say, 'Of course! Let Princeton create a junior college and one would have an institution of unquestionable excellence!' That may be correct, but it leads us down precisely the wrong path. If Princeton Junior College were excellent in the sense that Princeton University is excellent, it might not be excellent in the most important way that a community college can be excellent. It would simply be a truncated version of Princeton University. A comparable meaningless result would be achieved if General Motors tried to add to its line of low-priced cars by marketing the front half of a Cadillac (In Menefee and Cornejo, 1969, p. 40).

Thus, the institutional identity and success of the community college rests mostly on its own qualities rather than those of other institutions, but emulating other schools and colleges continues to be a temptation. Clearly, new and bold standards must be assumed by this institution before it reaches a zenith of mediocrity. In his 1963 message on education, President John F. Kennedy set the tone by calling for "a new standard of excellence in education, matched by the fullest possible access to educational opportunities, enabling each citizen to develop his talents to the maximum possible

The College

extent."

Still, the community college heedlessly adopts standard educational practices, most of which were designed by and for universities or secondary schools. It has yet to face seriously the problems of isolation, conformity, and rigidity in higher education. The new kind of excellence requires that its mission be truly different; certainly not a continuation of baseless change and empty promise. In Gardner's ever-renewing society there is no room for institutions that age, lose vitality and flexibility, and become calcified and incapable of meeting unexpected challenges.

The response of a community college president to an editor's conception of "cost-conscious colleges" reveals vivid insight into the kind of excellence that concerns community colleges:

> You suggest that the appropriate response to increasing demands upon community colleges is to 'upgrade academic programs' thus making it more difficult for students to qualify and presumably easier for them to flunk out. You label this process 'the road to excellence.'
>
> I once heard Dean Herbert Schooling of the University of Missouri speak of this as the 'bunny club' concept of higher education. He went on to point out the fallacy in equating excellence with exclusiveness. The notion that you can determine the quality of an institution by those it keeps out has been obsolete since post-World War II experience with returning veterans, many of whom would not have qualified for college admission by traditional standards. The World War II experience has been confirmed by the performance of veterans from both the Korean and Vietnamese periods.
>
> You speak of costs to sponsoring districts and to the commonwealth of providing public higher education, but you do not mention the costs identified by at least three presidential commissions and other agencies, associated with not educating students. Your paper speaks regularly of the staggering welfare budget, yet there seems to be no recognition ... that it may be less expensive to support people in idleness than it is to educate

them to the level of where they can support themselves (Richard C. Richardson in The Morning Call [Allentown, Pennsylvania], April 17, 1971, p. 6).

President Richardson of Northampton County Area Community College then proceeds to write about Pennsylvania's confused concept of excellence and its poor record of spending less than .6 per cent of its per capita income on higher education during 1967 and 1968. Concluding that Pennsylvania has suffered severely due to the lack of an educational system that could provide skilled manpower, he adds:

> ... We are in the process of building such a system through our community colleges, but our cause is poorly served by increasing the lack of public understanding as to what higher education is and who it should serve.
>
> Your suggestions, if followed, would have a number of direct and predictable results. The elitist approach to higher education which has a history of excluding [the minorities and poor people] would be perpetuated and expanded. Our Vietnamese veterans, a significant number of whom were high school dropouts and who, even under present conditions, are not taking advantage of educational benefits to the extent of their predecessors would be denied the chance to take advantage of their hard won maturity.
>
> Equally as undesirable, your suggestions imply that community colleges should concentrate on making academic programs more difficult and save money rather than developing more expensive career programs which better meet the needs of more students and which are closely related to the manpower needs of the community.
>
> Most colleges are interested in excluding students who might fail. In the process they must also exclude students who might succeed since prediction is a very inexact art when it comes to human beings. Surely there is room for one institution interested in including students who might succeed.
>
> ... You have printed several editorials on the

costs of educating citizens. Isn't it time that you devoted one to the costs of not educating them?

Only a different kind of excellence is capable of providing the educational response described here. To this end, it is highly speculative whether the community college is willing or able to live up to this challenge.

Many Things To Many People

Is it reasonable to expect any educational institution to provide innumerable services with limited resources? The basic concern is whether or not the community college is capable of accomplishing the multitude of tasks that are characteristically associated with it. This issue has polarized much thinking and reduced it to two primary positions-- either it can, or it cannot. According to Rislov (1957), the assumption that the community college can serve the needs of every student who enrolls is absurd. On the other hand, Governor Terry Sanford of North Carolina claims that the community college can undertake everything not being taken care of elsewhere.

The community college is too recent a phenomenon to have resolved questions that relate to its multifunction responsibilities, but it is safe to say that it cannot be all things to all people. The community college, however, is indeed already many things to many people. Among the more notable factors that supposedly characterize the community college are its comprehensiveness, open door policy, community services, adult and continuing education, counseling and guidance, vocational-technical career training, and its potential manifold opportunities to enrich home and community life.

The community college continues to perform more subtle functions too. For example, in community affairs the college has been known to be a catalyst for social action. People learn how to create change and improve their environment. In many cases, college programs develop genuine concern for people who would otherwise not have contact with an educational institution because of limited personal resources or different life styles. Preparing Americans for increasing periods of leisure and recreational activity is also a growing concern for community colleges. Even in 1928, the inability of Americans to cope adequately with leisure was seen as "the most important question in America" (Alderman, 1928, p. 1).

The concepts of leisure and education are inexorably entwined. Education for leisure involves liberal education in a way that has yet to be adequately defined. Certain assumptions become questionable. Leisure is not just free time left over when jobs are done, nor is it necessarily nonproductive. The community college will be challenged to develop what Freda Goldman calls "occupations of leisure" (In Whipple, et al., 1969, p. 75). Rather than being a peripheral program, learning for leisure must be integrated with the daily affairs of living in order to promote happiness and a sense of well being for society as a whole. Providing liberal education for leisure learning will require new methods and attitudes such that personal development, recreation, refreshment, and self-improvement become legitimate educational ventures. Current attitudes that view leisure time as insignificant--time to be spent, used, or filled--must necessarily be changed. (Goldman, 1969).

Educational experiences must provide leisure activities that relate to the nature of man, personal fulfillment, self-awareness, worldly affairs, intellectual stimulation, and public issues. People can relate to the arts, mass communications, technology, and self-sensitivity in new and daring ways and the community college holds a strategic position among all other institutions to effect this kind of learning activity. Quality of life can be improved if man changes his orientation from a work-centered to a life-centered style of living. But the scope of liberal education remains limited due to our failure to confront the means by which leisure time can be made a more productive part of contemporary life styles.

In a more simple and directly attainable fashion, the community college can provide educational opportunities for people who would normally have little or no opportunity to pursue more education. Specifically, it can provide a relatively low-cost proving ground for people to become "students" with some sort of trial and error being permitted and, indeed, encouraged. There is no reason why those who learn slowly should be constrained by "regulation" loads and rigid time schedules or otherwise restricted in their attempts to progress. Arguments that cite limitations on physical and financial resources are hopelessly trapped in the quagmire of traditional thought. Too much money has been spent on building physical plants that often are not conducive to learning. School rooms are not prerequisites to learning. Even when facilities do aid learning, they are usually unseen by most people, unused a great part of any twenty-four hour period, and shut down or in partial use during the summer months. If critical cost-analysis techniques were applied to education as they are to business and industry, they would most certainly show cost overruns of great magnitude. Accountability requires new and better ways of operation.

Community college functions necessarily interlock with the functions of all educational institutions. Reading and writing is often taught. Basic grammar, developmental courses, and high school equivalence programs are usually available. Courses that provide parallel learning at freshman, sophomore, junior, and senior levels can be found. Community college facilities are often utilized to bring graduate level and technical or specialized programs to the community college. The college can simultaneously serve bricklayers and Ph.D. candidates, housewives and dropouts, doctors and nurses, as well as those who are normally thought of as students.

Being many things to many people is a concept that allows the community college to go into secondary schools with its academic programs. Many students earn advanced college credit while completing high school. Even a reverse articulation function is emerging whereby four-year college students transfer back to community colleges for personal, academic, financial, or other reasons.

Few other institutions provide a second and third chance to academic dropouts. Yet, the "salvage" function is an admirable social service performed by the community college. And, as required by academic tradition, the "cooling out" function is performed on those students who think they are "academic." In a manner psychologically acceptable to these people, most community colleges get them to accept their "terminal status" in hidden ways. (Clark, 1960).

Adaptation to such a diversified clientele is making the community college role ambiguous while weakening the ability of administrators to maintain and defend goals (In Symposium, 1960). The ability to maintain and then broaden the current multifunction approach to higher education is a crucial test of further growth and innovation since the community college is still in transition.

Multi-Comprehensiveness

The degree to which a community college can attain a high level of comprehensiveness rests, to a great extent, on a state's plan for education. A number of states have not yet arrived at comprehensive master plans for postsecondary education and probably will not react until political considerations are raised by an ever-growing population. Coordinated master plans for education are basic to growth and development at all levels. Hurlburt (1969) suggests that a master plan for community colleges should be able to show concern for the education of adults and adolescents; define an organized system of education rather than a mere group of institutions; meet both universal and diverse needs; help community self-assessment of educational needs; remove college development from political and local pressures; establish priorities; insure coordination of all education; provide a basis for further planning; disclose areas of needed research; reveal inadequacies in current laws and plan new legislation; and bring together laymen and professional educators to make things work.

For some people, the all-purpose college and its curriculum are useless (Jennings, 1970); but for others the multipurpose, open door, guidance-oriented, geographically convenient, and relatively inexpensive college remains an opportunity (Johnson, 1964b). A master plan may either help or hinder an institution's comprehensiveness. For example, the 1964 Illinois Master Plan places "increasing emphasis on upper division and graduate level instruction and--relatively less emphasis on programs at the lower division level" (Browne, 1966). The 1966 Ohio Master Plan cautiously considers whether the community college or the university branch is the preferable organizational arrangement for higher education. Its illogical conclusion revealed that the community college is the organizational arrangement better suited to meet the needs of large urban populations but "the university branch organization must be considered primarily as the response of the State of Ohio to the declared legal policy of open-access to all higher education for all high school graduates" (Ohio Board of Regents, 1966, p. 132). Proposals to abandon all university branches or to convert them to community colleges continue to be fought by the university system.

The community college and the university branch extension are different in purpose and function and do not work

The College

well together. Poor coordination at the state level is often due to political influence beyond the reach of any formal plan. For example, in northeastern Pennsylvania, where one community college was recommended, three two-year colleges appeared. Political encounters between two adjacent counties and the dominance of the State university produced three independent, public two-year colleges within several miles of each other. An editorial view describes the "wasteful education war" as follows:

> War has been simmering since Pennsylvania decided to push ahead with its community college system.... The new community college system has been getting the freeze and its promising programs have been demeaned by actions--or lack of actions--traced to the state's biggest tax-supported institution, Penn State University. [Penn State] has been 'doing everything in its power to detract from the community colleges as institutions.' Penn State has offered no support and actually has 'sown seeds of doubt' about the new institution as a means of effective education.
>
> Penn State's hostility to the community college setup has been an open secret for some time, principally because it feels it should be filling the community college gap by expanding its own branch campuses.... The old Penn State extension schools and branch campuses have fulfilled an important need in their time ... but modern needs required this new state-community venture into education.
>
> ... The state must now end the damaging competition in this field with state-supported education. Taxpayers ... will find untold millions of dollars wasted if two competing institutional arrangements at the associate degree level are funded as presently provided. No state can afford funding one institution with one hand in competition and conflict with another institution it supports with the other (The Bethlehem Globe-Times, April 10, 1967, p. 6).

Within four years, one of the community colleges was temporarily closed when one of twelve sponsoring districts failed to approve a new gymnasium. "The community college was not planned to compete with four-year colleges" was the basis of the suit which is still being resolved by the State Board of Education.

A better idea of comprehensiveness can be developed in state master plans that demonstrate an understanding of community college expectations. For example, in 1956 the New York Regents declared:

> Two-year comprehensive community colleges ... offering both transfer and technical-terminal programs, are considered to be the best single means of (a) accommodating future demands for higher education, (b) embracing the increasing heterogenity of abilities represented in the students graduating from the secondary schools, and (c) providing the education necessary for an emerging group of semiprofessional occupations. Community colleges have a meaning and competence in their own right. They can provide, as well as technical-terminal education, competent preprofessional and general education instruction (In Doran, 1969, p. 6).

In a more sweeping statement in 1964, the Regents expanded their views on comprehensiveness as follows:

> 1. Comprehensive community colleges should be recognized and supported as the basic institutional approach to providing a broader public educational opportunity above the high school level in New York State.
>
> 2. These institutions should be open to all high school graduates or persons with equivalent backgrounds, operated at low cost to the students, and located within reasonable daily commuting distance of the students' place of residence.
>
> 3. The comprehensive community colleges should be expected to perform the following specific educational functions:
>
>> a. General Education ...
>> b. College or University Transfer Education ...
>> c. Occupational or Terminal Education ...
>> d. Adult or Continuing Education ...

e. Guidance and Counseling ...

4. Two-year and four-year colleges, in a planned, coordinated, and complete system of public higher education, provide essential and complementary, but distinctive, services in post-high school education. Therefore, existing two-year colleges should not be converted to four-year baccalaureate college status as an approach to the expansion of college programs in any region of the State (In Doran, 1969, p. 6).

The concept of comprehensiveness can be traced from state or regional levels down to local levels in all forms of administrative, organizational, curricular, and philosophical goals. An example of a public junior college that projected comprehensive goals for 1985 is seen in the development plan of Hillsborough Junior College, Florida (1969). The College established its comprehensive goals in practical terms which will make use of a systems approach in the areas of administration, curriculum, counseling, budget, personnel, and facilities. Also, the College expects to implement an instructional-specialist approach in algebra, English composition, and biology courses; to write entire curricula in terms of behavioral objectives; to identify cognitive styles and learning patterns; to develop the role of teachers in 1974 as managers of learning; and to institute an instruction resources center.

In order to develop and expand the comprehensive nature of community colleges, several institutions have formed alliances to redefine and carry out their mission. Recent examples are: The League for Experimentation and Innovation in Public Community Junior Colleges, which includes Cochise College (Arizona), Coffeyville Community College (Kansas), College of the Mainland (Texas), and Western Piedmont Community College (North Carolina); The League for Experimentation, a confederation of twelve colleges with headquarters at the University of California at Los Angeles; and GT 70 (Group Ten for the Seventies), a network of ten community colleges with headquarters at Miami-Dade Junior College in Florida. For different reasons, even private junior colleges have grouped together to form the National Council of Independent Junior Colleges to maintain their goals of remaining small residential colleges with superior teaching.

Open Door to What?

Without doubt, the most critical issue in all of higher education is whether higher education is a right or a privilege. The issue of who should go to college and, more importantly, who should decide who goes to college is charged with emotion. All institutions of higher education are involved in this great debate which has brought strong reactions from teachers, administrators, students, politicians, and citizens. But of all the institutional responses, only that of the community college is based on its credo for existing. Far too many people are only interested in the affair as long as it remains in the discussion or "talk" stage. And some have taken the discussion into the political arena, where it is still quite fashionable.

In practical terms, the open door issue is concerned with open admissions and equal access to universal postsecondary educational opportunity. The term "open admissions," like many others in education, is a generic descriptor having many shades of meaning with no single connotation attached to it in practice. In its most simple but troublesome form, open admissions refers to a policy that would permit anyone to pursue education beyond the secondary level. Obviously, few institutions, if any, have the capability and qualifications to implement this policy in its most basic form. All modify it one way or another and there is often little in common between two institutions that profess to operate with an open admissions policy.

The concept of open admissions is certainly not new. In their own manner, elementary and secondary education have had open, and even, mandatory admissions. In the midwestern states, high school graduates long ago had the right to enter their state university (Bush, 1929-30). Of course, land-grant colleges quickly developed a multitude of academic procedures that would relieve them of students who were unprepared to function at certain levels of accomplishment within certain periods of time. The "revolving door" is the popular form of open admissions that admitted all eligible students and then disgorged "a large number within a year or two," especially in "those institutions that did not depend on student tuition and that made some claim to scholarly excellence" (Assembly on University Goals and Governance, in The Chronicle, January 18, 1971, p. 10).

The nature of the university, and especially the

multiversity, is such that it can never provide an unadulterated open door policy. University involvement with open admissions has led to the politicization of higher education when, in effect, a democratization was being sought. Theodore Newcomb's suggestion is a good one. He says, "I think our institutions of higher education should either forget about open admissions or prepare to change themselves in fairly radical ways" (In Rever, ed., 1971, p. 55). The latter choice seems to be the more difficult of the two. It is easier for new institutions to cope with open admissions, especially if they are conceived and dedicated with that purpose in mind.

Daniel Moynihan seriously questions the ability of the university to operate with an open door policy:

> At the point of reaching universal opportunity for higher education, we reach the point of harder decisions. Unless we are utterly to debase the standards of higher education ... it becomes necessary to exclude a large number of persons from higher education on the grounds that they are not able to master it.
>
> That is not an easy thing to do.... It is a harsh thing to turn a young man away from a university because he is too poor to pay ... but I fear it may be no less harsh a thing to turn a young man away because he is too dumb. Society's injustice is succeeded by nature's (In Johnson, ed., 1967, p. 14).

Of course, these remarks are grounded in the tradition that made Harvard and Yale the major temples of American leadership. Producing about 15 per cent of the leaders in twentieth century America, Harvard and Yale, like the rest of us, have come into a new decade where the notion of leadership has been challenged and discredited all too suddenly.

A further discussion of open admissions makes it necessary to place several ideas in proper perspective. For one, the issue continues to polarize thought by producing at least two antithetical realms of meaning. Standards that the traditionalist fears debasing are not necessarily the same standards to which new institutions would subscribe. And excellence with which a traditionalist rightly identifies can not be the goal of institutions such as the community college.

It is mythical to think that we must all be of the same mold, pattern, and thought. Having experienced but one kind of educational adventure does not preclude the possibility of experiencing another, even simultaneously. There is need for the experience of scholasticism and research which only the university can generate, and a parallel need for the kind of experience that produces human equality, identity, and self-worth. Though these functions can be expressed differently, they are not mutually exclusive. Open admissions remains an ideal mechanism whereby societal distinctions of class and race are devitalized pragmatically through the educational process.

Open admissions has generated campus reform at all levels. In a practical sense, colleges must decide whether their open admissions policy refers to programs, courses, degrees, or the college itself. The distinction between admissions to the institution and admissions to the curriculum is real. A decade has passed since the two-year college popularized the open door metaphor and still the issue is left "swinging in the confusion of diverse interpretations and practices" (Huther, 1971, p. 27). In The Open Door Colleges (1970), the Carnegie Commission recommends that all states enact legislation to provide admission to public community colleges "of all applicants who are high school graduates or are persons over eighteen years of age who are capable of benefiting from continuing education." This does not mean, however, that every young person should attend college. Some may choose not to attend and others may find it difficult to profit from their attendance efforts. Accordingly, the Commission wisely favors universal access, but not universal attendance in higher education.

For open access to become a reality, free tuition is inevitable for the majority of students. There is a clear relationship between family income and attending college. But according to Gleazer, a true open door policy would make no financial demand on the student. He concludes:

> Once the principle of tuition is established, no matter how small the amount, almost inexorable pressures will result in a gradual but continuous increase. It may be that the degree of opportunity is reduced proportionate to the increase of fees (In Read, 1969, p. 14).

In general, there is agreement that at least two years

of postsecondary education ought to be available to all citizens, and that all barriers, including race and the inability to pay, must be removed. Postsecondary educational alternatives must include both formal and informal, and institutional and noninstitutional opportunities. Whether by use of loans or grants, this opportunity must be provided with little or no tuition except in some obvious cases where students can indeed pay their way.

Community colleges have generally accepted open door policies with definite limitations and reservations. Once admitted, the results of past records and testing often restrict the student from taking certain courses or entering certain programs. But some educators erroneously feel that simply "being refused to a program is not a serious blow to a student's personality" (Rogers, 1970). According to Gleazer (1968b), "Although publicly supported community colleges are predominantly open door institutions, admission to programs within the college is on a selective basis." Reynolds states the situation more clearly:

> [Even though] the institutional purposes proclaimed by the community college in its catalog may coincide satisfactorily with the definition of [the open door] ... in only a relatively small number of instances does the developed educational program reflect a full realization of what these stated purposes imply (In Johnson, ed., 1967, p. 12).

There is a clear dysfunction between the stated goals of the community college and the actual practices that are developed to support them. College catalogs are notoriously written in the area of goals, aims, and philosophy. Few colleges state their open door policy as candidly as the following: "At Berkshire we don't quite have an 'open door' but we do admit any high school graduate who looks to us like a reasonably good bet to do the job in one program or other at our college" (O'Connell, 1968, p. 5). The extreme diversity among community college admissions policies is so manifest that it now challenges the very concept of a "movement" (Huther, 1971).

For the American university, the question of admissions is basically a question of the best policy for the allocation of students among the different units of the university, rather than admission to the university as a whole. Thus, the City University of New York defined its tuition-free open door policy to mean the admission of all high school graduates who apply.

Open admissions is seen as a matter of educational desirability, social equity, and economic necessity in the city of New York. Relying heavily on the services of its community colleges, the Board of Higher Education in New York City said, "The question of increased enrollment is no longer one of how many students should be admitted, but whether and how soon the resources adequate to meet our commitment to all the people of our City will be forthcoming." Consequently, the Board asked the University Commission on Admissions to suggest an open admissions policy with the following provisions:

1. It should offer admission to some University programs to all high school graduates;

2. It should provide remedial and supportive services for all students requiring them;

3. It should maintain and enhance the standards of academic excellence of the colleges of the University;

4. It should result in the ethnic integration of the colleges;

5. It should provide for student mobility between the various programs and units of the University; and

6. It should not detract from the educational opportunity afforded to those under the old admissions system.

(From the Report and Recommendations to the Board of Higher Education of the City of New York, 1969).

With optimism amid controversy, several other university systems, including the State University of New York, have adopted open admissions as a goal. But unlike California's open access strategy which offers State university admissions to the top eighth of high school graduates, State colleges to the top third, and community colleges to everyone, the City University of New York opened all its campuses. One reason was that "community colleges have the image of ranking at the bottom of the academic pecking order and thus tend to set low expectations for both students and teachers" (Time, October 19, 1970, p. 65). Admitting disadvantaged students only to community colleges was seen as extending de facto segregation, so the University opened its doors to a freshman class of 9,000, more than one-third being nonwhite. As with any open admissions policy, the student clientele changed to include domestics, workers, cab drivers, carpenters, and the sons and daughters of blue collar workers, many of whom were the first in their family to enter college. Said Vice Chancellor Healy, "There are the original American revolutionaries ... they want a piece of the action."

The initial effects of open admissions policies are just coming to light. Amitai Etzioni, Chairman of the Sociology Department at Columbia University, feels that open admissions is not opening the system to disadvantaged minorities (In The Chronicle, March 22, 1971, p. 4). Open admissions policies have so far benefited "the children of the hardhats" more than minorities. Etzioni also concludes:

> Heads of universities, appealing for support of open admissions, have stated that there will be no change in the quality of higher education as a result. This is manifestly inconceivable. Open admissions means opening education to people who previously did not qualify.

William Moore (1970) sees the open door as being "mythic" even in community colleges that profess to admit disadvantaged students. He decries a "deliberate and systematic exclusion of the marginal student from quality education in many community colleges." Ironically, "while many people associate blacks with marginal programs, they are actually needed by a greater number of whites." Still, open admissions has incalculable potential and "given proper motivation, students can do well in college even though they have not taken the traditional courses, credits, tests, or other standard work deemed essential" (Fine, 1971).

Open admissions must be discussed in relation to its effects on society in addition to problems at the institutional level. It is obvious that if the input to our colleges is selectively made on the basis of traditional criteria, the output must also be better in the same sense. But segregating students on the basis of academic ability at the institutional level does not enhance the overall quality of the educational process. Even grading systems have been shown to make little difference in student performance at various levels of college selectivity because institutions make internal adjustments to compensate for their clientele.

Speaking at the Twenty-sixth National Conference on Higher Education [Chicago, 1971], Alexander Astin suggested that open admissions would reduce ability dichotomies according to race. Thus, such policies have less potential for race conflict than racial quotas which provide double standards by inevitably lowering the criteria for admitting blacks while raising admissions criteria for whites. Astin concludes that selective admissions is one way for traditional colleges to avoid the responsibility of educating students, since the college experience itself may have little to do with the high quality of its graduates.

Still to be reckoned with are those who see cataclysmic repercussions and impending doom for higher education as a result of open admissions. A community college president and former President of Hood College, Andrew Truxal, was quoted as saying that "the people who will run our complex society in the next fifteen years are those that have brains, and if you put those with quite low I.Q.'s in classes with the brains, you make it impossible for a professor to teach." In an interview with The Evening Sun (Baltimore, December 6, 1967), Dr. Truxal, a sociologist and ordained minister, insisted that "not every youngster is entitled to college." In the same spirit, Vice President Agnew identified open admissions and racial quotas as "strange madness," especially at the university level. He added:

> For these students I believe we must have more community colleges and special preparatory schools, to insure to the late-blooming, the underprepared, and the underachieving student every educational opportunity.
>
> But I make this distinction: preparatory and compensatory education do not belong in the university ... the goal of college education for everyone is now too widely endorsed both by white middle-class Americans and minorities to stop the high-schoolization of colleges simply by trying to uphold the old standards ... (In The Chronicle, April 20,

1970, p. 2).

Quoting Amitai Etzioni, the Vice President concurs with the prevalent but misguided view that the two-year college is a catchall or buffer for the university:

> If we can no longer keep the floodgates closed at the admissions office, it at least seems wise to channel the general flow away from four-year colleges and toward <u>two-year extensions of high school</u> in the junior and <u>community colleges.</u>

"And, of course, that is what should be done," concluded the Vice President.

Fritz Machlup, the noted academic economist at Princeton, also feels that higher education is too high for the average intelligence, and that longer education, even if it is not higher education, will overtax the interest, patience, and perseverance of most people (In <u>The Chronicle</u>, November 16, 1970, p. 4). He sees universal higher education as "longer education for everybody" or "universal postsecondary schooling" and not "higher education" which is:

> ... The level of scholarly teaching, learning, and researching that is accessible to only a small fraction of the people. Any level of education that is designed for a larger portion of the population is, if extended beyond the age of completing high school, in fact only continuing second-level education.
>
> An affluent society can offer continuing education to as many people as it may want to take it. But we should not kid them, and still less ourselves, by the fake assertion that this is higher education.

Machlup sees a clear and present danger in attempts to make college offerings and requirements more relevant to the interests of the academically uninterested. The "worst possible option," he warns, is "to admit all comers regardless of academic interest and capacity, and then either flunk them out after a year or lower academic standards sufficiently to get them through the mill and out armed with a degree that will have lost all use as a certification of academic achievement."

The fervor of the open admissions dilemma can be seen in a response to Mr. Machlup by the Vice President of Miami-Dade Junior College:

> Mr. Machlup is dead right. What this country needs is a good king, a natural aristocracy of the best ten per cent, a return to the rich order and stability of a feudal system. Democracy was abandoned by thinking people over 2,000 years ago....
>
> In my own case, I spent entirely too much time in school, and part of that was in reading Mr. Machlup's work. I found it too high for my intelligence, much too high for my interest, and vastly too high for my patience and perseverence, here and anywhere.
>
> So let me join you Mr. Machlup. If ever he decides to hold a diploma burning on the Princeton Campus, I'd like to throw in my Ph.D. next to his (In The Chronicle, December 7, 1970, p. 8).

It remains for the community college to provide a common base upon which further understanding of the open admissions problem can be discussed. One thing is certain, the issue of open admissions is no longer the exclusive trademark of the community college--nor are the solutions to resolve its perplexity. In the end, the public or politicians will decide the issue. Still, far too little of substance is written about open admissions (Kane, 1970), and researchers have yet to unfold the ways in which its various forms affect the individual, his institution, and society.

Community Service and Continuing Education

No single venture has done as much to alter the institutional nature of the traditional junior college as did its involvement in community service. What might be called the community dimension of the community college is what characterized that period of growth and transition since 1945. Community services are still an evolving function of the community college ideology and all too often the function is relegated to a subordinate or peripheral position. To a great extent, however, the success of the community college concept is measured by the ability to extend the college to the community with a full range of services.

Actually, any worthwhile endeavor of the community college may be called educational if its purpose is to produce change and renewal in an individual, a group of individuals, the community, or society in general. As early as four decades ago, public junior colleges began to involve themselves in activities that were aimed at comprehensive problems. In 1932, for example, California junior college objectives were to meet State expectations as follows:

> A fully organized junior college aims to meet the needs of a community in which it is located, including preparation for institutions of higher learning, liberal arts education for those who are not going beyond graduation from the junior college, vocational training for particular occupations, usually designated as semiprofessional vocations, and short courses for adults with special interests (California Commission, 1932, p. 64).

The community dimension has evolved around several different aspects of community service which include permeation, sensitivity, and commitment to local problems; penetration and integration of the college into the community; and education, the function by which all programs are legitimized (Myran, 1969). In every walk of life the comprehensive community college sets out to affect the thought processes, economic status, habits, values, customs, and mores with new forms of social interaction. In a sense, higher education has been "vertical" for many years, but with community service there is now the possibility of making it "horizontal" (Harlacher, 1969).

For some, the unique feature of the community college is the community dimension. According to the National Council on Community Services for Community and Junior Colleges, many experts consider the community service dimension to be the single most important characteristic distinguishing it from other institutions of higher education. The college becomes the logical vehicle for drawing the community into the process of making and changing educational policies and programs. In effect, the community becomes a laboratory for learning, and the college an institution without "walls."

In analyzing the community service function, it becomes apparent that community service and adult education are <u>not</u> synonymous. Further, community service is not synonymous with those programs which are designed to enhance public relations, however worthy. Adult and continuing education programs are but one type of community service. In addition to the academic aspect, these services include others which are personal, recreational, cultural, social, political, religious, nonacademic, or occupational in nature.

Historically, higher education has been concerned primarily with the young student. All school functions for adults, especially in the evening or on a part-time basis, were viewed as being peripheral to the central purpose, which they undoubtedly were. The second-class status was even worse for women, blacks, and other minorities. According to Robert Finch, the myth that education takes place only in schools has made our educational system an inappropriate vehicle for the older person who may have to change life goals.

In most, if not all colleges and universities, at least a part of the institutional purpose is concerned with providing community service. Yet, most of these concerns appear to be little more than warmed-up variations of what is offered to the younger students. Programs generally tend to be makeshift arrangements with little attention devoted to assessing the needs of a community or providing learning experiences to specialized groups who are quite different from traditional students. Part of the problem appears to be a genuine lack of concern for such programs. Another sound theory among adult educators is presented by Paul Miller who argues that there are two worlds in the university--"on the one side there is the faculty which tends to hold on tenaciously to the traditional, historic sentiment; and on the other side are the administrators who, in order to get support for the university, have had to accommodate the contemporary needs of society" (In Whipple, 1970).

Discontent with the university's efforts to provide effective community services has heightened the responsibility for the community college to take up the slack. Brubacher (1970) contends that the university cannot afford to overemphasize its service function without becoming a conglomerate of trivialities. He would rather see the theory which underlies a variety of social demands being taught as a form of service.

Birenbaum (1968) argues that the graduate model of higher education is inappropriate for most adult education programs because it is "too narrow or too special, too timid or too easy, too late or too irrelevant." University adult education too often takes the "form of a simple translation of assumptions, pretensions, and controlled content" of undergraduate education which fails to aim at the totality of adulthood. Universities will pay "lip service to the problems of the communities in which they exist; in fact," concludes Hodgkinson (1970a), "many city problems are caused in part by the existence of universities."

Concern for adults becomes a real challenge for the community college, especially after being viewed as a marginal activity at libraries, high schools, vocational-technical institutes and universities (Long, 1970). Community service and the popular forms of continuing and adult education have too long reflected the fear of adventure and the dominance of form and tradition in the academic establishment. "With the exception of cooperative extension programs, statistical data are unavailable, incomplete, and ambiguous in the whole sprawling enterprise of adult and continuing education" (Stern, 1970). In the monograph, Higher Adult Education in the United States (1969), Malcolm Knowles concludes that there are "no common yardsticks" against which institutions can measure their policies and practices.

Stern (1970) cites an information gap concerning public service continuing education because it is an amorphous activity that is not tangible and clear cut; it is a complex, diffused, and growing activity that is constantly merged with other activities. Working with other organizations in Washington, James Stinchomb of the American Association of Junior Colleges concluded that national organizations know very little of the community college role in community involvement and public service (Menefee and Cornejo, 1969). And due to the lack of dynamic professional leadership, much effort continues to be wasted with duplication of programs and services at all levels. Prior to 1955, statistical information concerning adult education was primarily fiscal data which represented combined expenditures for general activities at all levels. With more people involved in this type of education than in the institutional "core" or mainstream, the community college must absorb or complement other community services as offered by government training programs, industrial programs, educational television, poverty programs, manpower training, extension programs, and correspondence courses. Educators must coordinate these growing activities by forming a data bank which would gather and exchange factual information related to the nature of adult clientele, instruction, programs, fees, evaluation techniques, budgets, stipends, and so forth.

With this vast clientele to serve, the community college must try to present community services to adults in ways much different from current practice. Seven major trends which could serve as a program guide for community colleges are put forth by Harlacher (1969). Community service programs should:

1. Develop aggressive multiservice outreach programs that "extend" the campus;
2. Increase emphasis on community education at all age levels;
3. Utilize a greater diversification of media in meeting community needs and interests;
4. Utilize catalytic capabilities to assist the community in the solution of basic educational, economic, political, and social problems;
5. Be concerned about the cultural growth of community and state;
6. Place greater emphasis on interaction with the community; and
7. Recognize the need for cooperation with other community and regional agencies.

Easier transition into and out of the academic community must be planned for greater mobility. The community college should also capitalize on the experience of other service models which include work-study programs, experimental schools, Armed Services training, and apprenticeship programs. With more than thirty million American adults engaged in systematic instructional programs (Welden, 1969), much can be learned from existing programs that offer fundamental literacy education; vocational-technical and professional competence; education for health, welfare, and family living; civic, political, and community competence; and education for self-development. With increasing numbers of women returning to college, a whole new spectrum of educational programs can be offered which should be supported with such services as planned parenthood, child care, and consumer relations.

The Higher Education Act of 1965 and later Amendments are dedicated to assisting the people of the United States in the "solution of community problems." Title I is specifically intended to facilitate community service and continuing education programs. Attempts are being made to aid in the solution of community problems in both urban and suburban environments by increasing the quality of adult education programs. In 1968, about 14 per cent of the institutions that participated under these programs were two-year colleges. Also, in 1968, the W. K. Kellogg Foundation funded the Clearinghouse on Community Services with its own newsletter to gather and circulate information for improving community service programs in the community college.

Still, continuing education suffers from the attitude that there is first a period for education followed by a period for it to continue. James Allen often discussed the need for lifelong learning as "the repeated return of the experienced and developed adult to the learning process so that new knowledge can continually be applied to living and working. It is increasingly accepted that all workers must be retrained periodically to keep abreast of the knowledge explosion." The President's Committee on Education Beyond the High School supports a growing and possibly accelerated trend in this area:

> One of every three adults in the United States is engaged in some kind of continuing education during any single year. Rough estimates indicate that 50,000,000 persons participated in programs of adult education in 1955, a nearly fourfold increase in 30 years. Approximately 2,800,000 people were contributing some or all of their time to operating these programs (Second Report, 1957, p. 66).

In 1971, the White House Conference on Youth recommended that national, state, and local priorities be revised in order to fulfill a commitment to educating "all the nation's citizens." Asking that the dignity of every human endeavor be recognized, the Task Force concluded that "with today's rapidly changing technology, learning must be a lifelong process."

The community service dimension has been useful in coping with the urban crisis and providing learning opportunities for the disadvantaged. Harold Gore, President of Educational Facilities Laboratory, Inc., concludes that "education, and particularly the community college, may be the best hope of the inner city. The battleground is in the city.... The community college may be the only acceptable agency for saving the central city" (In Read, 1969, p. 12). In an address to the American Association of Junior Colleges in 1969, Cleveland's Mayor, Carl B. Stokes, concluded, "No group is better suited to aid cities in solving the urban crisis than junior colleges." These institutions are "on the move to meet the diverse needs of the complex urban community ... and to continue to provide comprehensive up-to-date educational offerings ..." (In Yarrington, ed., 1969, p. 129).

The idea of public service gives rise to many new occupations in urban development and is supported in a manpower report of the A. A. J. C. which aptly concludes:

> There is much that the junior college in large urban areas can contribute to the solution of the manpower problems in public service. The extent of this contribution depends upon: (1) the willingness and ability of junior colleges to engage in educational experiments, and (2) an acceptance of urban governments of the potential role of the junior college in preparing men and women for careers in public service (Urban Government, 1968, p. 21).

People are the community, and providing service to people is what the community college is all about. In Baltimore, "New Careers" students are employed by the community college to search out potential students in poor neighborhoods, and in New York City a university-wide College Discovery Program goes into the community to attract non-students. "Upward Bound" projects have experienced considerable success in placing students in community colleges, as have other programs of recruitment, remediation, and public service.

For too long, government and voluntary agencies have treated certain community problems in a primitive and childish way. To this end, community services are now defining and expanding the concept of community self-determination and community control. Giving a voice to the poor and dispossessed, community colleges are located strategically to provide community counseling, referral services, communication skills, volunteer work, and other educational services to ease manpower shortage and reduce racial tensions while developing new approaches for reaching the undereducated, underemployed, and unemployed. (Stokes, 1969).

Whether or not the community college can meet the new mandate will determine its ability to move above and beyond the former junior college role. As with university involvement in national, foreign, and international development, the community college is challenged to bring its untapped resources to aid community development. Urban areas and cities invite educational involvement in ways that have yet to be thought of, let alone tried. More than funding, education must increasingly become the key to providing new but effective responses to pollution, discrimination, congestion, poverty, fear, crime, and other social realities. Educational strategies must be developed which take into consideration the need for developing positive feelings toward self and the entire environment.

Too many responses continue to be characterized by singular goals which relate to academic, personal, or emotional development when they should relate to the whole person. It remains for the social sciences to develop programs with better success rates. As an urban center, the community college must take its informational services to the people in shopping centers, churches, storefronts, social agencies, businesses, hospitals, civic groups, prisons, industry, and homes. Using social dynamics, the community college must start hiring personnel to plan, develop, and implement social services for people outside the classroom. The failure to utilize faculty, staff, and students as agents of social change has limited the degree of involvement and maintained the town-gown separation.

Procedural barriers too often render the community college and its program of services inaccessible to the poor, the educationally handicapped, and others lacking the ability to cope with a bureaucratic system (Knoell, 1970a). For many potential "students," the problem is often less one of qualifications and costs than of conformity to established behavior patterns. The problem is also less one of achieving test scores than of arranging to take the test at a certain time and place with appropriate fees, forms, and approvals. With layers of bureaucracy, administrators, secretaries, and paperwork to separate people from other people, the community college has too quickly followed traditional patterns that are known to be ineffective at best, and dehumanizing at worst.

It is the responsibility of the community college to know its community and its people if appropriate resources are to be made available in an intelligent and useful manner. It is all too easy to relegate the function of community services to a director with limited resources while the faculty and staff go about their regular business. Community service is the regular business of the comprehensive community college and it cannot remain as a part-time, peripheral, second-class activity that occurs several times per year or at annual cultural fairs or career day exhibits. Faculty commitment is mandatory and teachers should be selected with this commitment as a prime qualification before being hired.

The community service effort of any institution will be assessed in terms of its impact on the community; in terms of how the community and its citizens are better off or have changed behavior as a result of the service. To reach the people, J. Kenneth Cummiskey (1969), Director of the Kellogg-supported Community Services Project, suggests the following steps:

1. Find out who is to be served;

2. Find meaningful ways to serve them;

3. Take services to them or bring them to the services;

4. Evaluate the results of expended efforts and adjust the programs on the basis of what is learned by asking, 'Who is being served by the college?' and 'How has the community benefited from the presence of the college?'

In reality, everything that a community college does becomes either a service or disservice. In a wide variety of organizational arrangements and institutional settings, community service programs are beginning to make an impact, both directly and indirectly. A typical program might be oriented to early childhood development, law enforcement, nursing, community health, or urban development. Public seminars, political forums, tuition-free courses, and town meeting assemblies have all been used to reach citizens. Even fulfilling educational and vocational needs and desires of former narcotics addicts in a residential therapeutic community is a form of public service offered by the community college (Morgenstein and Strongin, 1969). Other public affairs programs include the art of lobbying, the dynamics of public relations, community mental health, drug abuse, consumerism, news conferences, and panel discussions with political candidates. Additional programs involve creative dramatics, institutes for hospital administrators, discussions of the role of labor and management in a changing society, presidential politics, social science technology, and community counseling.

Much has been done in an impressive way by some institutions, but much more remains to be done if the community college is to develop its community service dimension on a high level.

Career and Occupational Education

The two-year college has long suffered from what Robert Finch calls the "liberal arts syndrome." The community college evolved with the promise of serving its people through programs characterized by diversity rather than by sheer intellectuality. Yet,

> It is obvious from [junior college studies] that the two-year college in America is focused more on transfer than the terminal function. If, then, the institution is adjudged unique solely on the basis of its special services to students who do not transfer, it fails to measure up (Medsker, 1960, p. 12).

The nature of the community college is predicated upon the assumption that it limit the emphasis upon transfer programs to those constituents who need them, without sacrificing the quality of these programs. It is no longer feasible to debate the relative merits of vocational and nonvocational education since the two are not competitive; they are mere phases of a single process. But although academic and vocational aspects of any program are complementary and compatible, the time has come for a clear and decisive emphasis on the vocational-technical, career-occupational role of the community college. The lack of concern for the 80 per cent who will not graduate from a four-year college causes a gross imbalance throughout education at all levels. The forces of industrialism and technology have already altered the meaning of "work" and man's relation to it. When dropouts from four-year colleges and graduates from two-year college academic programs fail to find meaningful entry jobs, they "experience underemployment rather than unemployment, and the underemployment of those with some college study heightens unemployment among those with no college work" (Venn, 1964, p. 14). Employment opportunities in the lower reaches of the job spectrum have become seriously limited, leaving no room at the bottom for those who try to enter.

In his Congressional message of March 19, 1970, President Nixon noted an imposing problem for the community college to help solve. He said:

> Critical manpower shortages exist in the United States in many skilled occupational fields such as police and fire science, environmental technology, and medical paraprofessionals. Community colleges and similar institutions have the potential to provide programs to train persons in these manpower-deficient fields. Special training like this typically costs more than general education and requires outside support.

The importance of career training was never more critical nor more problematic than at present. Department of Labor projections estimate that the youth of today will probably shift occupations some five times over the next forty years that he is in the labor market. Are any schools and colleges prepared to respond with flexible programs?

Brief attempts at college in programs with academic emphasis are insufficient for most youth. Large gaps appear in the availability of occupational curricula in two-year colleges and, taken as a whole, "American junior colleges do not give proper attention to the educational phase of their purpose. Less than a quarter of all junior college students are enrolled in organized occupational curricula" (Venn, 1964, p. 88). Perhaps we should ask, "Why?" The prolonged failure of these institutions raises doubts about their ability or willingness to meet the needs of people seeking occupational training opportunities at the postsecondary level. Many community colleges simply lack comprehensiveness and such states as New York, New Jersey, and Massachusetts have fared rather poorly in providing occupational education. The college still leans in the direction of higher education with its "symbols, procedures, folklore, and objectives." According to Gleazer, the status that the institution seeks,

> ... has to be won on another basis, because the assignment of the community college in breadth of educational services is similar now to that given another educational institution a generation or two ago--the comprehensive secondary school ... (In The Chronicle, February 26, 1968, p. 8).

The failure of educators to agree on the place of vocational education in the schools during the 1890's has increasingly encouraged a developing dualism that still isolates and disparages education that is not purely academic. Human dignity has yet to be adjudged for certain kinds of human activity. John Gardner (1961) recognized the dilemma of values in his famed treatise on excellence:

> We must learn to honor excellence, indeed demand it, in every socially accepted human activity, however humble the activity, and to scorn shoddiness however exalted the activity. An excellent plumber is infinitely more admirable than an incompetent philosopher, and the society which scorns excellence in plumbing because plumbing is a humble activity and tolerates shoddiness in philosophy because philosophy is an exalted activity will have neither good plumbers nor good philosophers, and neither its pipes nor its theories will hold water.

The National Advisory Council on Vocational Education was extremely critical of vocational education in American education in its first annual report ("Vocational Education," 1970). With representatives of many groups, including the two-year college, the Council concluded that there is a national prejudice against vocational training, and further, that more than 60 per cent of those who graduate from high school do not receive any additional vocational training, thus making them "ill-prepared for useful work." Federal funding continues to favor academic programs over vocational ones, with budgets in a ratio of about fourteen to one respectively. Where Federal funds are made available, they tend to be earmarked for material and equipment, but not for personnel to make full use of it (Bock, 1968).

The 1963 Vocational Education Act gave impetus to the community college by requiring that training under the Act be focused upon gainful employment as the goal of vocational education. The Vocational Education Amendments of 1968 are significant since they direct funds to aid ghetto and inner-city youth; to equip disadvantaged and handicapped persons with employable skills; to develop new programs; and to form a partnership with business, industry, and education with work-study occupational schools, some even with dormitory facilities. Notably, the newer legislation is providing for "people" categories in local communities and includes the disadvantaged, physically and mentally handicapped, and the socioeconomic disadvantaged, among others. Through its funding patterns, the Federal Government has increased social pluralism while reducing isolationism. The Federal influence has also raised the educational level of people and programs (Vaccaro, 1968). As the community college adapts to this pluralistic approach to community interests, the impact of Federal funding on program planning will have to be assessed very carefully.

In order to qualify for increased financial aid in career education programs, James Allen would have the community college operate under an open door policy and facilitate student transfer between occupational and academic programs, and between vocational and career education programs (In The Chronicle, November 24, 1969, p. 2). He suggests that community college programs be designed to blend with other relevant education programs and facilities, including secondary schools, colleges and universities, and community education programs. But coordination has often been a problem when industry cooperates with the two-year college (Hayes, 1969). Major difficulties with work-study programs have included:

1. A lack of coordinated supervision by the college and employer;
2. Little relation of college courses to job experience;
3. Conflicts in work and class schedules;
4. Student over-interest with salary; and
5. Occasional poor placement of students.

Paramedical programs have not enjoyed the support they deserve because "doctors do not understand the community college and are skeptical. They still equate length of training with equality of education" (Menefee and Cornejo, 1969, p. 9). Despite initial fears that paramedics might make errors of medical judgment, experience shows that this is not the case. California has already enacted legislation to permit physician's assistants to work, provided they are under a doctor's supervision. Getting the professionals and the public to accept technicians such as physical therapists and cobalt technicians is still a problem for the community college. In 1969, the one-year Certified Laboratory Assistant program was the only laboratory technician program to be fully recognized by the profession. Professionals who help to develop paramedical programs continue to differ sharply in their opinions of the tasks that are essential to practitioners. Until this can be overcome, Fullerton (1966) wisely suggests that common courses be identified and integrated as the basis for all paramedical education.

In some areas of training there is danger of overtraining or causing students to repeat courses if they transfer from certificate to degree programs. For example, the Registered Nurse training program is increasing in scope while the Licensed Practical Nursing program remains more basic and usually not acceptable to the degree program. Laboratory assistants are certified by an examining board, as are registered nurses, but the latter have a higher rate of failure in passing state nursing examinations--even higher than three and four-year trainees. To a certain degree, this is expected because associate degree nursing programs were primarily designed for bedside nurses. (Skaggs, 1969).

More concern is needed to make transition easier between different programs by designing each program as a stepping-stone to others where possible. Four-year colleges are even designing one-, two-, and three-year programs to which community college students may transfer. For example, Duke University offers paramedic studies which range from community health to bacteriology and psychosomatic medicine, plus techniques such as regulating intravenous infusions and operating respirators. The University of Colorado offers a child health associate program for candidates with two years of college. In this program, students take two additional years of training in anatomy, genetics, nutrition and other basics, then spend a third year interning at health centers and in doctors' offices. Colorado recruits intensively among minority and disadvantaged high school students.

In a different approach, the Office of Economic Opportunity is funding training programs for mature family health workers who need only the equivalent of a fifth-grade education. Many students are recruited directly from welfare roles. The trainees learn to incorporate some of the functions of the public health nurse, the lawyer, social worker, physician, and health educator. They make house calls and are trained to help people negotiate with welfare and other agencies to get the help they need. Bachelor of Medicine programs are also contemplated to qualify students for research and teaching positions. With this concern for training and staffing at all levels, the community college is desperately in need of trained, capable personnel to plan and coordinate appropriate programs.

New roles are developing at all levels in medicine to support the scientist, technologist, technician, and laboratory assistant. To some extent, the importance of the job is inversely related to job status. Thus, the laboratory technician becomes a vital link or specialist in the clinical process. Many of the diagnostic and clinical aspects of everyday medical treatment can be expected to be carried out by physician's assistants rather than the professional physician or specialist. Hopefully, salaries will be commensurate with responsibility.

With automation and specialization on the increase, care must be exercised in the selection of students for health programs. Having an autoanalyzer that can perform thirty-six blood and urine tests for twelve samples at one time, within a minute, is going to necessitate some paramedics to function as Biomedical Equipment Engineers. This will require that students have suitable temperaments and other personal abilities beyond the required academic ones. (Menefee and Cornejo, 1969).

Availability of suitable students and appropriate work experiences must be considered in planning career programs. Starting with Patient Care programs, the community college usually provides training for related programs such as Medical Secretary, Medical Record-keeping, Medical Laboratory Assistant, Emergency Medical Technician, and Hospital Ward Manager. Other areas in need of program development relate to dental surgery, emergency rooms, ambulances, and geriatric centers, with demand for personnel generally exceeding the supply. With more than sixty types of health-related programs offered in the community college, nursing remains among the most popular, with only about one-half of all qualified nursing trainees ever entering hospitals and clinics for employment. Usually they accept more lucrative positions in home nursing or industry. Even when Optical Technician programs produced technical assistants for opticians, salary and working conditions attracted them elsewhere. (Skaggs, 1969).

It is estimated that 20 per cent of our population need the services of mental technicians (Menefee and Cornejo, 1969). Further, two technicians are needed for every engineer or physical scientist; six to ten technicians for every doctor or health researcher; and four or five technicians for each biological scientist. The main thrust of science and engineering programs at the two-year level includes those for civil, electrical, mechanical, and chemical engineering technicians. To a certain extent, these programs have been able to meet the needs of students unable to follow rigid two-year sequences in programming. But very often, students who become technicians in the physical sciences go on to baccalaureate programs. To this end, Bachelor of Technology programs are beginning to emerge in several universities. (Menefee and Cornejo, 1969).

The range of career and technical programs is growing rapidly despite temporary problems. With growing numbers of vocationally trained persons, the National Commission of Technology, Automation, and Economic Progress recommended to the President and Congress that a computerized, nationwide service be established to match people with appropriate work experiences (Kellogg, 1967). The Civil Service Commission also took cognizance of the growing occupational force by instituting the Junior Federal Assistant Examination. This is in direct response to needs of community college graduates and other persons with equivalent combinations of experience and education. The GS-4 classification is designed for positions such as computer technician, tax examiner, statistical assistant, accounting technician, and library technician. (Read, 1969).

Improved public relations programs are needed to raise the image and prestige of vocational education with students, parents, and industry. With professionals already regarding vocational nurses, engineering technicians, and dental assistants as suspect, it was not unexpected that others would also question the more recent positions of library technical assistant and teacher aide. The professional has a "self-righteous approach" which presumes that the paraprofessional may go beyond his authority (Bock, 1968). For example, each program that set out to provide library technical training was affected by resistance and lack of professional support from various library associations and graduate library schools (Giles and McClaskey, 1968). The

American Library Association took the position that the training of library clerks or assistants should not be encouraged in the community college for several reasons, some of which include:

1. Poor success in existing programs;

2. Opposition of the New York Library Association Personnel Committee;

3. Lack of standards;

4. Demands of subject and language knowledge require a college education;

5. Courses would not transfer to undergraduate or graduate library training programs;

6. In-service or short courses were preferable; and

7. Library routines varied too much.

Part of the problem was the inability of the profession to clearly delineate its own tasks. The American Library Association, in trying to establish behavioral objectives for librarians, found that many fears grew out of uncertainty in role perceptions among professionals. (Bock, 1968).

Only eleven states have policies or guidelines pertaining to the role of instructional aides. With little agreement about what constitutes teaching and nonteaching functions, no clear directions have emerged in policies relating to teacher aides. One of Pennsylvania's first teaching aide programs failed at Harrisburg Community College because high school teachers were unable to agree on the role of the teaching aide and potential students never really learned the nature of the position. The use of temporary Federal funding also proved to be inadequate and detrimental in supporting teaching aide programs.

California's Instructional Aide Act of 1968 is a pacesetter. It decrees that instructional aides perform tasks which, "in the judgment of the certified personnel to whom the instructional aide is assigned, may be performed by a person not licensed as a teacher" (Tanner, 1969). In effect, the law permits school districts to employ non-certified personnel to assist teachers in the supervision and instruction of students (Roth, 1969). Some defined tasks would permit aides to grade themes and act as an intermediary for teachers and students. Instructional aides and auxiliary personnel are accepted as paraprofessionals who can perform various classical tasks, set up laboratories, grade objective tests, record grades, operate audio-visual equipment, tutor, counsel, and offer clerical-secretarial services to facilitate the teaching process. Many community colleges train these personnel as auxiliary aides as part of a general trend toward liberalizing staffing problems. A second purpose, according to Weisz (1968), is to provide "a career ladder for disadvantaged candidates who are chosen through schools, social agencies, and community programs on the basis of sensitivity, flexibility, self-esteem, social adaptability, sense of responsibility and leadership, and acceptance of authority."

The field of public service is becoming more significant to community college program planners since research shows that personnel demands in this area are not being met adequately. The U.S. Office of Education suggests a definition for public service occupations which actually merges the functions of community service and career training as follows:

> Public service occupations are those occupations pursued by persons performing the functions necessary to accomplish the missions of local, county, state and federal government. These missions reflect the services desired or needed by individuals and groups ... and are performed through arrangements or organizations established by society, normally on a nonprofit basis and usually supported by tax revenues (In Institute for Local Self-Government, 1969, p. 3).

One out of six workers employed are in government occupations, and recent projects indicate that state and local government manpower requirements will rise at a rate greater than that of the overall labor force. The community college finds itself as a prime agency to train, retrain, and upgrade needed manpower. At Berkeley, the Institute for Local Self-Government concerns itself with the role of the community college in providing public service education and training in the belief that:

... it is essential to fully utilize this educational resource for that purpose. The community college is uniquely suited to this purpose. They can provide for those interested in local government public services in technical and subprofessional occupations.

With one of the largest systems of higher education anywhere, California's community colleges created the unique position of Consultant in Public Service Occupations to explore and collect data related to job opportunities, employment, and future occupational needs as a service to the public. Related public service careers are defined in the <u>Directory of Occupational Titles</u> as "government services and any related occupations performed primarily in the public domain." In general, these careers fit two broad classifications: human services and municipal services. "Human service" programs involve training and education in knowledge and skills related to interviewing techniques, report writing, counseling, interpersonal skills and behavioral knowledge. In addition, graduates are trained to identify community resources, to understand intergovernmental relationships, and to know the local and expanded community. Specific human service positions include teacher assistant, instructional aide, special education aide, nursery school aide, library technician, library clerk, technical assistant, group counselor, social service assistant, counselor assistant, correctional program assistant, employment community worker, and instructional media specialist. (Institute, 1969).

"Municipal service" programs involve a specialty skill and on-the-job training followed by in-service experience. Educational training includes the social sciences and interpersonal relationships. Programs utilize the services of technicians and semiprofessionals in varied municipal service. Typical positions include city planning technician, urban development officer, travel agent, steward, professional guide, airport operations, stewardess, communications programmer, announcer, dispatcher, and technician-aides in safety, traffic, and recreation areas. Undoubtedly, the consultant in public service occupations will grow to become a position of national significance in meeting the urban crisis.

Many career programs receive undue opposition and fail to achieve national recognition because of misplaced convictions in the Department of Health, Education, and Welfare; U.S. Office of Education; Department of Justice; National

Science Foundation; Departments of Labor and Transportation; and the U.S. Public Health Service. While traffic engineering and several paramedic programs are recognized nationally, much remains to be done in training paraprofessionals for environmental control, general aviation, social welfare, marine technology, recreation, consumer and legal aid positions. (Menefee and Cornejo, 1969).

In 1958, no associate degree police science programs were found outside of California, but by 1969 there were more than two hundred. Local government is in need of trained persons for careers in traffic and fire science also. As might be expected, community college graduates in the vital areas of police science, criminal corrections, and traffic control are quickly absorbed into four-year colleges for advanced degrees and roles that remove them further from the people whom they were trained to serve.

New careers are being formed in the trucking industry which needs trained drivers, inspectors, and dispatchers. The apparel industry calls upon community colleges such as the Fashion Institute of Technology (New York) to train people for positions as designers, buyers, plant engineers, plant managers, models, and costing analysts. Even the largest mortuary science program for funeral directors can be found in the community college.

Still, the future of the 60 per cent of unemployed persons who never finish high school (Kohler, 1965) is uncertain. The unemployed constitute a national resource with untapped potential. The low and middle socioeconomic groups are even more likely to complete occupational programs than are those of high status, but this fact is not recognized in program planning. The community college is failing in the important function of helping academic program dropouts to reassess their goals rather than withdraw (Hakanson, 1967). Formal schooling periods are often lengthened as dissatisfied students pass from college to college while switching "majors" in an attempt to discover their limitations and abilities. To this end, the community college should be prepared to bring students to a better understanding of their aptitudes and potential in a manner which makes them cognizant of their own responsibilities for the degree to which they commit themselves. (Hakanson, 1967).

Some communities find that "certain vocational programs are not only unnecessary, but inadvisable." (Henry, 1956).

As with other college programs, occupational curricula must be matched to local needs and institutional resources. Industry and commerce should be asked to provide better work-study arrangements, some teachers, and additional part-time and full-time employment. The instructional staff could easily be strengthened with experts from business and industry, with many programs being held in factories, plants, banks, and hospitals rather than on campus. The under-utilization of industry and government, including resources and personnel, has been all too prevalent. Care must be exercised to insure that career programs remain flexible rather than prepackaged in a closed or terminal sequence. Above all, they must withstand the traditional fears of transferability which are often unrelated to the needs of the individual and his proposed work. (Menefee and Cornejo, 1969).

Occupational programs must still coincide with academic programs while satisfying the requirements of industry, community, college, students, and faculty. As students are attracted to programs, financial aid should be made available along with work-entry positions and a skilled career counselor. It is simply inadequate to place the responsibility for career programs in the hands of well-intentioned amateurs. Expertise is necessary to plan, coordinate, and articulate programs that work. The task is too much for one person and can hardly be made an extra assignment for a dean or director; nor should it be lumped peripherally with evening, summer, night, and part-time programs. Much of the failure that is encountered with unsuccessful career programs can usually be traced to inept leadership and a genuine lack of concern on the part of those who operate the programs. Only a systems approach to program development and implementation can provide the range of talent and resources necessary for improving quality.

Career programs must not get bogged down with licensing, certification, and degree problems. Above all, vocational, occupational, and technical programs must never sacrifice their general education component; liberal education will always include a technical education and vice-versa. Unless the community college can break with tradition to a much greater extent than demonstrated so far, new forms of education are inevitable.

Amid the popularity of career programs at the community college level, it must not be forgotten that this stage of learning is but one step on the career ladder. The step immediately below provides a firm foundation with its own kind of work opportunities for persons with less than four years of college. The Federal Government and private industry are quite determined to promote more than 25 Technical Careers You Can Learn in Two Years or Less. With only a year or two of technical training at technical institutes, area vocational-technical schools, or community colleges, productive technical careers can be started.

Even high school graduates are still afforded a chance to enter worthwhile careers directly after graduation. The Department of Labor discusses its position as follows:

> Workers having a high school education or less outnumber those having a college education three to one. Postsecondary training is becoming an increasingly common requirement for many technician jobs. However, many jobs will be open to well-qualified high school graduates. The job outlook is very favorable for service workers including hospital attendants, cooks, practical nurses, firemen, policemen, waiters, and beauticians. Particularly promising positions for craftsmen include business machine repairmen, air conditioning and refrigeration mechanics, TV and radio repairmen, and appliance servicemen. Skilled occupations will experience an acceleration in the demand for foremen and building trades craftsmen. While employment of sales workers is expected to rise fairly rapidly, employment in clerical occupations is expected to rise only for a substantial number of these jobs.... In 1975, the bulk of job openings will be accessible still to high school graduates with proper training (In Flanders, 1968).

It is simply not true that high school level vocational programs do not prepare students for the labor market (Buckels, 1970). It is true, however, that further training would open greater opportunities for these people. In planning for career education programs, we cannot overlook the needs of that 28 per cent who never graduate from high school and that 50 per cent of high school graduates who attempt to enter the labor market directly upon graduation from high school. Strong coordinated programs at high school and community college levels could provide these people with salable skills which permit various entry levels into business and industry.

The "bigoted, biased view of vocational education in this country today" must be recognized for what it is and what it is doing, concludes Kenneth Hoyt (1970), Director of Student Research Programs at the University of Maryland's College of Education. He calls on the community college to eradicate this prejudice with the following proposals:

    1. Eliminate the artificial requirements of liberal arts courses for those who wish vocational education.

    2. Eliminate the artificial length of course requirements for those in vocational education.

    3. Eliminate the artificial limited enrollment dates for vocational education students.

    4. Recognize and capitalize on the contributions of secondary school vocational education.

    5. Resist attempts to impose process-oriented accreditation standards on the product-oriented programs of vocational education in the community college.

    6. Campaign actively for a financial base of operation that recognizes the higher per student cost of vocational education.

    7. Eliminate the practice of basing vocational and technical education curricular offerings on local labor market needs.

    8. Engage in meaningful efforts aimed at evaluation of vocational-technical education in the community college setting.

    9. Work vigorously to both open doors of the community college wider and to ensure that every student is treated with equal respect and dignity (p. 37).

With too many community colleges concerned about raising standards they cannot define for reasons they cannot defend, Hoyt (1970) concludes that a national assessment would show urgent need for their improvement. Needless to say, if the community college is to change the current inequities in career education, it must continue to change itself also.

Student Personnel Services

Existing models of student personnel work are grounded in regulatory, servicing, therapeutic, and social aspects of schooling. Transposed directly from high schools and universities, current practices are often overly concerned with the traditional nonacademic functions of extracurricular activities, athletics, physical facilities, student welfare, and socialization. To a certain extent, these services extend adolescence and incomplete adulthood for young students by providing an artificial environment somewhere between school and society. While European higher education institutions continue to remove themselves from directly providing nonacademic student needs, the American institutions continue to get more involved. If the extent of student personnel involvement is an indication of student need, then there should be great alarm about the physical, spiritual, moral, and mental condition of our students. More and better student personnel services should be producing fewer and less urgent problems for students.

The prevalent model of providing student personnel services in the community college is through a series of scattered and often unrelated services for financial aid, registration, admissions, parking, student activities, student records, and health services, among others. Moreover, activities that do not fit elsewhere are often grouped with student personnel services. These often include dramatics, student publications such as a newspaper and yearbook, student government, and social organizations. Usually, a dean is given the responsibility for keeping the program in operation and his role becomes one of managing the resources and inertia of the entire process. After analyzing the many services and functions that are performed in the community and junior college, a national advisory committee concluded on a sad but realistic note:

> The conclusion of these studies may be put bluntly: when measured against criteria of scope and effectiveness, student personnel programs in community junior colleges are woefully inadequate (McConnell, 1965).

Student personnel services have too long been focused on program rather than process. The "whole" program takes on more importance than the "whole" student. There is a general failure to recognize that many students are capable of conducting their own programs as long as reasonable resources are readily available, not necessarily within the school. Student personnel services in the community college serve purposes that cannot be "sold" to students, especially since more than half of these students are well over age twenty-one and far removed from their availability. Indeed, many student services are clearly designed for eighteen-year-old, full-time, day students who comprise a prestigious minority to whom most faculty are dedicated.

The community college all too easily allows the related functions of guidance, counseling, teaching, and learning to grow separate and distinct. Teachers operate in separate areas independent of counselors who usually work out of isolated cubicles. Teachers remain ignorant of the guidance-counseling function and counselors have all but disassociated themselves from the teaching process to retain a sense of neutrality. More bluntly, teachers do not care very much for counselors, whom they see operating empathetically in a vacuum; and counselors hardly appreciate teachers, who bring about or relate to most student problems. In a certain sense, teaching and student personnel services are parallel, but separate and unequal.

Part of the problem that relates to obtaining more meaningful student personnel programs is the inability of those in the profession to agree on a sense of purpose and a professional program of training. Two critics once summed the status of training as follows:

> Three groups of guidance-personnel workers have taken, and still maintain, different stands on the question of training. One group supports a liberal education-oriented program; another advocates technical training, with an increased number of specialities; and the third, no specialized training in guidance-personnel work or education, but simply advanced academic preparation. Out of this lack have grown the modern issues ... the issues that arise out of the content of guidance-personnel training are apparent. What body of information and skills should every personnel worker have before he is considered to be trained? What should be

the balance in guidance-personnel training programs between the liberal and technical offerings? What information and skills from related fields are rightfully a part of the subject matter of guidance-personnel training programs? How can materials from other fields best be integrated into these programs? (Barry and Wolf, 1958).*

More recently, a Survey of Requirements for a Doctoral Program in Higher Education (Palinchak, et al., 1970) revealed that student personnel programs are nationally held in low esteem. Said one respondent, "I think this is an inflated field of dubious value; perhaps one course would take care of it." In general, serious concern is still raised about the value of the student personnel function throughout higher education.

Though many generalizations are made about community college students and many of these accepted as facts, there is still much to be uncovered with better data, evidence, and information (Berdie, 1966). Despite long-standing disagreements concerning its service, the need for improved guidance and counseling was generally felt to be greater in the two-year college than in senior institutions (Weersing and Koos, 1929-30; Kemp, 1930). Nevertheless, teachers, students, and counselors openly contribute to the current weaknesses in student personnel programs. Terry O'Banion (1969a) lists some of these weaknesses as follows:

1. Some personnel programs are peripheral and lack clear goals;
2. The dean of students often has too many other duties;
3. Staff members often feel a lack of professional identity;
4. There is inadequate staffing and funding;
5. Teachers do not appreciate the program;
6. There is little in-service training or innovation;
7. The staff lacks time for personal and vocational counseling;
8. Students are apathetic; and
9. Seldom are transfers or dropouts pursued with follow-up studies.

---
*Reprinted by permission of the publisher from Ruth Barry and Beverly Wolf, Modern Issues in Guidance-Personnel Work. (New York: Teachers College Press, copyright 1957 by Teachers College, Columbia University), p. 88.

The early factors that brought the positions of "monitor," "matron," and "warden" into student personnel work are no longer prevalent. Many of the needs that student personnel workers attempt to fill are, in effect, still brought about by faculty who abdicate much of their responsibility to students in the teaching-learning process. However, the student personnel profession is now seeking identity and prestige among professional educators in a manner similar to the community college's search for identity in higher education. For too long, student personnel workers have "assumed a stance and authority that is protected only by administrative sanction." Often pedantic and narrow in scope, the student personnel profession has produced little substantive research or innovation, thus causing others to view it as "anti-intellectual and unnecessary." Except for sporadic but notable exceptions, a growing conglomeration of student personnel services is rapidly becoming an end in itself rather than a means.

If student personnel services are to be an accepted part of the community college program, a major overhaul is in order. Students require a personalized college experience which can best occur when the teaching-guidance-counseling functions are brought closer together. The high school stigma that characterizes the guidance function must be dispelled by professionals who are trained to know the limitations of the function as it applies to vocational, personal, academic, and social problems of students. The testing and personal assessment function, while conducted by student personnel staff, is probably more useful to the faculty if only they could be sensitized to the information revealed.

The field of counseling still raises several questions about the competence necessary to perform this task. Jones (1969) seriously questions whether guidance counselors should practice psychotherapy and suggests that trained psychologists should be part of the community college staff. Vocational and academic counseling is a particularly vague area that needs greater coordination. In one sense, counseling must be seen as the generic tool of the personnel worker and, in a larger sense, as a philosophy and way of life. However, professional counseling is a demanding clinical experience that requires the expertise of doctoral-level counseling psychologists. Amateur approaches in counseling and sensitivity sessions should be avoided.

Counseling services are often overlooked for evening,

adult, part-time students and the growing number of those high school graduates who vacillate and make late decisions to enter a community college. That the students are "unsure" is demonstrated by the fact that only two-thirds of the transfer group and less than one-half of the occupational group ever make plans to attend a community college (Brue, et al., 1971).

The lower socioeconomic level of occupationally-oriented males must be recognized and aided with specific job and financial assistance. It must also be recognized that black male students demonstrate a dire need to express their masculinity and counselors must help them to adjust to new college and social structures (New Challenges, 1970). Personal dignity and personal identity are interpreted differently by different kinds of students and the counselor must adjust his actions to these differences.

Fragmented guidance-personnel services tend to disorient students while raising their anxiety. Many current student personnel programs might be improved if they were temporarily discontinued and then reworked to conform to demonstrated student needs. The changing needs of students can readily give rise to relevant services or programs which, in turn, could periodically be reorganized in a grass-roots approach rather than from the top down. To a great extent, many counseling-personnel functions are needed in the community to help people cope with social mobility, and bigness in labor, industry, government, and business (Marsee, 1968). The student personnel worker can also serve to enhance the open door policy by acting as a change agent with the professional staff and the public. As counselor to the community (Heiner, 1969), the community college will rely more and more on the student personnel staff to assert themselves in community problems and social issues by offering their services openly as a part of the college program. In this way, the college acts as a barometer to measure social pressure and as an outlet from which social action can be initiated.

Disadvantaged students often need help with personal, financial, and family problems, and this requires trained college personnel to interrelate with social, medical, psychiatric, and governmental agencies. As liaison between lay people and professionals, student personnel workers can recruit promising students in their own neighborhoods (Grant, 1968), and devise totally new remedial efforts to meet the needs of classless, forgotten, and disenfranchised people. Many blacks and minorities should be encouraged to become student personnel workers. However, to maintain credibility with the common academic community, student personnel workers should acquire a strong academic background in the traditional sense before entering the field of student personnel work.

Not all college trained graduates have the ability, tolerance, sense of purpose, and physical stamina to work in the student personnel area. The community college must define for itself what its tasks are and what kinds of people can best serve its needs. People without degrees or certification may be useful in this endeavor if they have a record of substantial promise or experience. With the individual in mind, student personnel workers must see that programs really work and people relate to overall college purposes. Faculty only see the college in a piecemeal fashion. Student personnel workers should relate as generalists among the specialists: seeing that the output of the community college matches its input.

The Committee on the Student in Higher Education (1968) concludes that most college students have three major needs:

> 1. Each student needs to acquire a positive and realistic conception of his own abilities in the world of higher learning and in the world at large.
>
> 2. He needs to reach the point of being able to see the structure and interrelations of knowledge in order to start forming judgments on his own.
>
> 3. He needs to see the relevance of higher learning to the quality of his own life and to see that life in relation to the new kinds of judgments he now makes (p. 10).

Both the faculty and student personnel staff share in this broad responsibility.

In reflecting on the superfluous nature of student personnel services, a university dean likened them to a fifth wheel on the educational cart. In a spirit of defensiveness, William Cowley agreed, but said it was the steering wheel. Out of new guidelines, "Many of the old, cherished ideas that guided student personnel workers are being questioned, remodeled, or cast aside as no longer 'relevant' to this day" (Ravekes, 1969). But, at the present time, community college "student personnel work is still in a state of confusion" (O'Banion, et al., 1970). The opportunity and necessity that favored a different approach for the community college are passing. Nevertheless, the urgency for a different approach to the student personnel service dilemma remains.

Like teachers, student personnel workers must develop new styles to match the needs of the open door college. But as the Southern Regional Education Board forcefully concluded, the open door concept has not met with success (New Challenges, 1970). With all of its ramifications, the open door philosophy has at the same time been accepted and rejected by the community college.

Chapter 4

THE STUDENT CLIENTELE

Those who are served by the community college best characterize its uniqueness. Yet, descriptive studies of the student clientele are often inconclusive and paradoxical. With the most diverse clientele in higher education, the community college serves people who are more representative of society than any other institution of higher learning: the many categories include young students, adults, veterans, skilled workers, the disadvantaged, blacks, and "transfer" or "terminal" students, among others.

It is incorrect and misleading to view this college clientele in the traditional academic sense. There is no "typical" or "average" community college student as often portrayed in the literature. Most research in this area has concentrated on the transfer aspects of student programs while generally ignoring comparative and remedial populations, dropouts, occupational students, adults, part-time, night, and continuing education students. It remains blatantly difficult to change traditional academic inquiries that seek to describe only those students who are young, academic, full-time, transfer-oriented, day students. Even when other than traditional college students are described, they are blandly categorized as ancillary components of a lesser and peripheral process. Standard academic values continue to relegate certain kinds of students to a second-class status, even in the community college. The frequent connotation attached to "student" is somewhat derogatory and disparaging.

The lack of a common base for analysis makes it difficult to develop a comprehensive profile of those who are served by the community college. Students get involved with community college programs for a multitude of reasons, only some of which are purely academic. Not all work for degrees and transfer status, despite the glamour attached to such programs in popular surveys. Our academic sense of values tends to ridicule and embarrass persons who might classify themselves as nonstudents or poor, marginal, dumb, disadvantaged, high-risk students. It is the calcified thinking of the standard academic mind that continues to promote a singular, monolithic excellence while relegating all else to a lesser status.

Within certain parameters, it is feasible to construct a general student profile based on such characteristics as educational aspirations, academic aptitude, socioeconomic background, and personality traits. While generalizations of this type are of limited value, they can serve to correct mistaken notions based on information of even lesser value. What follows is a brief review of several erudite studies that have specifically concentrated on the postsecondary student and are offered in an attempt to generalize a profile.

Developing A Profile

Open-door learning has generated a highly uncommon clientele. While this is appalling to many educators, Arthur W. Chickering suggests that:

> The most productive educational outcomes for the individual and for the country probably take place in those 'Podunk' colleges where the proportion of uncommon or non-traditional students is high and where, because of their numbers, they are recognized, encouraged, and helped (In The Chronicle, January 11, 1971, p. 1).

Further, he concludes that the success of a college is highly dependent upon what happens to those students who stay in college, particularly those who are not ready for the experience. He feels that "the college which helps such students to survive, and to accelerate their own achievement through their struggle to survive, makes a significant contribution."

In this new spirit, the community college has opened its doors to such great numbers of people that, according to a U.S. Census Bureau study, two-thirds of today's college youth have parents who did not attend college themselves (In The Chronicle, February 15, 1971, p. 3). The percentage of increase for students enrolled in all two-year colleges was 86.3 per cent in the period from 1960 to 1965. For four-year colleges during that same period, the enrollment increased only 49.7 per cent (Digest of Educational Statistics,

1969). Due to the number of returning Armed Forces veterans, an expansion of career programs, and a backlash against campus unrest in senior colleges, some 1,100 two-year colleges enrolled 2.4 million students in 1970 (In The Chronicle, December 14, 1970, p. 5).

Less than seven decades ago, it was recognized that different kinds of students would attend secondary schools for various reasons. Included were those who would:

1. Go to a traditional college;
2. Complete high school, then take a vocation;
3. Not finish high school, but take a vocation;
4. Quit after compulsory age or soon thereafter and take a profession;
5. Quit after compulsory age.

(Davis, 1911).

Aside from the first category, the community college was destined to be concerned primarily with alternative options in its mission to transform the dependent being into the independent, self-directed individual.

In 1969, the American College Testing Program surveyed more than four thousand community and junior college sophomores and found that the "typical" student attends high school just prior to enrolling at college and enters a transfer program. He sees his vocational interest to be of primary importance. The student reports few extracurricular activities and nonacademic achievements. He finances his education by working and by receiving outside financial support. As might be expected, a minimum of time is actually spent on campus. Still, working and commuting do not seriously interfere with learning activities and general satisfaction with college (A.C.T. Program, 1969a).

While still in high school, students of low socioeconomic status report experiences which reinforce handicaps to educational achievement (Bowles and Slocum, 1968). Vocational-business students generally reveal lower self-images when compared to academic, college-oriented students. Even though they are somewhat bored with high school, they still choose fields related to their interest or prior training. As many as 65 per cent of high school seniors expect to attend a post-secondary institution, according to Lins (1969). However, only 12 per cent expect to attend a vocational-technical-adult school. Fourteen per cent in the top quartile and 21 per cent in the upper half of graduating classes do not even expect to continue in post-secondary education immediately after high school. Twenty per cent indicate an interest in immediate employment while 10 per cent of the males plan to enter military service (Lins, 1969).

More than fifty years ago, Koos demonstrated in his investigation of junior colleges that 50 per cent more graduates go on to college if local facilities are provided. And, in 1946, Philip Cowen published A Study of Factors Related to Attendance in New York State, which revealed that "the presence of a college in a community seems to about double the percentage of youth who attend college from the local area." On the other hand, A Longitudinal Study of the Barriers Affecting the Pursuit of Higher Education by New York State High School Seniors (1969) concluded that the proximity of two-year colleges does not materially affect the college-going rate. Only when a two-year college and a four-year college are both available is the college-going rate raised significantly. Despite what appears to be conflicting evidence, it is quite safe to assume that attendance rates are generally higher among students from low socioeconomic backgrounds in those communities that have community colleges. Further, communities that only have university extension centers show about the same rate of college attendance as do communities with no college at all. Therefore, the community college is indeed attracting many students who would otherwise not pursue post-secondary education.

The Florida Community Junior College Inter-institutional Research Council (1969) reports that the "average" student attends a local college immediately following high school, takes more than two years to earn his Associate's degree, is gainfully employed, graduates from the college he enters, chooses transfer programs in order to major in education or arts-sciences, and feels positive about his community college experience. Two-thirds of these students expect to transfer to a baccalaureate program and more than one-quarter even anticipate entering graduate school ("Opinions," 1970). However, only one-third of the students actually transfer to a four-year college.

At present, the community college clientele resembles a group that encompasses all other educational systems more than one that fits between high school and college. Men still outnumber women and almost half of all students are married. About 50 per cent of the students are under twenty years of age, while 16 per cent are reported to be over thirty years of age (Read, 1969).

A major characteristic of all community college students is the fervent desire to explore and experiment with various programs and courses of study. And the factor most related to persistence is motivational in nature, as reported by Trent and Medsker (1968). A lack of general interest generated by unrealistic goals and low self-confidence proves to be a troublesome, but common, attribute of the postsecondary student. The institution is seen as a means to an end and interest in extracurricular activities inevitably is lacking.

A strong commitment to vocational-occupational education is generally demonstrated by older or mature students. The tendency for these students to comprise a growing segment of the community college clientele has created a bimodal age distribution with a median age of about twenty-seven. Furthermore, the number of students entering the community college directly from high school is rapidly on the decline in many parts of the country while the number of part-time students is rapidly increasing in proportion to the number of full-time students. It is not unusual for less than 40 per cent of the applicants for admission to come from members of the most recent high school graduating classes. Implications for the future suggest that less permanent types of facilities are in order, with the "college" going to the people within their own habitat. New styles of delivering instruction are critically needed to meet the new demands.

Academic climates are generally recognized to relate in some manner to the nature of student clienteles. Pace (1968) developed the Environmental Assessment Technique (E.A.T.) based on this assertion, which claims that the college environment is a product of its size, the average intelligence of its students, and the personality characteristics of students. From one of his studies, Pace concludes that "junior colleges" tend to have low scores on measures of Scholarship and Awareness; average scores on a Community dimension; and above average scores on Propriety and Practicality. The academic atmosphere is reportedly more congruent than divergent among two-year and four-year college populations according to data from the American Council on Education Psychological Examination (Medsker, 1960). As with other college students, the community college student is expected to exhibit "general ability, motivation, time, commitment, interest, aptitudes, and skills" to succeed (Cook, et al., 1968). However, such expectations are not always borne to fruition.

According to the American College Testing Program (1969a), the community college faculty must relate to a broader range of ability than their colleagues in a "typical" four-year college. Students with high ability are reported to be comparable in two-year and four-year colleges, but students with less ability are always found on the lower end of the community college continuum. With so much diversity found in the community college, good students at one institution may be poor students elsewhere. The A. C. T. report (1969a) also demonstrates a pressing need to correct deficiencies in skill areas such as reading, composition, arithmetic, listening, speech, and study habits. It is in this area that the community college fails to demonstrate much originality and creativity to meet an obvious challenge.

Serious problems still exist in articulation procedures related to transferability of courses, credits, and grades. Furthermore, transfer students generally experience other academic, personal, and social adjustment problems during their first semester after transfer (Flax, 1968); however, most differences tend to disappear during the junior-senior years when the transfer students perform comparably to native students. Unfortunately, with quality point averages, prestige, and status problems, direct rewards are often too slow in coming for this group's value system (Bossen, 1968).

Four general conclusions emerge from studies concerning public two-year college transfer students:

> 1. [Transfer students from community colleges achieve] records about the same as those made by transfers from four-year colleges and by native students, sometimes better, sometimes worse. They usually show a drop in grade point average in the first term after transfer but then recover that loss.

> 2. [Community] college transfers retain their relative scholastic standing after transfer that they held before transfer. Those that were high stay high; those that were low stay low.

3. There is clear evidence that [community] colleges are salvaging a large number of students for success in advanced studies. [These students] would otherwise have missed them entirely.

4. There is variation, sometimes wide, in the findings in different senior institutions and also between [community] colleges in the same state. Such variation presents problems to those institutions that seek to maintain a uniform policy for recognition of the [community colleges] of the state. [Generally, community] college transfers have [performed] so satisfactorily that doubts about the quality of [two-year] college preparation for advanced study no longer exist.
(The Public Junior College, The Fifty-fifth Yearbook of the National Society for the Study of Education, Nelson B. Henry, ed., 1956).

In response to a broad survey (A.C.T. Program, 1969a), community college students surprisingly revealed that the college is accomplishing its various tasks for the diversified clientele. To a certain extent, this response represents an incomplete view of the community college ideology and a false sense of satisfaction as held by students and others. For example, when the period of institutional development was at its height, student activism was highly dormant. But this has now changed. A report about The Scope of Organized Student Protest in Junior Colleges (Gaddy, 1970) reveals that 37.7 per cent of 613 two-year colleges experienced organized protest during 1968-1969. A total of 1,586 protests occurred at 231 two-year colleges. Most of these protests were at public community colleges and involved issues which placed students in confrontation with administrators. Grievances concerned institutional services, social and academic regulations, governance, and the role of students in making important decisions. Inevitably, major issues related to the military, the draft, civil rights and Vietnam.

Finally, recent studies are examining attitude and value assessment in an attempt to explain normative characteristics of community college students. For example, Abbas (1968) investigated the interpersonal values of three groups of students including: (1) community college students in a terminal course; (2) others in a transfer course; and (3) university students. Gordon's Survey of Interpersonal

Values was used to measure six qualities: Support, Conformity, Recognition, Independence, Benevolence, and Leadership. Both community college groups were reported to score higher than the university group on Conformity. On the Leadership scale, the university students scored significantly higher. No other significant differences were noted. It was suggested that community college students scored higher on Conformity because of their commuter and home status, whereas a university environment tended to foster more nonconformity (Abbas, 1968).

In a study by Mauss (1967), attitudes and values were reported to vary among selected student groups. Four student subcultures were identified and adapted to the community college setting. The method of study was selected because of its "concern for an interrelation of sociological factors in educational performance." Two values were measured: (1) identification with the adult community, and (2) involvement with intellectual ideas. Results from a large urban community college revealed the existence of four subcultures: academic types, 9.5 per cent; incipient rebels, 23 per cent; vocational types, 24 per cent; and perpetual teenagers, 44 per cent. The findings suggest that the environmental press of large urban community colleges is perhaps "anti-intellectual and somewhat adolescent" (Mauss, 1967).

Socioeconomic Background

It is misleading and inappropriate to rely on junior college socioeconomic data for effective use in the comprehensive community college (Thomas, 1969). Yet, junior college normative data is frequently all that is available. The following is an attempt to present the essence of a series of loosely strung studies and reports in such a manner that the reader may synthesize the results for himself. For the most part, such studies are local or regional, highly statistical, not readily available, and either reported or interpreted by second or third parties. Within these parameters, the reader must employ discretion.

For the most part, the community college does not attract a significant proportion of its students from the higher socioeconomic level (Astin, et al., 1967; Medsker and Trent, 1965). This trend should be recognized as a healthy one since it indicates that the community college is receptive to its most serviceable clientele as opposed to those from higher socioeconomic status who manage to attend college despite their ability or proximity to an institution of higher education. Becker's (1966) analysis of Project Talent data sheds further light on the two-year clientele which

> fell between the noncollege and senior college groups on every one of seven indices of socioeconomic status, including mother's and father's education, father's occupation, number of books in the home, whether or not the student had a room, desk, and typewriter of his own at home, and so on. Junior college students were, however, more similar to the four-year college group on these indices than they were to the noncollege group (Cross, 1968c, p. 16).

In contrasting ability with environmental factors, Cross (1968c) presents a conclusion by Schoenfeldt who, in 1966, concluded "that the ability of the student had more influence on whether or not he would go to college than did the socioeconomic status of the family." This is contrasted with the data of Medsker and Trent (1965) which indicates that "the occupation of the father showed somewhat more relationship to college attendance than did the ability of the student" (Cross, 1968c).

Fathers of transfer and occupational students are reported to have significantly different types of occupations (Brue, et al., 1971). More farm workers, laborers, or workmen are found among the fathers of occupational students while transfer students report greater numbers in managerial, official, or professional categories. As might be expected, the father's education and family income are also higher for transfer groups than occupational groups. Women students in transfer and occupational programs come from similar socioeconomic backgrounds and are reported to be more alike than different (Brue, et al., 1971). Therefore, a greater degree of flexibility can be exercised in program planning and vocational counseling for women moreso than men.

As might be anticipated, parental attitudes exert a direct influence on attendance and persistence at college. Trent and Ruyle (1965) attest to the parent-child relationship by noting:

> ... that there are statistically significant differences among the descriptions of parents given by

college persisters, college dropouts, and nonattenders. The persisters were most likely, and the nonattenders least likely, to describe their parents as loving, energetic, ambitious, orderly, and intellectual (In Cross, 1968c, p. 18).

Postsecondary educational plans also relate to such factors as innate ability, family attitude, and personal values. The greatest chance for college attendance is most likely to occur when the student's ability and parent's education are of high quality. But girls with similar ability and achievement as boys are still less likely to attend college. Phearman's study (1949) of college attenders and nonattenders also concluded that the possibility for college enrollment decreases as the size of the family increases. The community college alone holds the potential to rectify this condition.

While parents exert the greatest influence upon students to continue their education, clergy have been shown to exert the least influence (A Longitudinal Study, 1969). The study also indicates that both sexes rank siblings second to their parents in the degree of influence. Adult friends rank third for boys and fifth for girls, while peer influences rank fifth for boys and third for girls. Guidance counselors generally have little influence upon either boys or girls and rank close to the low influence of the clergy. The same is true for teachers who, as a group, rank seventh for boys and sixth for girls. A lack of identification with school personnel is clearly revealed by the faint degree of influence exerted upon noncollege-bound youth. In fact, the general absence of adult influence is reported to be a major characteristic of noncollege-bound youth. Students not planning to continue postsecondary learning typically seek help outside the school establishment and if the community college is to reach them, it too will have to go outside the established order.

Blacks and Minorities. The socioeconomic status of blacks and disadvantaged classes of people deserves special attention. Most colleges remain segregated and blacks still constitute less than three per cent of the total undergraduate enrollment at major universities (Willingham, 1970). The community college seems to represent a singular but notable exception to segregated higher education. Nevertheless, a summary report of higher education programs for disadvantaged students in New York State concludes that too few colleges are utilizing their resources to further the educational needs of disadvantaged people (Hood, 1969). A recent Office of Education Task Force surveyed the national scene and concluded:

> The poor youth's chance of attending a community college is only one-fourth that for the non-poor youth. Only 5.5 per cent of the junior college population comes from poor families.
>
> Opportunity would be fully equal only if 600,000 black students plus an undetermined number of Indians and Mexican-Americans were going to college now (Valien, 1970, p. 30).

The Task Force also reported that black students attend community colleges because of low cost, proximity, and educational programs. Their attendance and enrollment patterns understandably relate to "parental influences, especially from mothers; open door admissions; older friends already in the two-year college; and the desire to transfer to baccalaureate programs." Blacks generally believe that the community college is still inferior to senior institutions and "terminal" or nontransfer programs offer little relief to the press for status. They are more concerned about questionable teacher attitudes than they are about basic learning experiences. It is also reported that blacks are not accepted into campus life by whites and administrative personnel and procedures are not made to recognize the "real" black dilemma. (S. R. E. B., 1970).

Along with other students, blacks are rightfully critical of remedial and compensatory programs and standardized tests (S. R. E. B., 1970). They resent standardized tests that measure potential for college work in an unfair but traditionally "safe" manner. Also, there is a tendency for career counseling to be "culturally loaded and blatantly inadequate." Although black students from integrated high schools find fewer problems in adjusting than do students from predominantly black schools, the reasons are complex and not understood. All too often, the immediate drive to work and earn money causes black students to withdraw in order to fulfill short-term, but pressing needs. (S. R. E. B., 1970).

Harold Kastner of Florida's Department of Education, Community College Division, suggests that innumerable shortcomings prevent the community college from providing a direct response to blacks. He concludes:

The Student Clientele

> The community college and its community are seldom ready to undertake a comprehensive program for the disadvantaged student. Implementation of such a program requires that an educational environment be established which is conducive to its achievement. Administrative leadership is needed to develop an appropriate organizational structure and personnel commitment before such a program can be implemented fully (In New Challenges, 1970, p. 9).

All personnel responsible for creating the educational environment must adapt to this task. In a practical sense, non-instructional employees, admissions officers, secretaries and staff are the interpreters of the college to the community; for many, this is the first and last contact. Once more it is necessary to reassess existing policies, admissions procedures, curricular flexibility and appropriateness, motivation, teaching, learning, and evaluation techniques. The community college effort must inevitably merge with elementary and secondary school efforts to have any substantive impact on the black community.

The Southern Regional Education Board boldly explored New Challenges to the Junior Colleges: Their Role in Expanding Opportunity for Negroes (1970). The question "When does an educator begin to think black?" was raised many times. Claretha Carnegie's penetrating reply is most revealing and bears repeating:

> A black or white educator begins to think black when he accepts the fact that the open door policy does not have the same connotation for the black student as it does for the white. For the black student, the process of testing and screening is so complicated, complex, and misunderstood by him that he may have developed mental attitudes that help to defeat his efforts to successfully pass the tests. An educator begins to think black when he recognizes the testing problem and begins to seek ways to find the pass key that will get the black student through the testing door. An educator begins to think black when he can look beyond the veneer of complacency of the black student or understand the outward show of hostility of the black student placed in compensatory programs. Thinking black, the educator is able to understand

how the students, parents, and members of the
black community may view the black student's progress in the college. Being desegregated, but
isolated, in an 'integrated setting' is for them
segregation new style. Another impressive fact,
closely related to how the students view themselves
and how others view them, is the unfortunate psychological effect upon the aspiring, capable black
students in the compensatory classes. In these
junior college classes the black student often feels
that, regardless of his personal attainment, the
group with which he is now identified is viewed as
less able, less acceptable than some of the former
classmates with whom he has been associated in
an integrated high school.

The impact upon the self-image and motivation of
the student--as revealed in our on-campus interviews--is the most tragic outcome of this new
segregation. The challenge for the educator is to
use additional diagnostic tools to help in identifying
the capable student and move him into the mainstream of the college curriculum, and by similar
means to identify and retain the less able so that
he can get the individualized help for the elimination of his educational deficiencies. Thinking black
is seeing the black student as an individual with
varying anxieties. Thinking black is encouraging
the black student to enter campus political and social organizations. The black student as well as
the white student must realize that the interrelationships developed in competitive situations will
enhance his chances for successful endeavors after
he assumes his place in his own community.

The question was raised whether thinking black may
be conceived as a subtle attitudinal change that becomes overt in the form of actions bringing about
educational changes within the established order
which in the end will benefit black and white. Or,
thinking black, the educator seeks the unsought;
devises means to test the untapped knowledge; explores and challenges fully the untapped rich resources of the black student so that the junior college open door policy can become in reality a door
to the American way of life (In New Challenges,
1970, p. 8).

Interests, Attitudes, and Self-Estimates

As might be expected, the community college student exhibits a greater interest in nonacademic than academic areas. The traditional core derived from the trivium and quadrivium is less easily nurtured at the two-year institution than at most four-year institutions despite self-assertive faculty expectations. It is primarily in the areas of financial and business success that community college students generate more interest than their four-year counterparts (Cross, 1968c).

What little is known about personality characteristics of college attenders is succinctly sketched from a 1967 study by Medsker:

> [Community and junior] students are more conventional, less independent, less attracted to reflective thought, and less tolerant than their peers in four-year institutions (Cross, 1968c).

Comparative studies generally place the two-year student above non-college youth and below all other college youth on traditional indices of personality. The trend may be accurately reflected in Warren's study (1966) which portrays the "junior" college student as "the most cautious, prudent, and controlled, most apprehensive, and rigid" in academic matters (Cross, 1968c).

Common to most research conducted in this area is the indication that community college students tend to hold unrealistic aspirations for their future and as many as 89 per cent express an interest in earning a baccalaureate degree (A. C. T. Program, 1969a). It is this uncertainty that compels young people to attend a community college rather than a traditional four-year institution. In Glenister's study (1969) at a two-year technical college, he confirmed that students are definitely more interested in practical aspects of learning and less in the abstract or theoretical. The Study of Values Scale by Allport, Vernon, and Lindzey was used to detect values and attitudes in six basic interest areas: Theoretical, Economic, Aesthetic, Social, Political, and Religious. Male and female two-year college students reportedly earned higher scores on the Economic scale than four-year students. Likewise, the two-year students also demonstrated a higher mean score on the Social scale than did their four-year counterparts.

Glenister (1969) also reported that two-year college females are more interested in useful rather than Aesthetic aspects of everyday life. They demonstrate an interest in power while still respecting the intrinsic value of interpersonal relationships. The two-year college females' score on the Political scale tends to be significantly higher than the mean score of the four-year college females. However, males at both two-year and four-year colleges demonstrate comparable power and Political values. In the area of Religious values, no significant difference is reported between the two male groups, but the four-year females tend to rate higher than their two-year counterparts (Glenister, 1969).

Community and junior college students continue to reflect characteristics that are generally not known or understood by the faculty (Bossone, 1965). These students are reported to be present-oriented, receptive to the concept of equal opportunity, and lacking in basic communication skills. They generally live in unaesthetic settings with minimal privacy and are likely to be dissatisfied with their work, salary, and opportunities to advance. Parental attitudes reflect suspicion and fear in authoritative situations which may be a carryover not readily recognized or provided for in curricular and instructional planning for the community college student.

Educational Aspirations

It is slowly being acknowledged that college students at all types of institutions have educational aspirations that are unrealistically high (Davis, 1964). Whether this is an intrinsic quality or one generated by societal-environmental pressures is not clearly understood. Still, it must be recognized that most two-year college students do not complete their course of study in two years just as most four-year college students do not complete their program in four years. With increasing numbers of students irregularly changing programs and colleges, we are left with a fluid situation that cannot be isolated, let alone placed under the scrutinous eye of the researcher. Overall,

> ... at the end of four years, 28 per cent of the students entering colleges of all types have obtained degrees, but almost as many (24 per cent) are still in college and have not yet qualified for their degree (Cross, 1967).

But getting a degree or completing a program is a traditional measure or index that only partially fits the educational aspirations of the community college clientele.

With the median age rising above the mid-twenties and growing numbers of discontented four-year students transferring back to the community college (reverse articulation), new rules of college attendance and subsequent success have evolved. We are at least a decade short in our understanding of the new directions that have already taken place.

Parental pressures are notoriously evident in many young people who are subjected to the demise of being alter egos playing out unfulfilled missions. The uncompromising pressure to pursue further education after high school often makes a potential senior college student switch to a community college at the last possible moment. Inordinate amounts of pressure inevitably culminate as undue anxiety for many of the students who arrive at the community college and, in a sense, aspects of an involuntary campus tend to appear. All too easily, this dilemma is viewed by faculty in the light of lesser issues related to academic performance rather than the many complex reasons which underlie a greater unresolved dilemma.

Occupational Orientation

For students in the second, third, and lowest quartiles, Turnbull (1968) suggests that the safe and stable educational structures of the past are no longer appropriate, especially in the community college. He says:

> To look at the student body along the narrow dimensions of academic talent is, of course, grossly inadequate. For the students newly represented on college rolls, skills and aptitudes of quite different orders are probably the pertinent dimensions of comparison.... Clearly, in education, we are moving away from the relatively uniform academic program of earlier decades to a much more diversified assortment of offerings. At the higher education level, the community college in particular offers a ready example of an institution that has accepted just this responsibility (Copyright 1968 by the American Association for the Advancement of Science).

The community college clientele is best served with reputable alternatives within vocational, technical, and occupational career education. Only when the faculty is matched to this task as well as to the students will the community college maximize its effectiveness.

Most students who plan to enter post-secondary education tend to select vocations related to engineering, business, teaching, science, and health-related professions (A Longitudinal Study, 1969). Overall, a low degree of interest is reported in mathematics, the humanities, and the social sciences as formal disciplines. However, far more students are ready for nonacademic programs than the number that actually enroll in them.

In comparing community college transfer and occupational students, Brue and others (1971) report that occupational students express higher interest in skill and technical areas while transfer men indicate greater interest in business, music, literature, drama, and leadership activities. The only difference noted between occupational and transfer women is a higher interest in business demonstrated by occupational women. Behm (1967) also reports that "occupational men are less socially oriented than transfer men," which supports Stewart's contention (1966) that occupational students are less concerned in areas related to social service.

Occupational men are reported to be less original, aggressive, and independent than transfer men (Brue, et al., 1971). Further, they estimate their physical energy and health to be lower than that of transfer men. Occupational women see themselves with more ability in mechanical and mathematical areas than do occupational men. Occupational women also rate themselves higher on clerical ability scales.

The study by Brue and others also shows that occupational men generally decide to attend college during their senior year whereas transfer students make this decision earlier in high school. But despite lower academic test scores and high school grades, occupational students are reported to make higher college grades than transfer students. Occupational students also seek to experiment in their attempt to select a vocation much to the discomfiture of traditional academicians. Three-fourths of the occupational students indicate that they will continue in their field of study while an even larger percentage indicate that they have a good chance for success despite high attrition rates.

Students in the health-related fields are reported to score high on interest scales in health, biology, and home economics. Similarly, students enrolled in business-oriented programs measure high on interest scales in business and secretarial skills (Brue, et al., 1971). A more definitive picture will slowly emerge as new subgroups are identified and closely followed over longer periods of time.

Academic Aptitude and Grades

Higher academic ability is consistently demonstrated by the four-year college student when compared to the community college student. On a national level, Cross (1968c) reports that these results are confirmed by using the Preliminary Scholastic Aptitude Test (Seibel, 1965); the English, mathematics, social studies, and natural science tests, as well as the composite of the American College Testing Program (Hoyt and Munday, 1966); the School and College Ability Tests (Medsker and Trent, 1965); the College Qualification Test (Seashore, 1958); a rank-in-class index (Seibel, 1965; Medsker and Trent, 1965); and reported high school grades (Astin, Panos, and Creager, 1967; Panos, 1966; A.C.T. Profile, 1966).

Eight characteristic patterns can be identified to describe students who enroll in community or junior colleges (Riendeau, 1967): (1) engineering majors; (2) English grades less than C; (3) English grades B or higher; (4) those who had "few superior teachers"; (5) an interest in teaching or educational administration; (6) fathers with "less than eighth grade education"; (7) prior academic probation, and (8) holding awards for citizenship or leadership. These patterns tend to corroborate other reports which suggest that students entering two-year colleges are influenced more by practical considerations than intellectual factors (Cross, 1968c). In academic ability, this clientele represents 20 per cent from the first quartile, 63 per cent evenly distributed over the second and third quartiles, and 17 per cent from the fourth quartile (Cross, 1969).

Academic aptitude and family background are known to effect postsecondary educational plans. For example, vocational-technical education is reported to attract students with high aptitude and low family socioeconomic status, or low aptitude and high socioeconomic status (A.C.T. Program,

1969a). As a result, vocational-technical students are generally looked upon as underachievers with more aptitude than achievement. Still, two-year college students rate their instruction to be good overall. Teachers reportedly "emphasize factual information and exact answers" rather than broad, liberal understanding which may account for the positive perception of community college instruction.

Not surprisingly, high school grades constitute the best predictor of college grades. However, Thomas and Stanley (1969) point out that grades are also more beneficial to white students since they "do not consistently make the greatest contribution in predicting college grades for black students, perhaps particularly for men."

Students at two-year and four-year colleges are reported to receive about the same proportion and distribution of letter grades despite the lower academic potential generally attributed to two-year college students. Apparently, teachers make internal adjustments based on prior notions or standard perceptions by "curving" or fitting the student to commonly accepted grade patterns. If the two-year college student were placed in a parallel four-year situation, he would probably receive lower grades. Junior college grades and senior college grades are simply not comparable (A. C. T. Program, 1969a). With academic potential held constant, two-year college grades would be higher than four-year college grades. In general, however, high school grades and test scores are useful predictors of success in the two-year college. Also, grades in two-year colleges are reported to be as predictable as grades in four-year colleges, and grades in technical curricula are reported to be as predictable as grades in academic areas. Various measures of aptitude are not peculiar to either junior or senior colleges (A. C. T. Program, 1969a).

Academic Probation and Dropouts. The indiscriminate manner of filtering out certain undesirable or nonacademic students represents a significant loss of human potential and should be challenged. According to Arthur W. Chickering, "The most important index of a college's success and social contribution may well be the quality of its dropouts, not the quality of its graduates" (In The Chronicle, January 11, 1971, p. 1). Most students are reported changing in much the same way regardless of the college they choose or the kind of students they are. Compared with students who remain in college, Chickering concludes that "a substantial proportion of those who leave are more autonomous, more complex, and less concerned with practical achievement and material success."

Educationally and socioeconomically deprived youths are reported to have a nationwide dropout rate of 90 per cent in the community college (Valien, 1970). For all community college students it is estimated to be between 65 and 75 per cent. Meanwhile, high schools have reduced their graduating class dropout rate from 38 per cent in 1959 to 22 per cent (Kruger, 1969). But overall, approximately one-half of all students attending American colleges and universities leave before attaining a degree (Summerskill, 1962).

Less than one-half of community college freshmen return for the second year (Colvert and Baker, 1955); however, this rate is improving. Most educators recognize the deleterious effects of the "sophomore slump," but few are cognizant of the immediate and otherwise terminal effect it can have on a two-year college student. Even at Vassar, the "sophomore slump" exists as early as spring in the freshman year (Sanford, 1962). And it is also in the initial year that the shortcomings of most curricula display their deleterious qualities much to the chagrin of neophyte students. With half of all students who enter the community and junior college still dropping out before completing a two-year course of study, Landrith (1971) concludes that the dilemma lies with faculty who are oblivious and unaware of the institution's mission. With part-time students increasing in number, most will take longer than two years to complete the so-called "two-year course." On the other hand, students who come for less than two-year degree purposes should not be labeled as dropouts in the derogatory academic sense.

The majority of withdrawals or academic dismissals include personal, social, nonacademic, and academic categories. Many students are prone to select majors and programs of study which demand a higher level of skill than they are capable of demonstrating (Meyer, 1968). And many students are too quick to attempt higher education in the manner in which it was popularly conceived--with prestige, ivory tower, and status factors. The dropout problem is entangled in a myriad of financial, institutional, and nonacademic factors; yet, all too often, it is handled in terms of academic dismissal or academic probation. Almost one-half of those who withdraw eventually return to a community college after finding a positive solution to problems of a developmental, financial, social, or academic nature (Bossen, 1968). As a result, the dropout problem may not be as quantitatively harmful as is usually thought.

Cohen (1969b) reports that dropouts generally take less than twelve credits, tend to be gainfully employed, attend more schools before the high school period, and have mothers with minimal education. Suggestions to reduce the number of dropouts inevitably include offering courses with different objectives for different groups of students. Taught from a broader perspective, such courses could replace those which are taught as if they were the first courses for students majoring in the subject. With many college catalogs listing hundreds upon hundreds of courses, Max Marshall (1971) calls for a "mandatory reduction in the number of courses" by one-quarter. He hastens to add that the "stereotyped answers used by professors to support their courses are well-known and should be foretold and ignored."

Aside from some novel ways to cope with the concepts of academic dismissal and probation, little has been done to examine their validity and usefulness. Generally, most community colleges require a student on academic probation to enroll in fewer courses, take remedial instruction, attend on a part-time basis, enroll in evening or vocational courses, or change programs completely. Most students on probation perseveringly select liberal arts programs for transfer despite inadequate college preparation in high school and a need for remedial instruction in English and mathematics (Fitch, 1968). Quite often, these students come from other two-year or four-year colleges where they were previously disqualified for various reasons. But the performance of students who stay out of school for a semester or more is not different from those who do not (Bissiri, 1966). From a study by Muck and Undem (1965), it was concluded that neither a waiting period between disqualification and readmission nor a restricted number of credits each semester contributes to ultimate success. Mistaken notions in this area must be challenged by the faculty.

Community college students on academic probation are reported to be no less heterogeneous than the community population itself (Capper, 1969b). They "range from high-ability students dismissed from senior institutions to students with severe visual-motor handicaps." Certainly, not all or even most academic dismissals are due to pure academic deficiencies. Changes in penalty grading and probation practices bring about favorable results by switching the college's emphasis from punishing inappropriate behavior to rewarding appropriate behavior. Above all, a change of attitude is necessary in which the philosophy of academic dismissal and probation are viewed in a broader perspective with the academic component being but one dimension. In a very real way, everyone is on probation in the community college, not just the students.

Financial Barriers

While the ability to finance education is only sometimes singled out as the major deterrent to attending post-secondary education, it can become a serious factor by relating to persistence, motivation, part-time attendance, frustration, family tension, loans and mortgages, and withdrawal problems. Family income relates directly to college attendance. In his Congressional message of March 1970, President Nixon pointed out the financial barrier:

> Something is basically unequal about opportunity for higher education when a young person whose family earns more than $15,000 a year is nine times more likely to attend college than a young person whose family earns less than $3,000.

At the 1970 annual meeting of the American Association of Junior Colleges it was proclaimed that Federal aid programs show a complete lack of understanding of the composition of community college students. Financial assistance continues to be aimed mostly at full-time students with little concern for adults who may be over twenty-one years of age, economically deprived, and working full- or part-time. About 63 per cent of all community college students reportedly work in some capacity to support themselves and do not carry enough academic credit to be considered full-time. Thirty per cent of all community college students receive no parental financial aid (Read, 1969), and far too many students are unaware of procedures to obtain financial assistance even when it is available (Lins, 1969).

According to Cross (1968c), financial problems rank first among the reasons for withdrawal given by community and junior college students who transfer to a four-year college only to withdraw later. As many as forty per cent report financial difficulty as a primary reason for withdrawing (Cross, 1968c). Lack of money is also the major reason cited by blacks for dropping out of two-year college programs (New Challenges, 1970). Despite this, low cost is still among the major reasons for attending the community college.

About two-thirds of all potential college students indicate a willingness to borrow money while 16 per cent do not (A Longitudinal Study, 1969). Others remain undecided and unsure of how to approach the problem. As might be anticipated, parents are more hesitant to assume financial obligations for their daughters' education than for their son's.

Work experience is growing for all students as they pursue their education. In 1969, 39.3 per cent of all sixteen- to twenty-one-year-old high school and college students were gainfully employed, a rise from 30.5 per cent in 1950. And of the sixteen- to twenty-one-year-old part-time college students in 1969, 39.8 per cent were in the labor force, also a notable rise from 32.9 per cent in 1959 (U.S. News and World Report, February 8, 1971). The fact that more and more students seek ways to support or supplement their finances for education indicates that the financial barrier is subtle but real. Some students, however, choose to integrate the learning experience with career experiences even when no financial problems are pending.

The frame of reference in which each student views educational costs varies greatly (Cross, 1968c). Wealthy students at high-tuition institutions often react to educational expenses much in the same manner as low or middle class students who work while attending low-tuition community colleges near their home; each may not be overly concerned about finances. The financial barrier is often subtle and affects the individual indirectly with commonly accepted low class life styles and low rates of college attendance. While the barrier does not always thwart enrollment plans, it often relates to low motivation, persistence, and high attrition rates. Far too many "financial" dropouts are still perceived as academic dropouts.

In Conclusion

Those who are served by the community college will shape its future role and determine its potential as an instrument of change. With its open door policy, the college serves an extreme range of societal needs which fall within the generic heading of "education." The myopic view of the institution and its faculty is one that still misperceives the anomalous student clientele. Most characteristics that differentiate this heterogeneous group dispel the collegiate student model as a useful standard for the community college. Standard teaching styles, obsolete methods of delivering instruction, ineffective use of communicative media, traditional evaluation and grading practices, and a failure to recognize widely divergent individual characteristics among students are bringing more of the same to a different kind of student. Overall, the community college student remains a "nonstudent" in the traditional academic sense.

If the open door college is to meet its challenge, more emphasis must be placed on adapting educational programs and competent teachers to the entry level and intrinsic limitations of the new clientele. The concepts of readiness and motivation must be re-explored and continually redefined to adapt the institution to the individual. In short, it is the college ideology that is lacking in substance and practice. Compensatory programs are fruitlessly locked into academic courses of one sort or another, and student entry levels are firmly entrenched in middle-class values which are often lacking if not absent.

Professional educators have yet to define, let alone agree, on issues that underlie the student dilemma. Indeed, legislators and educational commissions are already charting completely new directions from above, due to the obvious lack of coherence, progress, and effectiveness at the lower, but operational levels. A sincere commitment remains to be made to support and promote the community college idea from within. Inherent to this commitment is the recognition of a new clientele and a new order of faculty who are in genuine accord with the community college philosophy.

Chapter 5

THE COMMUNITY COLLEGE FACULTY

It has been shown that the community college is justifiably described as a post-secondary institution with distinct characteristics. Further, it is charged with providing multiple functions to the most diverse group of students ever to experience post-secondary education. Yet, community college teachers are evolving more and more to the model of the standard academic mind. In a very real sense, these teachers are only slightly different from faculty at four-year colleges and universities; what differences do occur are more of degree rather than kind. With the faculty being the prime agents through which the life of the institution is expressed, much concern is voiced about subverting the institution from within. Either widespread reform is needed among faculty or their mission is now being most effectively accomplished (Cashin, 1969).

The Teachers

The faculty that teach in community colleges have fought long to be accepted on a colleague basis by their counterparts in four-year colleges and universities. A deliberate attempt was made to be different from high school teachers and more like college professors. The quest for status and identity differentiation included the use of academic rank, reduced teaching loads, affiliation with the American Association of University Professors, and traditional collegiate calendars. Other subtle changes included the use of "lecture-concert series" rather than assemblies, faculty councils, and generally increased authority in curriculum and policy making (Friedman, 1966). Even staying open during a snowstorm when public schools closed was to make a difference.

Attempts to remove the high school stigma from community college teachers resulted in an inertial overkill.

The Faculty

This inertia typically encourages teachers to take refuge in a spirited defense of the values of their own academic specialization and in attacks on the superficiality and lack of respectability of general education courses. Teachers become scholars in a manner that is difficult to overcome. Of these teachers, Joseph Seidlin writes:

> Many of our 'teachers' are not really teachers. They are mathematicians, physicists, historians, linguists, etc.--not teachers. Many of them are men and women of great stature; major contributors to science, technology, and the arts; but they are not teachers. On some scales of worth to humanity they outweigh the teachers; but they are not teachers. They might even be indispensable to institutions of higher learning; but they are not teachers. To them, students are means; to teachers, students are the end products--all else is a means. Hence there is but one interpretation of high standards in teaching: standards are highest where the maximum number of students--slow learners and fast learners alike--develop to their maximum capacity (The Committee on Higher Education, 1952, p. 25).

Among the many concerns that affect the outlook of the community college, selection of faculty personnel is probably the easiest to influence and direct. Yet, community college teachers, as a whole, constitute a troublesome concern which needs immediate redirection (Cross, 1969; Landrith, 1971; Cohen and Brawer, 1968; Stratton, 1969; Erickson, 1970; Hancher, 1962; Moore, 1970). Moreover, a tragic intellectual gulf exists between administrators and faculty ("Junior College Dilemma," 1967). Administrators are seen trying to perpetuate a "junior college level" while the faculty perform at the "lower university level." And where faculty emphasize abstract and intellectual college aims more than do students or administrators, the administrators tend to value all college aims while placing more emphasis on those which are practical. After many years of breaking the mold as inferior college teachers, the new order of community college teachers is "basking in dull, unearned respectability." According to Stratton (1969), they now feel safe as college professors. He adds:

> The longing to be identified with members of academic faculties at four-year colleges and

> universities may be as damaging to the community
> college movement as the desire not to be identified
> with the high schools was good. It is time that
> teachers ... in two-year colleges began to identify
> with themselves.... We are engaged in a different
> effort in higher education than others. Let us
> proclaim it, and receive the respect we deserve
> for what we are.

While the philosophical mission of the community college is usually stated by educational leaders and authors, the realities are accomplished by faculty. (Cross, 1969). Still, a high proportion of new community college teachers are only hazily aware of the nature of the institution in which they are teaching (Siehr, et al., 1963; Cashin, 1969). Instructors are expected to understand, appreciate, and support the role of the institution (A.A.J.C., 1966), yet they are hired as subject-matter specialists, generally on the basis of earned academic degrees. Seldom are they trained for teaching positions (Landrith, 1971), and what little training is available is highly inadequate (The New Republic, February 1965; The Nation, August 1957; Harper's Magazine, February 1967).

Cross (1969) concludes that community college teachers "reflect the hierarchical values associated with 'traditional academic respectability' and 44 per cent openly admit their preference to teach in a four-year college or university." From Medsker's study of four thousand teachers in two-year colleges, Cross provides data which confirms that "much of the traditional thinking about higher education lingers" within the professional attitude of this group. For example, while 90 per cent of the faculty endorse the standard transfer program and 85 per cent agree that community college technical programs are essential, suggestions to make these programs different from each other are considered dubious. "Only 50 per cent feel that career programs for skilled and semi-skilled trades are essential," and only 21 per cent give strong support to occupational programs that are less than two years in length. Twenty-six per cent even feel that the latter programs are inappropriate for the community college. Forty-nine per cent of the teachers think that excessive stress is placed on recruiting additional numbers of students and not enough emphasis on quality. Forty-five per cent of the faculty disagree with the philosophical tenets of the basic open door policy which would admit all high school graduates. And 88 per cent agree that prior grades and standard tests are good "criteria for allowing safe passage from high school to the community college." (Cross, 1969).

Not much research is available which describes community college teachers, their attitudes, or their training. Rather, studies tend to relate to the generic two-year college teacher inclusive of all segments of public, private, community and junior colleges. Private junior colleges, for example, still maintain their elitist position, with small residential colleges enrolling less than six hundred students in most cases (A. A. J. C., 1963a). These institutions often strive to maintain their exclusiveness or finishing school image and necessarily hire faculty to meet this aim. "Private junior college faculties tend to be somewhat parochial and professionally unaware" of the community college concept. Their allegiance to academic tradition is of high order and should be if it befits the goals of their institution. As a consequence, studies which relate to all types of two-year college teachers are generally of little value, except for the most basic types of data.

Medsker (1960) provides a commonly accepted profile of junior and community college teachers. Nearly 72 per cent are men, about 75 per cent have a graduate degree, six per cent have no degree, 64 per cent taught in high school, and 27 per cent attended a junior college. Most of these teachers are reported to come from white collar or farm-family backgrounds. About half believe general education is important enough to make up 50 per cent of vocational-technical curriculums. Little agreement, however, can be found on remedial education or adult education, both of which are central to the community college philosophy.

It is safe to conclude that community college teachers and administrators have reached the point of development that generally leads to the establishment of a rigid bureaucracy (Park, 1971) in which the problems relating to teaching and teachers are protected from exploitation, analysis, and change. Roscoe Martin aptly describes this condition as follows:

> It may be argued, indeed, that bureaucracy (in the invidious sense) is a natural concomitant of professionalism. Thus the most advanced professions are those affected by sclerosis; by certitude of the rightness of any professional course or stand adopted; impatience with any contrary view; and

suspicion of all criticism (In Park, 1971).

A community college teaching philosophy is not visible among community college teachers. Academic degrees make it easy for teachers to get in while tenure makes it difficult to remove them. "Dead" faculty members are not being "prevented or cured" (Evans, 1969). A majority even consider themselves to be average or below average in understanding and accepting the two-year college philosophy. Indeed, most of these teachers rank themselves as average or below in causing student learning (Park, 1971). These teachers are also seen retaining an aloofness and disdain for their own professional advancement. As a consequence, the National Conference on the Teaching of English in the Junior College (1965) concluded that the junior college teacher is a "fumbling amateur" badly in need of ways to bridge the gap between subject-matter respectability and professional training.

The role of the community college teacher is very demanding, especially with nontraditional students. De Nevi (1970) suggests that a retreading is in order:

> Most [community] college teachers in the ghetto live neatly compartmentalized lives. Man, they actually feel sentenced to teach slum youth. They only put up with it because they need the bread-- the bastards. Their teaching is passionless. Their empathy with those they teach, with the surrounding community is nonexistent. Their jobs, like their lives, are counterfeits: dry lectures substitute for teaching; confrontations with students replace counseling. Ghetto teachers flee back to their tidy suburban pads for what little redemption they can get from cocktails or nagging wives. What is needed are seasoned professionals who are not gelded, who listen and teach with a skill that lends warmth and hope to lives which often hang by slender threads.

The community college is simply not living up to its claim as an institution that offers excellence in teaching. The dysfunction between the stated goals and actual practice of the community college is, in great part, due to the faculty's lack of information and training. What might have been a relatively minor problem is evolving into one of a more serious nature.

The Faculty

Recruitment

Most two-year college teachers come from secondary schools (33 per cent), graduate schools (20-23 per cent), college or university teaching (17 per cent), and the business world (11 per cent), according to Wattenbarger and others (In Gaddy, 1969). The majority of new junior college teachers have long been recruited directly from the high schools and, to some extent, this has delayed transforming the junior college into a full-fledged partner within higher education. Some of the teachers who initially headed for high school teaching quickly found themselves attracted to the two-year college by better salaries and the absence of demand for research (In Sanford, 1962). For others, the new position was treated as a mere extension of their former position (Kelly and Wilbur, 1969). Indeed, a good teacher in the secondary schools was always potentially seen as a good teacher for lower division courses of higher education (Weeks, 1970).

From an extensive study on "community-college" teaching, Koos (1950) found that almost three-fourths of the teachers were recruited from secondary schools and only one-eighth had prior teaching experience at the college or university level. Studying the South, Midwest, and West, he found that these teachers had the same professional education courses that high school teachers had, with less than one in ten having had a course about the junior college. He reported that about three-quarters had their master's degree and, on the average, most teachers had an additional year of graduate study.

In 1964, Florida recruited 36 per cent of its new community college teachers directly from graduate schools (Cohen and Brawer, 1968). During this period, California found that 300 of 681 new teachers of academic subjects came directly from high school positions while only 98 came directly from graduate school training. And in 1967, Table 2 shows that California recruited 41 per cent of its new faculty from experienced elementary and secondary school veterans, with the next largest group (20 per cent) coming from the ranks of experienced community college instructors (Wurster, 1969). Of all community college teaching positions filled in California in 1967, nine per cent were filled with persons having no prior teaching experience and ten per cent by candidates with industrial and commercial backgrounds. With teacher mobility on the rise and doctoral

TABLE 2

SOURCES OF NEW FULL-TIME JUNIOR COLLEGE TEACHERS EMPLOYED IN 1963-64 AND 1964-65

Source	Percentage of Junior Colleges		
	All	Public	Private
High school teaching	30.3	32.2	22.3
Graduate school	23.7	23.0	27.2
College or university teaching	17.1	17.3	16.2
Business occupation	11.3	11.2	11.7
Bachelor's degree class	3.7	3.0	7.0
Other educational service	2.4	2.4	2.3
Miscellaneous, noneducational	2.1	2.3	1.0
Government service (civilian)	2.0	2.2	1.1
Research	1.5	1.4	2.0
Homemaking	1.4	1.3	1.7
Elementary school teaching	1.3	1.1	2.0
Military service	1.2	1.2	1.1
School administration	1.0	0.9	1.3
Religious service	1.0	1.5	3.1
All sources	100.0	100.0	100.0
Number of colleges reporting	547	356	191

(In Wurster, 1969, p. 12)

recipients too plentiful, secondary schools will soon cease to be the prime source of community college teachers.

New sources of faculty are being found among retired military personnel, industry, business, the professions, and part-time persons employed elsewhere. In Maryland, recently appointed part-time teachers had their master's degree or advanced study, and the amount of academic preparation tended to reflect the nature of the local communities. In Illinois, 78 per cent of the part-time teachers had preparation similar to that in Maryland, but where 18 per cent held the doctorate in Maryland, only four per cent had similar credentials in Illinois. With the nature of the teaching function slowly being questioned, the community college is looking to new sources which will include teaching candidates with no degrees but substantial records of successful work experience. Even now, community college teachers come from a wide range of sources and with a broad range of experience as shown in Tables 2 and 3. Overall, 75 per cent of all community and junior college teachers come from the high school, graduate school, college and university, and business-industry. Significantly, in the period from 1963 to 1965, 17.1 per cent of the 7,626 new full-time teachers employed in community and junior colleges came from four-year college and university staffs, while the latter recruited only 1.6 per cent of their 29,621 new teachers from two-year college faculties. (Wurster, 1969).

Many states have yet to develop or recommend adequate guidelines and policies which can be used in recruiting community college teachers. Job descriptions are generally written in nebulous terms and preclude characteristics which tend to differentiate the unmatched role and responsibility of the community college. Nevertheless, the ability to teach or cause learning is beginning to replace academic credentials as the prime characteristic sought in community college teachers. Increasingly, department chairmen and faculty are becoming involved in the actual selection process. In 1967, the National Science Foundation reported on the contrast between hiring practices at two-year and four-year institutions during 1964-65. The report concluded:

> The department chairman at the four year institution acted as recruiter in more than two-thirds of the cases; the corresponding official at the two-year institution, in fewer than one-third of the cases. Even in the larger junior colleges, the

TABLE 3

NEW FULL-TIME COMMUNITY COLLEGE FACULTY ENGAGED TO TEACH IN CALIFORNIA FOR SCHOOL YEAR 1967-68 LISTED BY EXPERIENCE LEVEL AT TIME OF CONTRACT

Experience	Total	Percentage
No prior teaching experience	115	9.0
Secondary teaching experience	470	36.0
Elementary teaching experience	25	2.0
Four-year college teaching experience	198	15.0
Community college teaching experience	249	20.0
Secondary practice teaching experience (no other teaching experience)	6	.5
Elementary practice teaching experience (no other teaching experience)	43	3.0
Research assistant experience	7	.5
Teaching Assistant at the University of California	53	4.0
Industrial or commercial experience (not in teaching)	144	10.0
		100.0

(In Wurster, 1969, p. 14)

responsibility for recruitment was delegated to the department chairman in 46 per cent of the cases (in the smaller junior colleges, 22 per cent of the cases) ... (In Gaddy, 1969).

Sociological studies have revealed several task adaptation patterns that characterize the three major sources of community college teachers. New teachers generally respond to their new demands by drawing extensively from prior experience and orientations. These teachers find new performance expectancies for which they usually lack pre-service training or special preparation. Consequently, those teachers directly recruited from the secondary schools immediately upgrade the extent and depth of their own knowledge, lecture more often, adopt "college level" textbooks, and shift from a "methods" to "subject matter" emphasis. Characterized as "high schoolers" by Friedman (1969), this group tends to have a minimum of five years of high school teaching experience. They also tend to be over thirty-five years of age with equal distribution between males and females. In addition to maximizing the utilization of classroom time, this group speeds up the content of courses by minimizing discussions and question-answer sessions.

As previously stated, many community college teachers come directly from graduate school studies for the master's degree, although a larger number are beginning to come directly from doctoral programs. They lack prior teaching experience, are usually under thirty-five years of age, and are mainly males. This second largest source of teachers is characterized as "grad students" who try teaching as a possible career. They usually suffer from some form of "reality shock" after finding that students are less academically able and less mature than expected. Also, these teachers prefer lecture-textbook styles and have difficulty condensing their field of knowledge and reducing it to an effective, communicable form; student performance is generally scaled down from prior expectations. (Friedman, 1969).

The third major source of community college teachers is the "profs" who, after prior positions in four-year colleges and universities, decide to try two-year college teaching. Usually over thirty-five years of age, this group includes both males and females who hold a strong commitment to teaching. They experience the least trouble in adjusting to course content and student ability, though much use of lecture and textbook technique is retained from prior experiences.

As might be expected, good and bad teaching occurs with all groups of community college teachers and more definitive conclusions cannot be drawn until a realistic understanding is reached concerning what they do, or better yet, what they ought to do. It may be that Kenneth Eble's (1971, p. 8) dictum has some merit: "Good and bad teaching, good and bad teachers, are matters no one knows anything about." We are hard pressed to find consensus within the teaching profession itself.

Professional Preparation

Little is being done to prepare teachers for community college positions (Read, 1969; Cohen and Brawer, 1968; Moore, 1970; Cashin, 1969). In 1950, William Wood reported that no college or university was offering teacher preparation programs for community college teachers. Cohen and Brawer (1968) see the paucity of teacher training programs as valid evidence that the community college is less concerned with teaching than with other matters. One of the earliest attempts to recognize the need for junior college teachers is the course entitled "The Junior College" which has been offered at U.C.L.A. since 1931. Specific programs for junior college teachers came in 1953 when the University provided for teaching-interns to be accepted and paid as faculty members in nearby junior colleges. (Cohen and Brawer, 1968).

Fewer than a dozen large universities have significant teacher-training programs for community college faculty (Moore, 1970). The expectation of programs to train teachers of high-risk students is even more dismal. Educators have simply bypassed the task or are clearly not able to fulfill it. As Pauline Hunter (1966) notes: "If professors think about the two-year college at all, they usually associate the institution with vocational education or with an inferior kind of education." Hancher (1962) cites a parallel situation in the 1870's when university professors felt it was "beneath their dignity to prepare teachers" for elementary and secondary schools and, as a result, the normal schools undertook the task. One might generally conclude that the professional interests of college professors do not willingly include the preparation of teachers in general.

Elementary and secondary school teachers are required to undergo certification and acquire special pedagogic techniques related to the psychology of learning and the learner. College teachers, on the other hand, are not required to know anything beyond their own specialization. Still, there is some truth that two-year college instructors are better than teaching fellows and assistants who carry a great proportion of the undergraduate teaching responsibility at universities.

Teaching roles are misperceived and distorted at all levels. According to Ralph Tyler, from the vantage point of the community college, "a professor in a four-year college does little work and is free to write, to think, to lecture, and to play" (In The Chronicle, November 17, 1969, p. 5). And Garrison heard the common recruitment problem: if the "word gets around the graduate schools about typical teaching loads and time pressure, what's going to make junior college teaching attractive to the bright, capable young people with a real future in education?" (In Read, 1969).

An overreliance on recruiting teachers from random sources can seriously stifle innovation and growth. Too many potential teachers are simply unaware of the nature of the institution, and the results of a recent survey in California indicate a need for substantial re-examination and redirection of appropriate training programs (Cashin, 1969). The master's degree should not automatically provide a teacher with life certification for community college teaching. Most teachers value information pertaining to the nature of the community college even though they do not receive it. As might be expected, the "better prepared instructors consistently place more emphasis and value upon professional preparation than those who are unprepared" or underprepared.

The uncommon, problematic nature of the community college provides a focal point around which training programs can be built. However, the stigma attached to professional training in methods and philosophy must be removed if teaching is to become a part of academic content training. Programs must be "de-educationalized" if they are to be accepted by academic disciplinarians. For teachers about to enter community college teaching, pre-service and in-service training should become a continual process developed at the local institutional level. Traditional forms of faculty orientation are generally inept and leave an urgent need for continuous upgrading of all community college personnel. This necessarily includes faculty, administration, staff, boards of trustees, and representatives from within the student clientele and the community.

It is wrong to think that the university must assume complete responsibility for educating people to the community college concept. Self-renewal within the community college itself will ultimately prove to be of greater value. Well-planned, faculty-based workshops constitute an immediate and worthwhile response to the lack of training of professionals and the lack of understanding of other concerned persons.

In 1968, approximately two hundred four-year colleges and universities recognized teacher inadequacies and proposed to establish new programs for training college teachers at all levels (Cohen and Brawer, 1968). Part E of the Education Professions Development Act (1967) directly encourages the training of educational personnel to serve in two-year colleges. To this end, attempts are now being made to attract persons concerned with the needs of educationally or socioeconomically deprived people. A grant from the Kellogg Foundation is enabling Columbia University and other institutions to prepare better community college administrators. By use of seminars and conferences for trustees, administrators, and faculty, persons from former disadvantaged backgrounds are being encouraged to train as teachers and deans, in the hope of bringing innovative ideas to the community college. In a similar manner, the Junior College Leadership Program at Berkeley is establishing new guidelines for community college research and development (Erickson, 1970). For the future, it will encourage different kinds of research on new students (including members of the minorities, the disadvantaged, and the disaffiliated); changing patterns of community college governance; the relationship between special programs for new students; and the entire decision-making process. (Erickson, 1970).

Training programs for community college teachers must necessarily include new methods of role delineation and self-perception in order to sensitize potential faculty to the area of human factors involvement. Faculty must be made more aware of the student point of view (Wisgoski, 1968) since past experience clearly shows that a teacher's training and experience distinguish the guidance-oriented from the nonguidance-oriented. Above all, the role of the teacher must be redefined at the institutional level in terms of other than degree and academic significance. Potential recruits must be made aware of educational accountability prior to accepting positions in the community college. Continued failure to recognize the problems related to teacher effectiveness can only serve to undermine the community college claim to excellence in teaching.

The Degree Dilemma

While master's degree programs are generally recommended as minimal requirements for the community college teacher, a growing consensus indicates that these are insufficient and even inappropriate (Committee on Preparation, 1969). Scholarship and subject mastery, by themselves, are not indicators of the kinds of training that are essential. The elements of quality teaching and effective educational research are generally left out of graduate programs which prepare teachers (Wortham, 1967). The inability of these programs to prepare teaching specialists for the community college has resulted in a myriad of new degree alternatives and proposals. Graduate schools have passed the responsibility of preparing college teachers to the all-university level which, according to Cohen and Brawer (1968), seems to indicate that it is no one's responsibility.

Behind all arguments that underlie proposals for new degree programs is the one which makes the Ph.D. the required license for teaching in most American colleges and universities. What Chase said in 1938-39 holds true: "The doctorate in philosophy has become a sort of union card necessary for entrance to the profession, but with little guarantee of quality." Consequently, the Assembly on University Goals and Governances now asks that this degree's near monopoly be challenged. Graduate schools still offer a limited track to all comers regardless of their diversity of interest, talents, or motivation. At a meeting of the Council of Graduate Schools, Herbert Weisinger, Graduate Dean at Stony Brook (S.U.N.Y.), noted the dilemma as follows:

> The spectacular growth of two- and four-year colleges has created the need for teachers who combine professional competence with teaching interests, but who neither desire nor are required to pursue research as a condition of their employment (In The Chronicle, December 8, 1969, p. 8).

Yet, as Carl Rogers (1970) bitterly concludes:

> Of all the various levels of education, from nursery school to post-doctoral work, graduate education is frequently the furthest behind the main

stream of our culture and is the least educational in any true sense.

The appropriateness of the Ph.D. as a teaching degree has been questioned since universities began in this country. Even the need for a systematic study of the kinds of teachers needed for two-year colleges was considered desirable more than three decades ago. The First Report of the President's Commission on Higher Education concluded that graduate school programs for college teachers were seriously inadequate because their "single-minded emphasis on the research tradition and [their] purpose of forcing all [their] students into the mold of a narrow specialism do not produce college teachers of the kind we urgently need" (In Troyer, 1948). As early as 1913, it was strongly suggested that "we distinguish carefully in our graduate schools between research students and the students preparing specially for teaching and that we offer two different degrees, [Ph.D. and A.M.] ... the A.M. being not of a lower but a different sort" (Schinz, 1913, p. 51). Thus, different kinds of degrees came to be an acceptable but ineffective method of providing alternatives to the Ph.D. As Packer (1970, p. 50) hopelessly concluded, "The Ph.D. is so deeply entrenched that it is better to reform it than to create alternative degree structures. Other degrees such as the Doctor of Arts and Master of Philosophy will be second-class degrees."

Still, the Ph.D. retains some serious shortcomings which Fred B. Millet describes as follows:

> What is shocking is what the graduate school does to the human material with which it works. On the whole, I should be willing to defend the proposition that most of the men who complete their work for the Ph.D. degree are less vital, less broad-minded, less humane, more narrow in interests then they were when they entered the graduate school. Anyone who has observed the passage of students through the graduate school will have noticed how frequently there takes place a slow drying up of the personality and its movement in the direction of narrowness and pedantry (In Troyer, 1948, p. 5).

Packer (1970) charges that the tradition of Ph.D. programs is being maintained in a manner that is inane, sterile, and irrelevant; generally overconcerned with triviality which produces boredom and degradation for students and teacher alike. The graduate programs for teachers are caught in a vicious circle which can only be broken with "another Johns Hopkins, this time designed to train teachers for our colleges" (Sewal, 1947).

In a report to the Council of Graduate Schools in 1969, Michael Brennan wisely concludes that entirely new Ph.D. teaching programs are essential. Further, he charges that current Ph.D. programs continue to give "lip service to the value of good teaching." Evidence now shows that most Ph.D. recipients never publish or use their research training. And according to E. Alden Dunham, Executive Associate of the Carnegie Corporation:

> Every ill besetting our colleges and universities is related in one way or another to the Ph.D. degree--student alienation, irrelevant curricula, uninspired teaching, ironclad adherence to what may be outmoded traditions, absentee professors, extravagantly high costs of research and graduate education ... (In The Chronicle, March 16, 1970, p. 1).

Thus, critics of graduate programs, and the Ph.D. in particular, continually call for the improvement of teacher training programs. The overwhelming size and growth of the community college movement has merely served to sharpen and rekindle the argument.

In the early 1920's, junior college teachers generally held a master's degree or some graduate study beyond the bachelor's degree. California, however, required its junior college teachers to hold the California high school credential which required at least one year of graduate work beyond the baccalaureate. Exceptions to this requirement were made for persons who taught music, domestic science, and manual training (Proctor, 1923). Only a decade earlier, Professor Alexis Lange proposed the conferment of a special degree in education to recognize the increasing importance of graduate work and, in particular, scholarly proficiency in subject matter. As a result, the University of California designed programs which led to the Graduate in Education (1915) and the Doctor of Education (1921).

More recently, Birnbaum (1966) conducted a study in New York to determine the educational preparation and professional background of faculty teaching career or transfer courses. Table 4 illustrates the manner in which he found degrees distributed among two-year college teachers. As might be anticipated, the master's degree is still predominant among two-thirds of the teachers. However, while the doctorate is gaining popularity among the "transfer faculty," it remains low with "career faculty" due to the nature of the discipline within the world of academe.

Wurster's study (1969) of degrees held by 2,783 new teachers at 429 community and junior colleges throughout the United States shows a lesser emphasis on higher degrees (See Table 5). With a median age of thirty-three, 75 per cent were married males in the twenty to thirty-nine-year-old age bracket. Seven per cent of the respondents held the doctorate; 73 per cent held the master's degree; 19 per cent held the baccalaureate degree; and one per cent had no bachelor's degree at all. A third of the respondents planned to remain in community college teaching while more than a quarter aspired to four-year college teaching. Seventy per cent of the new teachers were males with the overall percentage with master's degrees still increasing. Until recently however, teachers with doctoral degrees remained fairly consistent at seven per cent.

A task force in Florida recently reported that its community college faculty also had an assortment of degrees: 12 per cent held the doctorate; 77 per cent held the master's degree; and 11 per cent held neither doctoral nor master's degrees. In California, Wurster (1969) reported that about ten per cent of all community college faculty held the doctorate; 63 per cent held a master's degree; and 19 per cent held a baccalaureate. But eight per cent held no degree, which indicates a growing trend to recruit noncredentialed but capable and experienced persons as teachers.

Most attempts to reorganize new degree programs for community college teachers have failed to make adequate use of existing Doctor of Philosophy or Doctor of Education programs. "New" variations have been proposed which include the Doctor of Arts and Master of Philosophy, both of which were suggested decades ago. As a modification, the National Faculty Association of Community and Junior Colleges designed a subject-oriented doctoral degree which emphasizes excellence in undergraduate teaching (Stratton, 1969). This program would last three years beyond the master's program, but the last year would require full-time residency in

TABLE 4

EDUCATIONAL PREPARATION AND PROFESSIONAL BACKGROUND OF FACULTY TEACHING CAREER OR TRANSFER COURSES

Degree Held	(In per cent) Transfer Faculty n=1008	(In per cent) Career Faculty n=1024
Doctorate	16.6	5.5
Master's	67.0	61.1
Bachelor's	16.4	27.0
Associate	0.0	3.2
Less than Associate	0.0	3.2
	100.0	100.0

(In Birnbaum, 1966, p. 35)

TABLE 5

DEGREES HELD BY COMMUNITY JUNIOR COLLEGE FACULTY

Degree (Figures in per cent)

Year	Doctor's	Master's + 1 year	Master's	Non-Masters	Men
1957-58	6.2	22.1	43.6	28.1	72.0
1958-59	7.9	18.6	45.8	27.7	69.1
1959-60	6.6	17.7	47.8	27.9	68.6
1960-61	6.1	17.1	48.5	28.3	67.5
1961-62	7.0	18.4	53.6	21.0	69.1
1962-63	7.2	20.7	51.5	20.6	70.9

(In Wurster, 1969, p. 6)

a community college to demonstrate high competency in a variety of instructional skills. A similar program presented to the Council of Graduate Schools would provide a Ph.D. for persons interested in undergraduate teaching. In lieu of the dissertation, candidates would teach for two years in a two-year or four-year college and receive their doctorate upon the successful completion of this experience. Another proposal would include a one-year teaching internship supervised by experienced and dedicated teachers. "In place of the dissertation, one could present an expository dissertation of modest length." This project would be expected to display "a clear, well-organized presentation of a problem, theme or idea which draws not only upon a major discipline, but also upon knowledge of other relevant disciplines" (The Chronicle, Dec. 1969).

Some efforts are again being contemplated to make a Ph.D. in teaching an honorable alternative. But if such programs are ever to emerge as viable and respected alternatives, they will need "strong and aggressive administrative leadership, effective representative support from the teaching faculty, and a political place of power within the university structure." Ann Heiss, of the Center for Research and Development in Higher Education (Berkeley), correctly concludes:

> If none are willing to speak for teaching, or if those who speak are defeated by the wall of silence which confronts them, patchwork efforts at reform will continue to be applied in place of new and different doctoral programs that educate integrated teachers, not just specialized scholars (In The Chronicle, March 16, 1970, p. 5).

Allan Cartter, Chancellor of New York University, who predicted the current Ph.D. surplus more than six years ago, now predicts that the shortage of positions for Ph.D.'s will get even worse in most disciplines during the next twenty years. Hodgkinson (1970a), however, feels that less and less college and university teachers will have the Ph.D. due to the rapid expansion of the community college. But if the community college were to absorb the excess number of Ph.D.'s, it would rise to what William Birenbaum often depicts as new levels of ineptness. Adding Ph.D.'s to community college staffs just because they are available would constitute a serious blunder.

Programs to train community college teachers will

necessarily have to include aspects of learning theory, evaluation, community college philosophy, and the nature of student clientele. Also, the long-standing damnation of education courses will have to be reconciled. Bruce Dearing is quoted in Current Issues in Higher Education (1965) as saying:

> As a group, college teachers have been loftily contemptuous of courses in education and absurdly vain about their innocence of any formal instruction in curriculum design, testing techniques, and formal classroom procedures.

Thus, the new spirit of teaching calls for change, both internal and external; both in those who need it and in those who provide it. Bold new ideas are needed to raise the level of the teaching profession.

The Carnegie Corporation publicly supports the use of such degrees as the Master of Philosophy now in use at the University of Toronto and the Doctor of Arts currently in use at Carnegie-Mellon, the University of Washington, and elsewhere. At Carnegie-Mellon, the Doctor of Arts differs from the Ph.D. in that it does not require a foreign language or written comprehensive examinations. Oral examinations and a dissertation are required, but the dissertation may be traditional or creative, the latter category including such options as a group of poems or new curricular designs.

State agencies such as the Illinois Board of Higher Education are recommending use of the new degrees. A joint study of community college English departments by the Modern Language Association and the A.A.J.C. has also called for the establishment of the Doctor of Arts program, as has the University of California. "We need the specialists in college teaching far more at this moment in American higher education than we need our growing supply of research-oriented Ph.D.'s," said Michael Shugrue, the Language Association's Secretary for English (In The Chronicle, March 16, 1970, p. 1).

The Carnegie Corporation has provided ten $100,000 grants for institutions to plan and develop the Doctor of Arts as an equal alternative to the Ph.D. Support and guidelines are being developed by the American Association of State Colleges and Universities and the Council of Graduate Schools "to prepare students for a lifetime of creative and meaningful teaching at the college level," and to reverse the trend of current doctoral programs which "continue to produce research-scholars with little or no special emphasis on preparation for college teaching." Even external examinations for granting the Ph.D. are becoming a reality due to the lethargic response of traditional university change (Rogers, 1970).

The U.S. Office of Education has ruled that candidates for the Doctor of Arts degree are eligible for grants under Title IV of the National Defense Education Act. In effect, this decision recognizes the Doctor of Arts degree as "equivalent in quality though different in character from the Ph.D." Even so, community colleges would do well to seek and develop programs specifically related to their individual needs. For example, the University of Miami, with the cooperation of Miami-Dade Junior College and other nearby institutions, introduced a new doctoral level teaching program for community college teachers. Called the Diplomate in College Teaching (D.C.T.), the new degree includes courses about the students, instruction, community college programs, and a teaching internship (Besvinick and Fryer, 1969).

In a certain sense, the overpowering stability of Ph.D. programs has compelled teaching reform to take other alternatives to provide better training for community college teachers. More than likely, this same overpowering stability will reduce all other degree alternatives to a lesser status. Time and performance will undoubtedly make some of the new degrees more acceptable than others, but only alternatives within the current Ph.D. structure can quickly and effectively bring about the desired outcomes on a high level. Without serious options to prepare teachers in some current Ph.D. programs, teaching will remain relegated to a novel but lesser status than might be desired.

Problems

Siehr and others (1963) have studied the problems of new faculty members in community colleges. Studying some 309 public community colleges and "120 private community colleges," data from more than three thousand two-year college teachers was gathered. Seventy-two common problems were ranked by frequency, difficulty, and persistence. The question, "Which problems are perceived as more critical than other problems by new faculty members in community

The Faculty

colleges?" can best be analyzed in terms of the responses which ranked highest in all categories. They include:

1. Lack of time for scholarly study.

2. Adapting instruction to individual differences.

3. Dealing with students who require special attention to overcome deficiencies.

4. Acquiring adequate secretarial help.

5. Understanding college policies regarding teaching load.

6. Challenging superior students.

7. Obtaining needed instructional materials.

8. Grading or marking students' work.

9. Understanding college policies to be followed in curriculum development and revision.

(Siehr, et al., 1963, p. 26)

Of these nine major problems, none is unique from the point of view of the community college as a distinctly different kind of educational institution. Of course, the authors' inclusion of "private community colleges" tends to distort the sample and invalidate any explanation outside their loose interpretation of community college. Still, with this in mind, it is observed that five of the nine major problems are instructional; three are administrative problems related to the structure, policies, and procedures of the individual college; and one is a problem of professional improvement. In general, new teachers stated that their problems tend to be more persistent than those of teachers who had taught at the college for several years.

The study also reveals five procedures which can be particularly helpful and effective to new teachers. These procedures call for the following:

1. Further materials such as schedules, course outlines, texts, and faculty handbook should be supplied upon appointment.

2. An orientation conference with the department head should be arranged upon appointment.

3. A lighter teaching load should be set up for new faculty members.

4. Regular departmental meetings should be held.

5. A faculty sponsor should be provided for each new faculty member.

(Siehr, et al., 1963, p. 64)

Other problems for community college faculty relate to general issues in faculty governance, tenure and academic freedom, changes in faculty life styles, unionization, and militancy. Organizational structures are constantly being revised, thus permitting a great deal of flexibility to experiment with shared authority forms of college governance. The most effective internal organization, according to the American Association for Higher Education's Task Force on Faculty Representation and Academic Negotiations, is an academic senate that includes faculty and administrators, with a clear majority of faculty (Wright, 1967). To a certain degree, however, the community college still suffers from older governance techniques, not unlike those associated with the secondary schools in which faculty are treated as "employees" of the board rather than professionals.

The extent to which community college teachers learn to eliminate internal divisiveness and to raise their acceptance as a profession will determine the extent to which militancy and unionization take hold. In the absence of internal academic or faculty senates, external faculty pressures increasingly become more prevalent. At times, the close association with secondary schools provides an easy access for unionization to become a welcomed faculty tactic. Since a majority of community college teachers still come from high schools, where militancy has become prevalent, it is likely that former attitudes will be carried over into the new teaching assignment. The collective negotiating procedures of the elementary and secondary schools have already spread through the community college into four-year and graduate institutions. As with other groups who collectively negotiate, faculty concerns are primarily with salary and conditions of work. Unfortunately, the collective bargaining model for faculty and administrative interaction, as contrasted to the collegial approach, encourages an adversary relationship. With added pressure from the oversupply of teachers and dwindling budgets, some faculty members will be let go in order to pay for those who stay. And, as in other segments of education, community college teachers will continue to call for a greater voice in all college matters while not actually wanting to participate (Dykes, 1968).

The Teaching

The community college has long exploited the fact that teaching is notoriously worse in universities than in lower colleges. But now, the community college is openly challenged to verify its historical claim as an institution of teaching excellence. And like all other educational institutions, the community college is being forced to be more accountable for what it portends to do. In a real sense, the institution is being challenged to live up to its own standards.

Instruction and Learning

Koos (1925) and Eells (1931) both reported on the "superior instruction" and "superior instructors" that were found in the early junior colleges. But the Silver Anniversary issue of the Junior College Journal (April, 1955) and the Peterson study (1965) in California both found the most important problem to be concerned with the effectiveness and improvement of instruction. Excellence in teaching is no longer solely the trademark of two-year colleges. Indeed, hardly any educational institution fails to lay claim to superior teachers and excellent teaching. Still, we agree on so little concerning the learning process, creativity, good and bad teaching, and motivation. As Francis Wayland (1830) pondered a similar dilemma, he asked:

> If there be any art as the art of teaching, we ask how it comes to pass that a man shall be considered fully qualified to exercise it without a day's practice, when a similar attempt in any other art would expose him to ridicule? (p. 13).

In many ways, college teaching is still a primitive profession for, according to Kenneth E. Clark (1969):

> There are no standards to insure that only qualified practitioners enter the 'guild.' The stereotype

format assumes that only those with certain formal credentials are qualified as teachers. Teachers should be selected on the basis of natural communicative abilities rather than credentials alone, and should be further trained in the art of teaching.

Institutional practices in the community college typically consist of teachers "talking at students who remain quiet" (Cohen and Brawer, 1968). Individualized instruction often amounts to mass instruction, individually. In reality, the art of teaching as practiced in the community college is no different from that found in four-year colleges and universities. With teachers at all levels becoming more and more alike, it is inevitable that teaching practices will also become homogenized. Unfortunately, with the student clientele becoming more diverse in the community college, the commonly accepted modes of traditional teaching are simply not adequate.

More external influence can now be expected. For example, legislators are conducting studies and making educational decisions such as those that set working conditions for teachers; private enterprise is selling guaranteed learning; and private commissions are providing sorely needed leadership for educational change. All too easily, community college teachers blindly adopt the methods of the university and high school. They work under "unproven assumptions" which consider that there is a direct correlation between what a teacher says in the classroom and what the students learn. A second "fallacious assumption" is that a low student-teacher ratio is a sign of quality education. Still another "assumption that impedes progress" is that the student learns best when he is physically in the room with the teacher (Eurich, 1970b). Overall, teaching that favors indoor, seated, nonverbal, passive types of learning is still prevalent. As Cicero once stated, "The authority of those who teach is very often a hindrance to those who learn." And, in a more fashionable manner, Commenius wisely concluded that "the beginning and end of our Didactic will be to seek and find a method by which teachers teach less and learners learn more."

Social necessity demands that citizens acquire the ability to be self-motivated and self-directed within the confines of their innate abilities and resources. In a sense, then, "the final goal of any student's education should be the

The Faculty

capacity to learn without the teacher" (Eurich, 1970b). The first step toward self-education is to make the student aware of the "unpalatable truth that we do not know, and are unlikely to know, the answers to the questions that are of the greatest concern to us" (Toynbee, 1968). The teaching-learning and teacher-learner roles must be revised and even exchanged at times. The whole process must be restructured and based upon clearly stated, guiding principles which incorporate a personalized credo of education.

Shawl (1970) recommends a sound rationale for community college instruction which is based upon the following principles:

> 1. Teaching is the prime function of the community-junior college.
>
> 2. Teaching is the process of <u>causing learning</u>.
>
> 3. Learning is <u>changed ability or tendency</u> to act in particular ways.
>
> 4. Both teaching and learning may be assumed to have occurred only when observable changes are demonstrated by the learner.
>
> 5. Changes may be observed only if there has been a determination of student ability prior to instruction.
>
> 6. Specific, measurable objectives must be set in order that learning may be appropriately guided (p. 49).

This is in keeping with Skinner's <u>Technology of Teaching</u> (1968) which points out, "The first step in designing instruction is to define terminal behavior." We know that learners must perceive a sense of purpose and meaning to the activities they engage in, yet, communication of objectives in the community college is a rarity. "Students are not given the purpose of their endeavor or directions in which the activities are designed to lead" (Cohen and Brawer, 1968, p. 56). Put more simply, Shawl (1970) concludes that "<u>teaching</u> is causing learning, no more, no less." Teaching occurs only to the extent that learning takes place. "If no measurable evidence of learning can be exhibited," says John Roueche, "we must infer that no teaching occurred" (In <u>The Chronicle</u>,

March 30, 1970, p. 8). The essential concept is that teachers are greatly accountable for the results of their teaching.

This style of teaching necessarily demands more time and effort from teachers and will require new ways to define work loads. Present work routines generally prohibit teachers from seriously developing criterion-referenced instruction (behavioral objectives) of sufficient quality and satisfactory breadth. Still, the need for educational reform dictates that this style of teaching be developed. Behavioral objectives are commonly referred to as instructional objectives, performance objectives, or defined outcomes instruction. Perceived by most teachers as a "new" approach, teaching programs based on "desired outcomes" have long been an ideal for many educators. In 1929, Selvidge suggested such an approach in which the teacher selects and arranges learning experiences so as to produce desired outcomes. It was explained as "a case of analysis and synthesis." Perhaps the best source for the practitioner is Ralph Tyler's Syllabus for Education 360, which later became Basic Principles of Curriculum and Instruction (1949). Capper (1969a) summarizes the guiding principles as follows:

> The major course goals indicate what generally is to become of students taking the course by specifying actions to be taken, skills to be learned, abilities to be gained, or attitudes to be held or modified as a result of having taken the course. The objectives indicate specific, observable student actions or the products of such action, and to be properly utilized, should also indicate the circumstance under which the action will be taken and the degree of accuracy to which the student is to perform (p. 1).

Evaluation

Faculty performance and effectiveness must be evaluated if good teaching is to be encouraged and bad teaching discouraged. Unfortunately, there appears to be no consensus regarding the specific criteria for judging effective teaching. As B. Lamar Johnson (1970) concluded: "Evaluation of instruction is largely a missing entity in the junior colleges of our nation, as it is indeed in most of American education." For the most part, teachers use assessment for promotion or merit increases; to satisfy administrative curiosity about the quality of instruction; and for the improvement of teaching (Boyer, 1970). All too often, however, instructional evaluation does not relate to instructional techniques or the results of instruction. Cohen and Brawer (1968) conclude that "evaluation would be more meaningful if it related to instruction as a discipline rather than to the person of the instructor." But the teacher and the teaching are interlocked in the same process and more effective results are obtained if evaluation techniques are general and pervasive.

John Gustad (1967) compared methods of instructional evaluation that are used in two-year colleges. They are rank-ordered as follows:

1. Dean evaluation
2. Chairman evaluation
3. Classroom visits
4. Course syllabi and examinations
5. Informal student opinions
6. Grade distributions
7. Colleagues' opinions
8. Long-term follow-up on students
9. Student examination performance
10. Self-evaluation
11. Systematic student ratings
12. Committee evaluations
13. Alumni opinions
14. Enrollment in elective courses
15. Scholarly research and publications

Teachers should seek multiple forms of evaluation and not be subject to any single plan. Regardless of the methods or techniques employed, however, certain principles should be followed. Morin (1968) suggests six that are of some value:

> 1. Evaluation is a complex and vital process and must not be treated casually ...
>
> 2. The evaluator must employ 'scientific' procedures in an effort to collect objective data.
>
> 3. Evaluation of individual instructors should focus primarily on definable segments of observable behavior--both of the teacher and of the students.
>
> 4. To determine the desirability of changes in student behavior, some prior descriptions must be

prepared in operational terms of the type of performance desired.

5. Both instructor and evaluator must be cognizant of, and accept as legitimate, the stated objectives of the instructional procedures, and

6. The evaluative procedure must be inherent in the total scheme for instructional development.

Ascertaining the value or worth of the educational process should presuppose the establishment of explicit goals or objectives in addition to the usual implicit factors. Accordingly, "the ends of instruction must be agreed upon before effective evaluation procedures can be established" and teaching-learning effectiveness assessed more validly. It is this process, more than evaluation, that causes most problems for teachers. Only much time and deliberate planning can produce a complete instructional format. (Boyer, 1970).

An evaluation technique that merits additional study is the team approach in which a collective group of teachers integrate their skills and competence in all phases of instruction. Evaluation then becomes a process in which colleagues directly "influence each other's activities," eventually becoming "an integral part of the instructional development of the college" (Boyer, 1970). This collective approach includes administrative and student input.

Students must necessarily be a major factor in all aspects of community college education. Shawl (1970) suggests that we evaluate what students learn and not what teachers teach; the ultimate criterion of teaching success being student growth. This would necessarily place more emphasis on what students do while de-emphasizing what teachers do. Students enjoy a day-to-day relationship with the overall instructional environment that teachers and administrators simply cannot perceive. Student evaluation of instruction is considered among the most valid and constructive since there is little bias due to age, sex, or grades received. Even the most simple approach can capture the spirit of student evaluation. C. Gilbert Wrenn, Distinguished Professor from Macalaster College, would ask students only to respond to two basic questions:

1. What, if anything, do you *like* about me, my teaching, and my relations with *you* as a student?

In what would you encourage me to do more?

2. What, if anything, do you not like about me, my teaching, and my relations with students? What do I do or not that hinders your learning? (In The Chronicle, May 10, 1971, p. 8).

Evaluation is a natural part of the education process and occurs in both formal and informal ways. It is the responsibility of teachers to view evaluative techniques as useful components of their role performance. A well-defined self-conception of the teacher role is helpful even in the absence of formal evaluation procedures. Instructor self-appraisal thus establishes a workable and frequently interesting method in which teachers seek to improve themselves without the direct influence of administrators and colleagues. As a first step to more pervasive methods, self-appraisal can develop confidence and improvement in a self-operated manner, with reinforcement or feedback as a built-in component.

Grading

Present concerns about grading arise from a large body of firmly held opinion and little objective evidence. Yet, community college teachers generally rely on standard teaching and grading practices, even though the student clientele is remarkably diverse and not befitting the standard academic model.

Grades tend to serve the interests of faculty, certifying agencies, college catalogs, registrars, and upper division colleges more than they serve the student--for and by whom the original intent was initiated. There is no conclusive evidence that grades measure what they are supposed to, even if agreement could be reached on what it is. Like projective test items, grades or other letter-numerical symbols allow us to read into them whatever we wish within wide latitudes (Yelon, 1970). Too often, grades are erroneously equated with the larger and necessary concept of evaluation. Few, if any, recent research reports have supported the standard grading system. As one researcher aptly concluded:

> One of the greatest obstacles to effective education in the United States today is the traditional marking system. Abolish the pernicious practice of sorting students into arbitrary fixed grade

categories and a host of educational handicaps is reduced or disappears: extrinsic motivation, cheating, poor student-teacher relations, the test crisis syndrome, and failures imposed by the marking system (Manello, 1969, p. 305).

The composite qualities that grades are meant to reflect within various disciplines and activities are timidly being explored. Even when these qualities are identified and isolated, there is a general fear of relating to them in other than traditional ways. With its inconsistency and unintended effects, the traditional grading system proves to be embarrassing to teachers and frustrating to students. Faculty generally avoid discussing grading practices with each other and, from the student's point of view, the important thing is to understand the game and play it for survival (Birenbaum, 1969).

Evaluation is most often made manifest by the awarding, giving, or recording of grades--a ritualistic process with an endless variety of interpretations. Nevertheless, grading is but one visible aspect of much larger issues. Still, more than half of the literature about grades in the period 1965 to 1970 was concerned with their form and their predictive relationship to later grades (Warren, 1971). Some important but neglected issues remain:

1. Do we know the effects of grades on the educational process?

2. Can grades be justified as incentives to learning?

3. What aspects of student behavior are reflected by grades?

4. What function do grades serve in selection procedures?

5. Can alternative devices serve the functions of grades and eliminate their shortcomings? (Teaf, 1964).

With all the complexity and diversity in higher education, grading procedures are monolithic and remain basically at a standstill. Given that the community college is charged with different kinds of educational tasks and nontraditional students, unique instructional and grading forms have yet to be developed to suit the purpose. As the community college faculty becomes more and more like all other higher education faculties, the chances for real reform increasingly diminish.

Grading can be seen as the process by which symbols are assigned to some level of achievement as determined by the prior process of evaluation. The critical problem occurs in the process of translating the results of evaluation into symbols. In this sense, the fidelity of grades is poor in that they transmit only a small part of the information of the more important evaluation process. Unfortunately, many dissimilar kinds of affective and cognitive skills in all disciplines are collapsed onto the singular dimension of a grade and, even worse, a single grade-point average. Conceivably, the inability to read can be "averaged" by the ability to write. (Warren, 1971).

Grades serve administrative and educational functions (Ericksen, 1967) which often conflict. They are used to sort and select students, maintain existing class structures (Lauter and Howe, 1970), provide admission to some programs, and restrict admission to others. Grades are also used for employment selection, draft status, motivation, financial awards, and academic status or prestige. And while grades are generally predictive of future grades, they do not correlate well with occupational success (Hoyt, 1965, 1966, 1968). Very often, grades favor students for such qualities as sensitivity, compliance, and agreeableness more than for those kinds of activities that optimize learning (Becker, et al., 1968; Warren, 1971).

Grades become a motivation tool to coerce students, often punitively, to perform in a certain manner, even if only temporarily. They also attach a social status and a competitive spirit which raise anxiety levels for students while producing conformity, undue mental stress, and cheating. For students, grades become supreme ends; learning becomes an anticipated by-product. Wrote Woodring (1968):

> ... no one can seriously believe that grades are the goal of higher education. And the assumption that those who make high grades are the ones who profit most from their education and are most likely to make the greatest contribution to society after graduation should be re-examined, for it must withstand a considerable amount of contradictory

evidence (p. 42).

Educational research is just beginning to reveal the effects of grading. Many colleges are considering alternatives which include abolishing all grades and indicating only satisfactory completion of courses or objectives. Other more popular alternatives include descriptive grading; nonpunitive grading; pass-fail, pass-erase, or pass/no record grading; and systems which use ABCX; ABC; Excellent, Very Good, and Qualified; and Clear/Not Clear with respect to evidence of academic or skill competency. (Warren, 1971).

With students from first generation college families, the community college allows traditional grading systems to push out those who fail to learn what is traditionally expected. The first college year is generally an experimental one in which an individual learns to adjust, think, try different courses, and consider several careers. But he often acquires a quality point average which, to most teachers, reveals that he cannot "cut it," the assumption being that this grade index is an accurate reflection of what he has learned. Also, the concept of academic dismissal is based upon the assumption that a student with low grades is not profiting from his educational experience. There is little evidence to support this assumption, and some recent testing evidence actually contradicts it (see Astin, 1971).

Students with the ability to direct their own learning have a good chance to succeed despite educational barriers. But for those with unrealistic goals or no goals at all, the educational process should not merely terminate their attempts; rather, it should re-channel them into more productive alternatives. Grades should reflect the positive aspects of learning and show what was accomplished rather than what was not done and how "well" it was not done. The nature of the community college suggests that academic dismissal and punitive grading systems should be abandoned and replaced with more simple and meaningful practices. To be sure, "failure" itself cannot be eliminated; but the present system, with its unintended and debilitating effects, can. Expecting nonstudents or poor students to perform in the traditional academic environment is not only unrealistic, it is dehumanizing. With appropriate resources and trained personnel, all but a few of these "academic rejects" can be brought to acceptable or even exceptional levels of performance in academic, skill or career areas. Human self-renewal is a legitimate goal for the community college!

What appears to be radical or heretical in these observations is not. In reality, most revised grading policies are modest. Even the one that employs A, B, C for success, and no other grades, is coming into use with little confusion or concern. It is the overall grading system with excessive symbolism (A, B, C, D, F, I, W, W-P, W-F, S, U, P, CR, N-CR, X ...) that has perjured academic intent. Academic failure is recorded freely for improper withdrawal from courses, misregistration, tardiness, and absence, as well as traditional academic shortcomings. The grade "D" is used knowing that, in most cases, it does not have transferability, yet it allows a teacher to "pass" students who gainfully try to balance its effect with other grades. Lawrence Smith (1969) summarizes the dilemma of the "F" grade as follows:

Pro

1. A potential "F" is incentive to do better work.

2. Failure occurs in life and cannot be excluded from the academic world.

3. "D" and "F" grades bring academic dismissal making more room for qualified students.

Con

1. An "F" is a double penalty requiring better than average grades to counterbalance it.

2. Fear of an "F" may impair performance of anxiety-prone students.

3. "F" grades discourage experimentation outside one's own interest.

The logic that still supports relative grading on a competitive curve after half a century can only serve to debase the concepts of individuality, self-identity, intrinsic motivation, and self-directed continuing education. This logic also serves to enhance the custodial function in the community college.

Education without grades presents problems which, according to Warren (1971), "may be far less serious and more amenable to solution than the problems grades contribute." It remains for the community college to develop programs suited to the entry level of its students without the immediate possibility of placing these same students in a position where their efforts are graded with cold academic finality. Institutional practice must be made to conform to philosophical intent if the community college idea is to succeed. More than any other group, it is the faculty who shall determine what success is. Allowing the intellectually favored or endowed to get ahead by putting down the less favored constitutes an undemocratic process for the community college.

Research: A Missing Function

Teaching and research are interlocking components of the educational process; they cannot be completely divorced from each other. With a false sense of security and pride, the community college has chosen to claim the former by altogether disregarding the latter. According to Gaff and Wilson at Berkeley's Center for Research and Development, more than nine out of ten professors who nurture research at the university level say teaching is "the major source of satisfaction in their lives" (In *The Chronicle*, April 5, 1971, p. 4). But research in general is not a source of satisfaction to community college teachers. According to Johnson (1970), "The community college is a teaching--not a research --institution. Its effectiveness is dependent upon the quality of its instructional programs." Community college teachers are under heavy pressure to achieve efficiency and improvement in all aspects of operation. As a result, they become consumers of research rather than producers of it (Rislov, 1957). In 1962, however, Johnson noted that: "Both the quality of research and effectiveness of reporting varies widely from college to college. In all too many [community] colleges the quality of research is distinctively inferior" (In *Institutional Research*, 1962, p. 28).

The type of research that the community college should undertake can hardly be of the substance and kind that takes place so well in the university. Rather, the uniqueness of the community college suggests a different type of research: one that would require a systematic study and investigation to establish facts and principles to sustain further growth and development. Research is innovation and experimentation of substantive quality in areas related to open admissions, teaching techniques, new modes of learning, student motivation, behavioral objectives, evaluation techniques, and student performance. Research means understanding more about dropouts, slow learners, nonlearners, programmed learning, dial access learning, new grading systems, experimental learning, and new styles of community action. Community college research also means finding new ways to take learning to the people, and new ways to assess learning in other than fixed time, credit, and courses. Research can also suggest ways to attack illiteracy and redefine literacy to include the ability to read, to write, and to use a computer. Other possibilities are numerous and wait to be explored. The void of educational research at the practitioner's level can only be filled given the impetus and spirit of a moonshot endeavor.

The trichotomy of research in the community college involves the institution, the faculty, and the student-community. Scott (1970) provides a clear differentiation:

> Institutional research is defined as problem and student-oriented research either general and theoretical or specific and practical, depending on the ability of the researcher. It consists of systematic and organized fact-finding activities which are focused on current and pragmatic problems, with institutional improvements as an anticipated outcome.
>
> Student-community research is defined as the combination of student learning experiences with participation in the solution of socio-technical community problems.

It is inconceivable that any institution could provide teaching excellence without actively and aggressively exploring the state of the art. Faculty research may be more discipline-oriented than institutional research, but both are worthy endeavors. The whole area of student personnel services awaits experimentation, testing, and overhaul with faculty participation. But although teaching and research are not antithetical, "faculty members have a proclivity for denying that research findings about learning apply to their own discipline, to their own behavior in the classroom, and to the creation of academic policies" (Milton, 1971, p. 3).

Thus, the implicit disavowal of the research function is contributing to the chaotic nature of community college development (Knoell, 1969). The inability of the institution

to provide or stimulate faculty participation is causing much
waste of professional resources. The absence of a research
base for community college planning necessitates the use of
linear, status quo projections of growth that occasionally
produce what Knoell calls "absurd or economically unsound
estimates of quantitative measures needed in planning."

In a simple but effective manner, community college
faculty can contribute to the body of research concerning
their institutions. There is still no definitive evidence that
specification of behavioral objectives makes a difference
(Alkin, 1969). Nor is there evidence to support small
classes as being most effective. Since no one method of
instruction is best, controlled studies of parallel methods
with differentiated groups of students would be welcomed.
Several individual colleges may investigate learning as an
internal and personal affair while others explore methods to
enhance self-directed, independent learning. As long ago
as 1958, John Gardner and others noted the paucity of such
studies:

> It is important to accept the desirability of a rigorous reappraisal of present patterns and courageous experimentation with new patterns. This must include ... at the level of higher education the trying out of approaches which place more responsibility upon the student for his own learning (p. 25).

Yet, Arrowsmith (1968, p. 125) concluded ten years later,
"Apart from a few noteworthy experiments, there is so little
real innovation."

An example of what can be accomplished is the result
of a collective research effort among several community colleges in Texas. Over a period of time, under close examination, it was found that the use of deficiency reports at
mid-term would stifle further progress for students with an
"F" grade, but would permit significant improvement for
those students only receiving a "D" (Creamer, 1969). An
"F" seemed to be more of the same for students who did
not "measure up" in junior and senior high school. Thus,
the "F" notice apparently discouraged the marginal student
from improving, by depriving him of self-motivation. As a
result of this experiment, many of the participating institutions discontinued the use of deficiency reports. Widespread
projects should now be initiated to promote and validate the

results of such research.

The best current source for research productivity is the Educational Resources Information Center (E. R. I. C.) Clearinghouse for Junior Colleges. A joint project of the U. C. L. A. School of Education and the Powell Library, this E. R. I. C. Clearinghouse began operating in 1966. Its main purpose is:

> ... to process studies so that information would become available for people making important decisions in junior colleges. Accordingly the clearinghouse set out to acquire, index, and abstract research documents and research-related materials and to disseminate them to the field in a variety of ways (Cohen, 1967).

Thus, with a grass-roots approach, the community college is challenged to accept an educational research function at the local and regional level. The unprecedented style of community college education depends upon such research efforts receiving national dissemination.

In Conclusion

More than any other group, the teaching faculty of the community college express the institution's credibility and life style. The college cannot long endure if it allows its ideology to become mismatched with those who would express that ideology in a subversive manner. If this happens, the institution will lose its unmatched sense of purpose. The lack of tradition and freedom from institutional restraint that the faculty once knew is gone. In a similar fashion, the opportunity to be different in theory and practice is passing; the ideology of the community college appears to have already peaked. It remains for the faculty to revitalize their own style of renewal or forever submit the institution to the standard academic mind. Being unable to adapt to the consequences of an open door, too many teachers are already committed to closing it. Seeking protection from unwanted or disappearing jobs, too many faculty have taken refuge in the community college and may just be passing through.

A unique student clientele requires an unprecedented educational response that only dedicated faculty can provide.

Learning styles must be seriously explored without getting overly involved with popular but passing fads. Behavioral objectives cannot work for all teachers or all students, but parallel kinds of diverse learning activities can exist simultaneously, with students adapting in a manner that makes them more responsible for their own learning. The research function must be revitalized if the new order is to provide an adequate response to diverse needs within communities. Teaching loads must be redefined in terms of new styles of teaching and learning yet to be discovered and implemented. The faculty must resist the temptation to operate in a style which seeks prestige and status at any cost. It is antithetical for the community college to seek uniqueness while at the same time striving to be like other colleges.

In a wasteful way, the community college has failed to utilize sufficient numbers of its own graduates. Many assistants and aides can be trained internally to provide service in laboratories, classrooms, media centers, computer centers, and libraries. More than one-third of a teacher's duties are concerned with subprofessional tasks that community college graduates can fulfill (Bock, 1968). Indeed, graduates who develop the necessary expertise, with or without the baccalaureate, can become productive teaching assistants in the community college.

The manner in which the faculty develop and respond to such issues as collective bargaining, governance, the oversupply of Ph.D.'s, social problems, and economic restraint, will undoubtedly affect the future of the institution. Changes in faculty attitude, professional preparation, pre- and in-service education hold the key to real innovation. Meanwhile, leadership must be sought in new administrative styles and selectivity must characterize the process of recruiting, retaining, and nurturing community college teachers.

CHAPTER 6

SUMMARY, CONCLUSIONS, IMPLICATIONS

The community college has evolved from what William Cowley (1970) calls a "historical accident" to become what Robert Hutchins (1936a) calls the "characteristic educational institution of the United States." Economic, educational, vocational, social, and value changes have continually served to intensify rather than alleviate the needs which the community college serves. In short, this institution is the product of interlocking revolutions that have evolved along with society over the past century.

This study supports the thesis that the community college has evolved into a distinct educational form which has undertaken unique tasks that differentiate it from the conventional junior college. Only after a long struggle did the community college become more closely identified with higher education than secondary education, although many of its educational and social tasks are still secondary in nature. No longer a mere bridge between secondary and higher education, the community college overlaps and encompasses certain features of both, while retaining unique features of its own; its unprecedented dual status remains viable.

The institution's relative growth and success are, in great part, due to inherent inequities and deficiencies in traditional education. Higher education has accumulated a poor record with space-time utilization of physical, financial, and human resources. All too often, administrative convenience has taken precedence over teaching policy and learning effectiveness in an attempt to preserve the faltering concept of an uninterrupted, four-year college career. As the twentieth century land-grant institution, the community college is supposed to provide alternatives for all classes of people within reach of its programs and services. Barriers to higher education are seriously being challenged for the first time.

The inability of traditional higher education to resolve the problems of mass higher education in a technological society adds credibility to the idea of the community college. Education has grown to become the nation's largest industry with more than sixty-one million people involved as students, teachers, or administrators. Still, there is too little enjoyment in the educational process and each step in the disjointed continuum raises anxiety about qualifying for the next step. The obstacle of certification is unduly hindering the educational process with an "overriding assertion" that people must be "certified" by colleges in order to "succeed." The necessity for a degree or credential far outweighs the need to become educated. Value orientations have been distorted and college easily becomes a prelude to acquiring an essential, productive education.

More than ever before, there is a great urgency to identify and provide viable career opportunities. But academicians have incessantly belittled vocational-occupational-technical education despite the growing demand for people with competent skills in a variety of fields. In some unknown manner, social and cultural values have continued to enhance the status of those positions more closely related to pure mental activity, as opposed to those that utilize more obvious forms of trained or highly skilled physical activity. Ironically, lower working classes have supported this attitude which is antithetical to the very condition of their life styles.

Inherent to the community college ideology is a philosophy that is supposed to reduce the many dichotomies that have accumulated in higher education. Reflecting social uncertainty, these dichotomies pervade our educational thinking:

> quality versus quantity
> pedantic versus realistic
> work versus play
> elite versus mass
> private versus public
> idealism versus pragmatism
> thinking versus doing
> teaching versus research
> academic versus practical
> research versus service
> standards versus democracy
> white versus black
> excellence versus mediocrity
> privilege versus right

rich versus poor
theoretical versus applied   (Rever, 1971)

Because of things that have gone wrong and unfulfilled promises, the community college must continue to renew itself even though it adopts what appear to be contradictory tasks. Being relatively new, the institution is still defining its many roles and establishing priorities for its primary constituencies which include students, taxpayers, administrators, boards of control, minorities, teachers, and community representatives.

Providing a variety of personal and social assistance to multiple cultures has generated a new community dimension, with academic and nonacademic services constituting the educational program. The community becomes a work-study learning laboratory and change characterizes the defined outcome of its mission. The college is potentially free to be many things to many people, if only it will. It is challenged to face the common problems of higher education with the expectation that it will provide different but better solutions. Too often, however, the college continues to exhibit a fear of failure by sanctioning its programs within the safety and conformity of tradition.

The real strength of the community college lies with the people it serves. More diverse than any other clientele in post-secondary education, those who are served by this institution reflect divergent characteristics from a broad range of society and mirror the community in which each college is located. The usual connotations associated with students are inadequate and inappropriate in describing this heterogeneous group. With a median age of twenty-seven and rising, the new clientele turn more and more to part-time, continuing education that will require new modes of delivering instruction. As a group, they defy simplistic generalizations and make it necessary to realign much of the traditional thinking about what students should be like. It must be recognized that we are all career-oriented individuals who often find it necessary to drop in and out of the core system at various times and for various reasons; continuing education must be legitimized as a substantive attribute of all life styles.

The community college has changed the emphasis from being overly concerned about where students go to a concern with conditions from which they come. With the premise that each individual should be given a chance to develop equality, identity, and self-worth, the college strives to operate with an open door philosophy. But open admissions remains illusory for some. Once admitted, individuals are often subjected to an academic atmosphere which presupposes entirely too much about prior attitudes, interests, and academic preparation. New programs are often mere rearrangements of the traditional forms that they were designed to replace. Students still come to the college at fixed times to observe teaching techniques which often disregard the nature of the learner. In short, teaching continues to preempt learning.

The college must concern itself more with graduation competencies and admission weaknesses of applicants. Faculty must be cognizant of the fact that people are willing to accept life-learning styles that fit their lives; education adapted to the interests and convenience of teachers and administrators will not suffice. The college must provide for people to learn in relation to where they are, whenever convenient. Programs must reach into secondary schools, prisons, hospitals, and storefronts. Indeed, educational programs must find entirely new arrangements to accommodate changing needs of mobile learners as well as those who prefer to learn at home or on the job. Commencement must truly reflect the beginning rather than the end of an education.

Karl Marx concluded that the contradictions of a society are felt most sharply by its marginal classes. In this sense, the mission of the community college is directed to help all people, including nonlearners, classless and disenfranchised persons. Knowing that social dropouts and academic dropouts share similar problems, the community college must strive to reduce race and class distinctions, for no other institution has the vast potential to do so. Education remains the chief means of social mobility and the future is being charted by the kinds of education that each group receives now. Still, Daniel Bell (1962) forewarns that in the future post-industrial society, class lines will be predominantly color lines. Other futurologists maintain that current educational systems are growing obsolescent and new patterns of power are in the making, with the influence of teachers and politicians yielding to mass media; adults over forty to those in their thirties and younger; generalists to specialists; and men to machines (Syracuse Herald-Journal, August 27, 1970, p. 52). Divisions in society continue to

Summary, Conclusions, Implications

grow "between rich and poor, young and old, black and white, and those who understand the language of technology and science and those who don't." Being close to the people, the community college is openly challenged to render its services and resources in such a manner as to ameliorate these differences and inequities.

While much has been done to revitalize the standard academic thinking in higher education, in no way is the new order limited to expression in the community college. In fact, the spirit of change and innovation seems to have leveled off for this institution. More and more, the community college resembles other higher education institutions. Community college faculty have fought so arduously to be like other faculty in higher education that they have produced an overkill situation. Time-honored aspects of faculty, such as academic rank, tenure, A.A.U.P. membership, faculty governance, and an overconcern for academic or self-interests, tend to make all faculties more alike despite their necessarily different roles. Administrative practices are approaching the standard collegiate model in which a multi-layer, organizational structure is formed, with deans, associate deans, vice-presidents, divisions, and departments. As in senior colleges and universities, fractionated subject matter is overpowering sound pedagogy, with teachers, in their role as subject-matter specialists, contributing to a proliferation of courses, credits, requirements, and prerequisites for students. The community college tends to act as an unofficial extension of the state university. Indeed, many states organize their community colleges in a subservient manner to an older, well-founded university and its branch campus extensions. Such policies are distinctly inferior and should be reversed in all but a few special cases. A community college is simply not a junior college, nor is it a university center or branch campus. Differences are real and educators must become more cognizant of them.

Faculty are being recruited haphazardly, often without regard to their teaching capability and effectiveness. Sterile thinking that equates teaching competence and salary with degrees is the same thinking that equates student success with grades (and more degrees). But while teaching is in need of improvement at all levels, it remains vital to the community college ideology. To this end, the college is falling short of its claim for excellence.

Faculty generally view the community service aspect

and student personnel function as peripheral parts of the dominant academic program. Furthermore, they fail to seek and encourage research projects that would produce a better understanding of students, program planning, evaluation, institutional development, experimental learning, instructional techniques, grading practices, and so forth. Faculty, like colleges, are in need of direction, assessment, evaluation, and redirection. Academic and administrative leadership must merge and reduce the traditional dichotomies and adversary relationships among faculty, administrators, and students.

The community college is in the midst of change, as are all other educational institutions. In a concerted effort, its philosophy must be better developed and articulated at local levels. The absence of comprehensive conceptions of the institutional and educational functioning of the community college frustrates all attempts to understand its roles, practices, and problems (Cohen and Quimby, 1970). State and national aspirations can best be developed in new forms of professional and institutional arrangements, such as leagues for innovation, research compacts, and overlapping organizations of teachers, students, and administrators.

As community colleges evolve, they strive to unfold innovative efforts to match a series of extremely difficult tasks. Nevertheless,

> ... far from upsetting the status quo of American higher education, the [community] colleges shore it up. Far from contributing something new and substantial, the two-year colleges strengthen the status quo in a higher educational system desperately in need of reform. There is real and present danger that the expansion of the two-year colleges along present lines may serve mainly to subvert and postpone urgently needed changes in our higher education (Birenbaum, 1971, p. 11).

It is time for the community college to drop its defensiveness over its long-standing, identity crisis. Efforts to make the college "fit" into the current hierarchical structure are misguided and unnecessary; its uniqueness lies in the fact that it does not fit. As a substantive alternative to the educational dilemma, the community college must become a local resource agency which provides educational services of broad latitude. If the college is to produce significant and material change, it undoubtedly will have to change itself first. In essence, <u>the community college must move away from the collegiate model to a less institutionalized, social service arrangement.</u>

Principles For Action

Based upon the summary and conclusions that follow from earlier chapters, it is possible to list a series of implications and recommendations as a basis for developing individual models or standards for the future development of community college education. By their very nature, the following principles cannot be all-inclusive or uncompromising.

<u>The Institution</u>

1. The community college ideology is so entwined with all other aspects of education that it is inappropriate to propose solutions for only one facet of its existence.

2. The primary function of the community college is to develop and enhance human potential; this must be done in a social or educational climate that focuses on the individual regardless of who he is or where he is.

3. The community college is more than a two-year institution. Programs and attendance patterns range from several hours to two, three, four, or five years in length. "Two-year" thinking must be abandoned as a primary rationale for this institution.

4. The community college is the twentieth century land-grant institution, the people's college. It is inherently different in purpose and philosophy from the junior college or university branch-campus-extension.

5. The political climate is a major factor that affects autonomy for the community college; this can be beneficial or detrimental, depending on individual situations, and must be surveyed with caution.

6. The reasons why community colleges exist must continually be defined and articulated at the local level; the <u>idea</u> of the community college must be less ambiguous than is reflected in current educational thinking.

7. If the community college fails to determine its mission in a collective fashion, other forces will. State control is already on the upswing and must be counter-balanced with stronger local influence.

8. Nonpolitical boards of control should be representative of broad constituencies including faculty, students, citizens-at-large, administrators, minorities, and other professional persons.

9. Community relationships are vital to the existence of a community college. The college and its community must form a symbiotic relationship whereby each benefits from the other. The community is a rich resource for personnel, faculty, work-study arrangements, off-campus and shared facilities, specialized needs, and societal dilemmas as well as popular support.

10. The community college must directly enhance the social and cultural climate of its community. This will require genuine involvement as an active center for art, music, and drama, in addition to open forums for political and intellectual discussions.

11. The community college can easily be adapted to serve rural America as well as the inner city.

12. The community college has blindly borrowed too many educational concepts from other institutions and must reverse this trend, lest it become part of the problem which it seeks to resolve.

13. University requirements represent excessive control factors which place undue restrictions upon the role of the community college. A further analysis and clarification of institutional roles is necessary to promote accountability to the public.

14. The strength of the community college lies in the potential diversity of its responses to contemporary problems.

15. Among community colleges, different missions could be recognized or emphasized. Some colleges may choose to serve more limited clienteles, such as veterans, part-time students, transfer students, occupational students, etc. Still, the preferred model is one which favors

Summary, Conclusions, Implications

comprehensiveness to the greatest attainable and practical degree.

16. Post-secondary education has already changed the standard academic meaning of "college" and "collegiate." State master planning must reconcile a continuum of post-secondary educational activity regardless of its perceived hierarchical level. At the same time, pluralism should be encouraged as a desirable feature of American education.

17. Rampant growth places restrictions on the unique functions of a community college. No campus-type community college operation should exceed four to six thousand students (by full-time definitions) and a similar number on a part-time basis. Size is a major factor in determining differences among institutional purpose and effectiveness; being too large leads to problems already well-known.

18. Community college development demands that state legislators recognize the historical and evolutionary nature of post-secondary and higher education. Recognition, articulation, and coordination must be strengthened on state and Federal levels without the now prevalent bureaucratic entanglements. Basic to overall planning are several guarantees: (1) responsiveness to local need via local control; (2) equal stature with other post-secondary institutions; (3) continued financial support, with a minimum burden on the student; (4) coordination through a single state agency, and (5) research and development to establish state priorities and long-range planning to anticipate and meet future needs. The main growth period for community colleges is leveling off and these institutions must now learn to live on less without sacrificing their mission.

19. Community college thinking must be freed of natural and contrived limitations with reference to geographic location, ethnic and racial distinctions, quality of prior schooling, inflexible programs, restrictive admissions, irrational grading policies, and age of financial barriers. For the new idea to prosper, the college should attempt to stop organizing and classifying its operation around useless and discriminating distinctions such as evening school, part-time students, continuing education, transfer or nontransfer programs, off-campus studies, remedial programs, and so forth. The college must learn to operate equitably within a twenty-four hour period all year. It must be free of superficial separations that make certain people or programs

more legitimate and thus implicitly favored over others.

20. The community college has little tradition; this is an unrecognized but invaluable asset that should be asserted in creating change.

21. Despite its newness in higher education, the community college must relate cooperatively to the traditional bastions of academic excellence without faulting on its own evolving mission. The institution of today is incapable of satisfying future needs; change must be a permanent part of its mission.

22. By their very nature, social institutions are designed to maintain order, preserve the status quo, and resist change. Thus, the community college must strive to be based in noninstitutional arrangements yet to be developed.

Programs

1. Vocational-technical education is still viewed as second-class training at a time when it should have major stress in curriculum planning.

2. Even though academic and vocational aspects of any program are complementary and compatible, the time has come for a clear and decisive emphasis on the vocational-technical, career role of the community college.

3. Career education must involve the full range of educational endeavors from preschool through graduate, professional, adult, and continuing education. Priorities must be realigned if a concerted effort is to be developed to guide an individual toward a better understanding of what he does with his life--his calling. Given the present state of postsecondary education and the multiple needs of society, the community college holds the greatest potential for middle and lower America. In particular, there is much promise for blacks, disadvantaged, and other minority groups.

4. Specialized, vocational-occupational training costs much more to operate than does general education. While increased Federal and state support is necessary, Federal aid provisions demand inordinate proposal writing and are tradition bound, prejudicial, and inhibit community college efforts. These provisions must be restructured, simplified, and made more operable.

Summary, Conclusions, Implications 259

5. The credentialing process tends to hinder motivation and force imitation; it should be lessened in scope. Accreditation indirectly enforces conformity and should be carefully weighed against institutional purpose and local need. Accreditation agencies must review their procedures and allow for nontraditional areas that a community college pursues as legitimate ventures.

6. Public and community service needs should be met at the working level, i.e., close to the people. Community service and continuing education programs should therefore be major components of the community college philosophy.

7. Program planning must provide for effective use of leisure time in other than locked-step, formal sequences. Programs outside the formal educational core must be strengthened and brought into the community.

8. Planning career programs is equally as important, and difficult, as offering them.

9. As the college adapts to the learner and the community, programs will increasingly go to the people by means of alternative teaching environments (television, correspondence, dial access, meandering mini-college, go-anywhere courses, etc.). This will deinstitutionalize the community college and, hopefully, reduce the need and cost of fixed facilities as found on a traditional campus.

Student Clientele

1. The community college should open its doors to the nonstudent and be prepared to advance the individual from his level of entry to as far as his abilities and interests permit.

2. Concern for adults and part-time students should become a priority for the community college.

3. The community college must emphatically address itself to racial imbalance and societal injustice with specially designed programs. Faculty expertise should be tapped to provide specific medical, legal, mental, or other social referral services.

4. Human self-renewal is a goal for the community

college; on a larger scale, this applies to community and society.

5. The "salvage" function is a unique contribution and should be continued.

6. A primary mission of the community college is to develop independent, self-directed individuals. Any other method of learning is less effective and temporal.

7. The community college must shift from emulation to self-direction based on clientele and region to be served; public confidence will be strengthened by more visible forms of public relations and accountability.

8. Excellence in the traditional-elitist sense should not be a major part of the community college philosophy; an institution so different is not necessarily inferior.

9. While low or free tuition is desirable for most persons, there are a growing number of affluent students taking unfair advantage of this benefit as state and private institutions raise their tuition beyond practical limitations. Tuition should be assessed in some proportion to those who can afford it and financial aid made more accessible to those who need it.

10. The transition of "career" and "academic" students between institutions must be simplified and arranged so that earlier experiences match with later ones in order to advance one's self (the career ladder concept).

11. A complete re-examination of the dropout concept is in order. Current data are misleading and based on traditional, statistical analyses which are confusing and contradictory.

12. Student evaluation and grading practices must suit nonstudents who find their college experience to be experimental and full of uncertainties. Nonpunitive forms of grading should be explored and student transcripts should only record progress in those areas where the student has demonstrated and met acceptable, pre-defined levels of competence.

13. Student government is traditionally designed for young resident students who are campus bound in their needs, acts, and academic life styles. Transposing this form to

Summary, Conclusions, Implications

the community college is a useless venture that tends to be unproductive, except for a small minority of full-time, young, day students. The more numerous, older, and mature students have little need for the artificiality that supports a given amount of power in the hands of a popular few. Student governance must necessarily be merged with faculty-administrative governance, i.e., college community governance. To retain one form of governance as a token or competitive part within the larger, more important structure is baseless. In short, college governance must be participatory, with an all-inclusive constituency represented through the mechanism of an open forum or senate.

14. Student personnel services must be reorganized to meet all student needs, not just those of the full-time, day student. More and more students will attend part-time in the future as work-study relationships are made more respectable and workable.

15. Students who have the need and ability to be served directly by traditional colleges and universities must not be allowed to crowd out those individuals who have no such alternative; selective admissions in the nonelitist sense may become necessary as physical and financial resources become limited.

Faculty Preparation and Development

1. Teachers, more than any other constituency, hold the key to success or failure of the overall community college idea.

2. Faculty must be selected for potential teaching competence and performance aptitude as matched to job expectancy rather than for assumed competence based on credentials, degrees, or so-called "equivalent" experience.

3. Faculty must perceive their roles as teachers first and subject-matter specialists second. The traditional academic mind can only serve to subvert the community college, especially from within.

4. A firm commitment to involvement in student and community affairs should be expected of faculty prior to their employment.

5. Faculty members too often perceive student

attendance at the community college to be a privilege when its founding principles dictate differently. They must be educated to the ramifications of equal access and open admissions.

6. Counseling, remediation and referral services are primary concerns for all community colleges; teaching must be better reconciled with guidance and counseling services, with the student as common denominator.

7. Community college teachers should have prior teaching experience; the need for grants, supervised internships, pre- and in-service training should be recognized as essential to teacher training programs. The college itself could become a teaching laboratory if properly supervised.

8. There should be a comprehensive mechanism to assist the personal and professional development of teachers. This should be a continued in-service function of each college.

9. The concept of evaluation and educational assessment must be recognized and accepted at the broadest levels of application. Nurtured by a teaching-oriented faculty, evaluation principles must be discussed and developed as they are applied to students, teachers, administrators, and institutions.

10. Unless the faculty is already convinced that change is desirable and the potential results of change definitely outweigh the liabilities, little will visibly occur. The community college cannot afford extensive deliberations, excessive coordination, and consensus before effecting change.

11. Faculty exchange with other institutions, both educational and noneducational, should be encouraged.

12. Five- to seven-year renewable contracts should replace standard tenure policies in order to prevent professional incompetence from stagnating an otherwise productive process that must continually respond to change. Mandatory, paid sabbaticals should be a part of this endeavor.

13. Teachers must assume a new kind of research role; one that makes a systematic and objective inquiry as to the effects of teaching and learning, modular scheduling,

student attitudes and values, new calendars and grading systems, teacher effectiveness, evaluation of goals, and so forth. Such inquiries should be centered in an office of institutional research with built-in participation from faculty.

14. Teachers have a responsibility to be committed to the idea of the community college if they choose to be so employed. Professionalism also requires that they collectively reduce the amount of misinformation and uninformed opinion that currently dominates the educational scene.

15. Community college teachers should be trained in programs that not only give them subject-matter expertise but also a degree of knowledgeability concerning learning theory, program planning, curricular strategies, evaluation techniques, collective bargaining, educational law, and professional ethics. Only a special Master's program plus additional study or a Ph.D. program related to community college teaching would attack this problem directly. To this end, the university has offered little hope, mainly because it collectively fails to recognize the problem. The community college must therefore initiate in-service graduate programs for its faculty in cooperation with a university-based consortium. Faculty rejuvenation must be part of the community college philosophy.

A Need For Further Research

While many facets of the contemporary community college have been discussed throughout this book, the summary and conclusions lead to undeveloped concepts in need of further exploration. An analysis of new trends and developments in fiscal structures, leadership, control and organizational structures, new modes of delivering instruction, governance, and decision-making policies is strongly recommended.

It is not yet clear how collective negotiations will merge with professionalism and faculty participation in governance. Nor is it known what the best source of trained leadership will be. Therefore, it will be of interest to observe how the resolution of this dilemma affects graduate schools and upper-division universities. It is also uncertain how open door colleges will be financed in the very near future.

There is an obvious need to pursue further research on emerging trends which relate to the library college, increasing state control, the open university, independent self-study, credit by experience or examination, leisure learning, governmental-industrial sponsored education, external degrees, colleges without teachers, teaching without grades, off-campus multi-media learning, and other alternatives to standard academic excellence.

Much more knowledge and understanding will be needed before viable decisions can be made which will affect the future lives of dropouts and others with low motivation or socioeconomic shortcomings. A welfare crisis will develop unless we advance our commitment and concern for strong leadership to maintain and enhance hard-earned accomplishments at a time when state and national funding procedures are proving to be inadequate, inequitable, and perhaps even unlawful.

The implications of this book point to a series of problems that must be researched further if the community college is to retain its unique institutional phase of democratization. This quality permeates the entire spectrum of post-secondary educational opportunity by making it a national priority. It is imperative in this attempt that the community college remain faithful to the local environment by providing its community resources as an educational laboratory. It is feasible to envision a Center for Research and Planning with which a group of community colleges form a consortium, whereby each can benefit from the strengths and weaknesses of the others in a cooperative effort. Through such arrangements, strong pre- and in-service training experiences should be provided to develop stronger conceptualizations of academic leadership throughout all levels of teaching, institutional, and state influence. Only with such a concerted effort will the idea of the community college be strengthened at a time when most social institutions are seriously being challenged by the immediate effects of future shock and social uncertainty.

Appendix

REVIEW OF RELATED LITERATURE

The community college is still in "the unenviable position of being an institution about which little of substance is written" (Cohen, 1969a). Indeed, much of the prestigious literature of higher education fails to mention the community college at all. As a result of insignificant dialogue from within the profession, Cohen charges that others, such as laymen, sociologists, and journalists, are defining how junior college educators should conduct their affairs.

In part, the literature reflects the confused status and ambiguous identity of the community college movement. Virtually all of the literature relates to current change and transition in formal and traditional higher education. Only a few publications are available in which authors consistently recognize differences between the many two-year institutional forms and their intended purpose, function, philosophy, or effectiveness. Thus, the literature reflects an overlapping of terminology, ideology, and expectation as it applies to the status of the public comprehensive community college. This institution can simply no longer be confused with technical institutes, private junior colleges, state junior colleges, religious two-year colleges, independent, proprietary or profit-oriented junior colleges, and university branch-center-campus type junior colleges.

The literature also reveals weaknesses among educators, legislators, and laymen alike. There is a failure to recognize and articulate a comprehensive or consistent set of goals for postsecondary education. Continued disagreement is reflected in areas of general and liberal education, career and occupational education, "terminal" and "transfer" programs, and, to a greater extent, issues related to the purpose and accessibility of all postsecondary education.

While many of the defects found in the literature are due to problems of terminology and educational jargon, a greater concern is the absence or failure of an ideology. Other problems are typically found in misleading or inappropriate titles and a general tendency for publishers to produce outdated literary products which often do not relate well to contemporary issues. A proliferation of outlets for publication, coupled with the publish-or-perish syndrome, continues to produce an intolerable situation. "There is as yet no good way of identifying and retrieving" the meaningful from the mass of superficial material, according to Mayhew.

Among the best sources for current material, although it is of varying quality, is the Educational Resources Information Center (E.R.I.C.) Clearinghouse for Junior Colleges which operates under contract with the U.S. Department of Health, Education and Welfare, Office of Education. Under the direction of Arthur M. Cohen, this information center provides publications in microfiche and hard copy forms. Abstracts make use of generic "descriptors" which cover most phases of two-year college operation.

The Junior College Research Review is a recent publication of consistent quality. Most issues relate to the community college with specialized topics such as "Paying for Junior Colleges," "Faculty Recruitment," "Boards of Trustees," "Paraprofessional Training," "Occupationally Oriented Students," and "Studies of Student and Staff Attitudes."

Perhaps the best known source for reports from within the general movement is the Junior College Journal, which first appeared on October 1, 1930 at Stanford University. As the official voice of the American Association of Junior Colleges, this journal has changed its focus from appealing to lesser interests within the profession to broad, regional, and even international aspects of the generic two-year college. In an attempt to gain strength and support, the Association and its journal freely depict all forms of two-year colleges (public and private) as institutions of a singular nature. While this facilitates editorial concerns, it also proliferates much confusion. Articles and reports generally use various descriptives, including "two-year," "comprehensive," "junior," "community," and, as a catchall, "comprehensive community junior" college.

General publications and monographs from the American Association of Junior Colleges are usually quite good, but often confusing because they also aim to please all forms

Related Literature

of two-year colleges. Some recent publications include Principles of Legislative Action for Community Junior Colleges (1962); A New Social Invention: The Community College, What It Is (Gleazer, 1962); Starting a Community Junior College (Johnson, 1964); Guidelines for Law Enforcement Education Programs in Community and Junior Colleges (Crockett and Stinchcomb, 1968); Teaching In A Junior College (Garrison, 1968); The Computer and The Junior College (Sedral and Hill, 1969); State Master Plans for Community Colleges (Hurlburt, 1969); Community College Programs for People Who Need College (1970); Your Career and Two-Year Colleges (Pratt, 1970); and the 1971 Junior College Directory.

State departments and professional associations produce much literature of varying quality and limited circulation. Much can be learned from these sources since they usually address themselves to sound treatments of current and general issues which require popular support for legislative revision. The pacesetter in this area is A Master Plan for Higher Education in California 1960-1975 (California State Department of Education, 1960), which is the result of the 1959 Legislature's request "to prepare a Master Plan for the development, expansion, and integration of the facilities, curriculum, and standards of higher education...." The Bureau of Junior College General Education distributed A Guide For California Public Junior Colleges (1967) in which general information is presented about admissions policies, philosophy, tuition, curriculum programs, and accreditation.

The Michigan Department of Education produced an excellent series including Laws, Statutes and Constitutional Provisions Affecting Community Colleges (1968); The Metropolitan Community College in Michigan (1968); A Recommended Community College Districting Plan (1968); College Admissions Handbook (1969); and Financial Requirements of Public Baccalaureate Institutions, Public Community Colleges (1970). These publications discuss the community college concept within the fiscal, legal, legislative, and constitutional parameters of the State while at the same time setting forth a coherent philosophy. Similarly, the Illinois Board of Higher Education published a series of high quality which relates to developmental aspects of higher education. This series includes Two-Year Colleges (1963); College Enrollments (1963); Illinois Financing of Higher Education (1963); A Master Plan--Phase II (1966); Committee On Preparation of Junior College Teachers (1969); Admission and Retention of Students (1969); and Teacher Preparation (1969). It is interesting to note that the Board of Higher Education uses the term "junior college," although recognizing that "community" is "a more complete title to use since it is descriptive of the broader services which it is hoped this institution will render to an area."

The Ohio Board of Regents distributed a comprehensive Master Plan For State Policy In Higher Education (1966), and more recently, Ohio's Newly Developed System of Two-Year Colleges (1969-1970). Ohio law designates three distinct organizational forms within which the two-year college operates: the community college, the university branch, and the technical institute. A fourth has developed and is known as the urban university center. The development of the community college is recent in Ohio and it is useful to study the dilemma that is being faced as this college form is made to fit and coincide peacefully with the more dominant university branches and centers. Similar situations are found in Pennsylvania and other eastern states where the community college is a recent but dynamic force. The two-year college is proving difficult to cope with, especially when more traditional forms of higher education are firmly established and sanctioned by strong vested interests.

Concern with the history of junior college development is often minimized by those states that entered the community college phase directly, especially during the past seven or eight years. Legislative authorization for "county colleges" was given in New Jersey during 1968. Regulations Governing County Community Colleges was issued in 1969, and the general Goals for Higher Education in New Jersey was formulated by the Board of Higher Education in 1970. An analysis of enrollment trends in New Jersey and other states is presented by the New Jersey Commission for the Higher Education Facilities Act of 1963 in Meeting New Jersey College and University Facilities Needs Through 1980 (1968). Another type of publication that reveals official policy and attitude toward the community college in the light of other institutions is the Department of Higher Education's Facts About New Jersey Higher Education (1969).

Delaware cites its need for "a system of two-year open door comprehensive community colleges" in Delaware Technical And Community Colleges, First Report By The Board of Trustees (1966). The latest report is entitled Delaware Technical and Community College, Second Report

(1969) and describes the State's two facilities, in addition to current and projected needs.

States that have long records of both public and private growth in higher education present interesting case studies which reveal significant forces that affect the acceptance and development of the community college. States such as New York, Pennsylvania, Ohio, Massachusetts, and New England in general, fall into this category. For example, the bimonthly Pennsylvania Education often discusses how Pennsylvania made early attempts to initiate public junior colleges, but with little success. The Community College Act was passed in 1963 and contains rules and regulations which permitted the first college to open in 1964. The Standards, Rules, and Regulations for Public Community Colleges in Pennsylvania (1965) reveals later modifications. Reporting only a dozen community colleges by 1970, Pennsylvania's shortcomings can be traced to the entrenched branch campuses of the State university.

The State Education Department and the Regents of New York provide an abundance of literature which traces a similar account of limited community college development. With such a strong and effective private sector in higher education, New York has long delayed the acceptance of the community college ideology by providing stronger support to other types of institutions. The Regents Statewide Plan for the Expansion and Development of Higher Education, 1964 (1965) shows twenty-five community colleges to be operational among thirty-five private two-year colleges and six large two-year agricultural and technical colleges. The strength and vitality of New York's private institutions are given added momentum in New York State and Private Higher Education (1968), a report presented to Governor Rockefeller by McGeorge Bundy, James Bryant Conant, The Rev. Theodore M. Hesburgh, and others. Higher Education Planning (1968), a bulletin concerning the 1968 statewide plan for the expansion and development of higher education by the Regents of the State of New York, identifies major issues such as education of the disadvantaged, manpower needs, continuing education, teacher preparation and effectiveness, and interinstitutional cooperation, all without any reference to the community college. Other studies of particular interest by the State Department of Education include Enrollment Projections 1968-80 N.Y.S. Higher Education, New York State College Enrollment Simulation Model (1969); A Longitudinal Study of the Barriers Affecting the Pursuit of Higher

Education by New York State High School Seniors (1969); and Major Recommendations of the Regents for Legislative Action 1970 (1969).

Reports which describe the community college and higher education in Massachusetts include the Board of Education's Enrollment Study for Massachusetts (1969); General Laws And Procedures Relating to Collegiate Authority (1969); and the 1969 draft of An Economic Analysis of the Potential and Realized Demand for Higher Education in the Boston S. M. S. A. [Southern Massachusetts Service Area], the last-mentioned study being a current sociological investigation.

Rapid transition and change in higher education has prompted the Oklahoma State Regents for Higher Education to publicly review higher education goals, student enrollment and projection patterns, demographic and economic trends, and problems related to function, organization, and articulation. Publications include The Status and Direction of Oklahoma Higher Education: Guidelines for Policy Decisions (1968); Handbook for the Establishment and Operation of Community Junior Colleges in Oklahoma (1968); the Counselors' Guide (1969) to higher education; The Role and Scope of Oklahoma Higher Education (1970); and Junior College Education in Oklahoma (1970). The latter study presents an excellent account of the factors that must be weighed as two-year colleges become senior colleges (both public and private), and how needs arise that call for state junior colleges and/or comprehensive community colleges. The process of institutional transition is proposed as one means of responding to unsettled societal needs.

Like many other states, Michigan's Department of Education provides a Directory of Institutions of Higher Education (1969-70) which describes procedures, programs, governance, and different types of institutions in addition to defining terms used in higher education. Other publications include the Occupational Program Inventory (1969), which presents an assessment of educational programs designed to lead to immediate employment; the State Plan for Higher Education in Michigan (1969); and the Statistical Supplement to the 1969-70 Report to the Legislature on Financial Requirements of Public Four-Year Institutions and Community Colleges (1969).

The need for a clarification of institutional roles in higher education advanced sharply with the development of the

Related Literature   271

community college. The Missouri Commission on Higher
Education cites the following needs in its higher education
system: the need for a State master plan, the need for a
clarification of the junior college role, the need for improved
establishment criteria, the need for emphasis on vocational-
technical program offerings, and the need for a change in
the State coordinating agency to enable a greater degree of
effectiveness and efficiency to be developed. Useful reports
include the Final Report, Missouri Public Junior College
Study (1968); A Summary of Missouri Constitution and Laws
As Affecting Higher Education For Use Of The Commission
On Higher Education And Its Staff (1968); College Attendance
Plans (1968); and a confidential report entitled Specifications
for a Higher Education Information System (1968), which is
a study of information systems capable of providing data for
future planning in higher education. The reference on information systems provides resource material which is sub-
divided into the following subsystems: student, program,
financial, personnel, and facilities.

A similar group of publications is found in Maryland,
where reports eminate from the State Department of Education, the State Board for Community Colleges, the Maryland
Association of Junior Colleges, the Maryland Council for
Higher Education, and the State Teachers Association. Among
these are Maryland Standards For Two-Year Colleges (1969);
Master Plan for Higher Education in Maryland: Phase I
(1969); 1969 Legislative Program, The Higher Education
Journal of Maryland, The State Board: Its Roles and Responsibilities (1970); Maryland Community Colleges 1970-71;
and Legislative Program 1971.

Several compacts, regional laboratories, and development centers produce an assortment of research literature
which is relatively unknown. Thus, the Conference for Educational Development and Research (C. E. D. A. R.) emerged
recently by uniting the Conference of Regional Education
Laboratories and the Conference of Research and Development Centers. Reports relate to vocational education, adult,
and higher education and are of particular interest to this
study. Of fourteen centers, the Regional Education Laboratory for the Carolinas and Virginia is among the few that
produces research reports for two-year colleges. [This
Regional Laboratory has become a National Laboratory for
Higher Education.] The Junior College Division, under the
directorship of John E. Roueche, released such publications
as The Educational Development Officer: A Change Catalyst

for Two-Year Colleges (1970), and Developing Individualized Instructional Material (1970), a self-instructional format itself. In one respect, it is unfair to expect this type of research to be well circulated. The centers and laboratories are relatively young; their products are recent and their concern is with production, not dissemination. The D. & R. Report, a newsletter of The Conference for Educational Development and Research, is slowly changing this situation by coordinating and publishing research summaries on the national level.

Another experimental publication comes from the Midwest Committee of the College Entrance Examination Board. With its Higher Education Surveys, the Board recently published Admission of Minority Students in Midwestern Colleges (Willingham, 1970), which reports the experience of 129 four-year colleges in recruiting and enrolling minority students. This report suggests that the community college has the greatest success in serving minority youth, but it "cannot bear the full responsibility for educating those who have not been educated." A discussion of the "open door" is also presented, with implications for admissions policies.

Other regional associations that often produce material of high caliber include the Southern Regional Education Board (S. R. E. B.), Western Interstate Commission on Higher Education (W. I. C. H. E.), New England Board of Higher Education (N. E. B. H. E.), and the all-inclusive Compact for Education which releases relatively unknown but high quality publications through its governing body, the Education Commission of the States (E. C. S.). The most useful documents in this series are the Guide for Evaluating State Programs in Community Centered Post-High School Education (1968), and the follow-up report entitled Analysis of State Programs in Community Centered Post-High School Education (1968). The Guide is a self-study instrument which allows for analysis and action concerning the provisions for post-secondary education in each state; the Analysis presents the Education Commission of the States' general assessment of recent state programs in community-centered postsecondary education. Results of this continuing study reveal that three-fourths of the states participating in the survey are in "need of major improvement in their programs of community-centered post-high school education." Selected characteristics of a sound post-secondary educational program are presented which offer a challenge similar to the one accepted by most comprehensive community colleges.

Compact is the Education Commission of the States' editorial outlet and includes articles that relate to interinstitutional coordination and articulation on the state and national level. Other E.C.S. publications that warrant further investigation are Vocational-Technical Education: Changing The Contexts In Which Occupational Education Takes Place (1967); State-Federal Relationships (1968); State School System Development: Patterns and Trends (Fitzwater, 1968); Background Material On Collective Bargaining For Teachers (Linn and Nolte, 1968); The Politics of Elementary-Secondary and Higher Education (Usdan, et al., 1968); and Higher Education In The States (1970), the first of a monthly series consisting of a bibliography of publications of state and regional higher education agencies.

W.I.C.H.E.'s Annual Reports, and The Changing West: Implications For Higher Education (1965) provide insight about statewide and regional community college problems. Some pertinent articles include "The Rising Problem of Depersonalization" by Louis Benezet, "Technical Education" by Arthur Singer, Jr., "Junior Colleges for Tomorrow" by Eugene Chaffee, and "Continuing Education for the West's Adults" by Paul Sheats. Like other regional organizations, W.I.C.H.E.'s goal is to "improve the quality of education beyond the high school," and to this end it recognizes that several diversified levels of higher education are necessary in addition to the traditional four-year colleges and universities. This outlook is refreshing and evident in all its publications.

The periodical press must be scanned in depth for cogent articles related to the development of the community college. Only an occasional or incidental treatment is given to this institution in such journals as Liberal Education, The Journal of Higher Education, The Journal of General Education, and Daedalus. The Educational Record and School and Society tend to present what was previously stated elsewhere. Older volumes of The School Review are excellent, however, for tracing the early beginnings and development of the junior college movement and revealing the ideas of the most prolific junior college historian, Leonard Vincent Koos.

The California Quarterly of Secondary Education and The North Central Association Quarterly are two prime sources for analyzing various institutional transitions which most two-year colleges pass through. The journals present a continued account of organizational conflicts, accreditation issues, and other problems that exist between the high school and two-year college. The Spring 1969 issues of Improving College and University Teaching is completely dedicated to the purpose and structure of community and junior colleges and suggests a thematic approach which other periodicals may find useful. Pedagogy, certification, teacher training, and remedial learning are discussed from many viewpoints.

The popular press affords more coverage than might be expected. A link between the educator, legislator, and citizen, this source constitutes a major outlet for revealing daily changes in higher education at local, state, and national levels. Almost any newspaper is a source of community information and, to a great degree, the college relies on the press for popular support. Good sources include The Evening Sun (Baltimore), The New York Times, and The Morning Call (Allentown, Pennsylvania), among others. Each is in a geographical area which is significantly involved with current issues in two-year college development.

Less than a decade ago Frederick Rudolph, in his well-written history of The American College and University (1962), noted that the junior college was even then too recent a major phenomenon to have built a body of historical literature. To a great extent, some of the best sources of literature are those which were written between forty and seventy years ago. Leonard Vincent Koos produced The Junior College in two volumes by 1924. Walter Crosby Eells entered his version of The Junior College in 1931. Both studies are early documentaries of the "junior-college" movement.

Other publications of historical significance include University in Education (Tappan, 1851); University Addresses (Folwell, 1909); The Junior College Movement (Koos, 1925); "The Junior College in the States' Program of Education" by George F. Zook in National Education Association Proceedings (1930); The Chicago College Plan (Boucher, 1935); Present Status of Junior College Terminal Education (Eells, 1941); and Higher Education For American Democracy (Commission on Higher Education, 1947).

Some periodicals also provide interesting accounts of the early junior college growth period. A review of this literature is necessary if one is to understand the difficulties that confront the community college today. Of particular interest is "The Junior-College Movement in High Schools" by

James Angell in The School Review (1915), and "Problems Peculiar to the Junior College," also by Angell, in The School Review (1917). However, the first notable reference to the junior college in the Readers' Guide to Periodical Literature appears in Volume III (1910-1914) where the "junior college" citation refers the reader to "See High Schools." Interesting reports from Frederick E. Bolton include "What Should Constitute the Curriculum of the Junior College or Extended High School?" in School and Society (1918); "Some Probable Effects Upon Higher Education Due to the Development of Junior Colleges" in Educational Administration and Supervision (1944); and "Suggestions for the Post-War Development of Junior Colleges" in University of Washington College of Education Record (1944).

Other reports representative of the early junior college include "The High School of the Future" by William Rainey Harper in The School Review (1903); "The Six-Year High School Plan at Goshen, Indiana" in The School Review (1905); "Standardizing the Junior College" by Jesse H. Coursault in The Educational Review (1915); "The Junior College in California" by A. A. Gray in The School Review (1915); "The Junior College" and "Standards and Principles for Accrediting Junior Colleges," both in The Educational Record of 1921; "Conditions Favoring Integration of Junior College with High Schools" by Leonard V. Koos in School Life (1927); and "The 6-3-3-2 vs. the 6-4-4 Plan of Organization for the Public Junior College" by J. B. Lilliard in School and Society (1930).

Other pertinent articles which describe the secondary nature of the junior college include "The Junior College or Upward Extension of the High School" by C. L. McLane in The School Review (1913); "The Junior College As Relief" by William Magruder in The Educational Review (1921); "Junior College Graduates in the Universities" by G. M. Okerlund in School and Society (1929); and "Public Schools Through Grade 14" by Hugh Price in the National Education Association Journal (1959).

In following the growth and transition of the two-year college as portrayed in the literature, it becomes apparent that this type of institution has gone through a long period of evolution, moving slowly at first and accelerating sharply only within the past decade. A standard reference, The Two-Year College: A Social Synthesis (Blocker, et al., 1965), is already outdated. But a book of greater importance today than when it was first published is Man, Education, and Work (Venn, 1964). This perceptive report illustrates the failure of all segments of education, including junior colleges, to provide career and occupational opportunities beyond the limitations of traditional academic programs. In The Junior College: Progress and Prospect, Medsker (1960) sharply supports the contention that two-year colleges are primarily concerned with transfer programs at the expense of occupational curriculums. Similar positions are taken in Industry And Vocational-Technical Education (Burt, 1967). The whole area of postsecondary vocational and technical education is currently in transition and this undoubtedly affects the status and direction that the future community college will assume. The evolution of the community college is as yet incomplete, and the future form of this institution will undoubtedly differ from current arrangements.

One of the more astute textbooks for an introduction to community college teaching is Teaching in the American Junior College (1970) by Win Kelly and Leslie Wilbur. This text is more recent and comprehensive than To Work in a Junior College (A.A.J.C., 1966); Junior College Faculty: Issues and Problems (Garrison, 1967); and Teaching in a Junior College: A Brief Professional Orientation (Garrison, 1968). Other useful publications in this series include Problems of New Faculty Members in Community Colleges (Siehr, et al., 1963; College Teaching as a Career (American Council on Education, 1965); Personality Characteristics of College and University Faculty: Implications for the Community College (Brawer, 1968); Preparing Two-Year College Teachers for the 70's (A.A.J.C., 1969); Measuring Faculty Performance (Cohen and Brawer, 1969); Research on College Teaching: A Review (McKeachie, 1970); Orientation for Faculty in Junior Colleges (Kelly and Connolly, 1970); and The Improvement of Junior College Instruction (Johnson, ed., 1970).

Books which encompass more than limited or specialized viewpoints on community college education are difficult to locate. Even comprehensive historical overviews, such as the following, are all but lacking in any serious reference to the community college: The American College and University (Rudolph, 1962), and Higher Education in Transition (Brubacher and Rudy, 1968). It seems that the idea of the junior college was best inspired in the works of Koos, Eells, Harper, Lange, Bogue, and Jordan--all in the early decades of this century, some even earlier.

A movement is underway to restore the imbalance of literature on behalf of the community college. Some of the better books in this endeavor include The Junior College: Progress and Prospect (Medsker, 1960); Ten Designs, Community Colleges (Lacy, 1962); The Community College Movement (Fields, 1962); Islands of Innovation (Johnson, 1964); The Community Junior College (Thornton, 1966); The Community College Commitment to the Inner City--Implications for Facilities (Weidenthal, 1967); Community Colleges: A President's View (O'Connell, 1968); and Islands of Innovation Expanding: Changes in the Community College (Johnson, 1969).

Of special interest in the recent literature is Arthur M. Cohen's Dateline '79: Heretical Concepts for the Community College (1969). This is a very refreshing analysis of the future community college. The future is explored in terms of new styles of teaching, instructional archaisms, integrated curricula, and a defined outcomes or behavioral objectivist approach to institutional and individual change. A similar but shorter treatment is "The Community College in 1980" by Joseph Cosand in Campus 1980 (Eurich, 1968). Also exciting, but somewhat challenging and bitter are Overlive: Power, Poverty, and the University (Birenbaum, 1969) and Against The Odds (Moore, 1970). In each of these books the authors cite weaknesses in the current structure of higher education and forewarn of continued failure unless the community college accepts the challenge to educate all kinds of people, especially minorities and disadvantaged groups.

Other books that demonstrate the need for understanding the community college concept, especially in the light of mass education, revised curricula, and the open door philosophy, include Burton Clark's sociological study entitled The Open-Door College: A Case Study (1960); Universal Higher Education (McGrath, 1966); Beyond High School (Trent and Medsker, 1968); The Community Dimension of the Community College (Harlacher, 1969); and The Comprehensive Junior College Curriculum (Reynolds, 1970).

Additional references that directly relate to the broad but nebulous scope of community college education include Hanbook of Adult Education in the United States (Knowles, 1969); "Are Public 2-Year Colleges Secondary or Higher Education?" in State Formulas for the Support of Public 2-Year Colleges (U.S. Office of Education, 1962); To What Do the Technical Programs of the Two-Year Colleges Lead? (Beatty, 1963); Universal Opportunity for Education Beyond the High School (Educational Policies Commission, 1964); The Sheepskin Psychosis (Keats, 1965); Conference Proceedings on Administering the Community College in a Changing World (Martorana and Hunter, 1966); "Comprehensive and Higher Education: A Sociologist's View of Public Junior College Trends" by Normal L. Friedman in A.A.U.P. Bulletin (1966); and The Academic Revolution (Jencks and Riesman, 1968).

Literature which reflects research on the community college student is generally of lesser quality than expected. With too many generalizations, this literature tends to treat all post-secondary students as being of the same mold. That the community college student has a distinctness or uniqueness of his own is slowly being recognized. Among the better books and reports are Promise and Performance: A Study of Ability and Achievement in Higher Education (Darley, 1962); Toward Educational Opportunity for All (Knoell, 1966); The Youth We Haven't Served: A Challenge to Vocational Education (Kemp, 1966); Profile of the School Drop-Out (Schreiber, 1967); Your College Freshmen (Hoyt and Munday, 1968); The Junior College Student: A Research Description (Cross, 1968); the Students' Guide to the Two-Year College (Richardson and Blocker, 1968); The College Environment (Astin, 1968); Salvage, Redirection or Custody? Remedial Education in the Community Junior College (Roueche, 1968); Student Activism in Junior Colleges: An Administrator's Views (Lombardi, 1969); and The Two-Year College and Its Students: An Empirical Report (American College Testing Program, 1970).

The only definitive treatment of the entire student culture in the community college is The Community College Student (Koos, 1970). However, it is burdened with statistical information that tends to be outdated or indiscriminately merged with generic junior college data of overlapping periods. Other research reports concerning the community college clientele include Who Should Go To College? (Hollinshead, 1952); "Beyond Ability" by K. Patricia Cross in The Research Reporter (1967); the two-year college edition of The A.C.T. Guidance Profile (American College Testing Program, 1969); "Occupationally Oriented Students," also by K. Patricia Cross in The Junior College Research Review (1970); and Open Admissions and Equal Access (Rever, 1971). Related to this excellent series are the College Entrance

Examination Board's C. G. P. Reports which describe the Comparative Guidance and Placement Program. This program is designed for educational and vocational counseling at the postsecondary educational level and is just beginning to gain national recognition.

A highly respected source of literature is the Carnegie Commission on Higher Education, which issues a series of special reports. Of interest to this study are those reports that analyze equal access and open admissions for post-secondary education. The series includes A Chance to Learn: An Action Agenda for Equal Opportunity in Higher Education (1970); The Open-Door Colleges: Policies for Communities (1970); Less Time, More Options: Education Beyond the High School (1971); and the Preliminary Findings from National Surveys of American Higher Education (1971); the latter being a report based upon the largest survey ever conducted to determine the views and characteristics of persons actively involved in the life and work of America's colleges and universities. The essence of these reports clearly establishes the legitimacy and importance of community college education among a multitude of changes which are currently being expressed in "new" forms of post-secondary education.

Other sources that often relate to community college development include The Research Reporter, which is issued by The Center for Research and Development in Higher Education (Berkeley); the monographs and general collection of the E. R. I. C. Clearinghouse on Higher Education (George Washington University); research reports sponsored by the Kellogg Foundation and reported by The American Association for Higher Education; College and University Bulletin; and Current Issues In Higher Education.

Other general studies and reports are found in the American Association of University Professors Bulletin; news releases from Jossey-Bass and McCutchan; proceedings from the national conferences of the American Association of Junior Colleges and the American Association for Higher Education; Syracuse University Publications in Continuing Education and the E. R. I. C. Clearinghouse on Adult Education (Syracuse). The continuing education publications from Syracuse University represent a high-quality series with such titles as Liberal Education Reconsidered: Reflections on Continuing Education for Contemporary Man (Whipple, et al., 1969); Dilemmas of American Policy: Crucial Issues in

Contemporary Society (Cook, et al., 1969); Community Service and Continuing Education: A Literature Review (Whipple, 1970); and Essays on the Future of Continuing Education Worldwide (Ziegler, ed., 1970). The relationship between the community college and the needs of adults is vividly portrayed in this series which recognizes that "community colleges are a new kind of animal with a mandate ... to serve community needs. But community needs are needs of adults' continuing education" (p. 69).

A literary source that deserves special recognition for broad but concise coverage is The Chronicle of Higher Education. Coverage includes the open door admissions policy of the City University of New York's community colleges; Vice President Agnew's running commentary on open admissions; Malcolm X College of Chicago's city colleges; and Ralph Tyler's "The Changing Structure of American Institutions of Higher Education," a paper which projects emerging educational patterns of the next decade. Also found in The Chronicle are current legislative reports that affect community college development, and such documents as the "Newman Report" which was produced by a task force initiated by the Department of Health, Education, and Welfare. The Newman Report is highly critical of the current national system of higher education and suggests many possible changes for the future growth of the community college.

Additional sources of information concerning the evolution of the community college include general publications and bibliographies of varying purpose and quality. These include The Two-Year Community College (Morrison, et al., 1963); and the Need for Administrative Leadership in Junior Colleges (1960), a symposium report based upon the Western Conference on Junior College Administration held at the University of California, Los Angeles. An introductory approach to the two-year college is presented in Facing Facts About the Two-Year College (1968), a publication of the Prudential Insurance Company.

The list of general publications from the American Association of Junior Colleges is exhaustive and often outdated. Included are Junior Colleges: An Introduction (Gleazer, 1963); Junior Colleges: Their Present Status and Some Future Needs: A Brief Statement (undated); An Introduction to American Junior Colleges (1967); and the more recent collection of older and revised articles, Junior Colleges: 50 States/50 Years (Yarrington, ed., 1969). General bibliographical sources include Lewis Mayhew's annual survey of The Literature of Higher Education; Roger Kelsey's annual A. A. H. E. Bibliography on Higher Education; The American Council on Education's Publications Catalog; the E. R. I. C. Clearinghouse on Higher Education's Current Documents in Higher Education: A Bibliography; and the vast entry of the E. R. I. C. Clearinghouse for Junior College Information as listed in the monthly issues of Research in Education.

Unpublished reports, documents, and dissertations constitute a partial vacuum in the literature of higher education and community college development in particular. Even with erratic quality, this type of potential publication warrants further editorial and bibliographical analysis if it is to receive any worthwhile use. Two additional books of high quality were received well after this study was underway and merit further attention. They are Accountability and the Community College: Directions for the '70's (Roueche, et al., 1971), and Breaking the Access Barriers: A Profile of Two-Year Colleges (Medsker and Tillery, 1971).

The review of literature presented here is comprehensively related to the past, present, and future status afforded to junior and community colleges. To a great extent however, the literary form still lacks substance as it relates to the idea of the community college. To an even greater extent, the literature remains confusing, antithetical, and written from so many points of view that it is difficult to find a common basis for understanding and meaningful dialogue. It is this kind of dilemma that makes the community college indistinguishable from other kinds of two-year colleges. One can only hope that the community college discovers its uniqueness among other post-secondary institutions before the very forces that sanction its existence bring about new educational forms to replace it.

BIBLIOGRAPHY

Abbas, Robert D. Interpersonal Values of the Junior College and University Student. University of Missouri, N.D.E.A. Institute, November, 1968.

Agnew, Spiro T. "Toward a 'Middle Way' In College Admissions." Speech given in Des Moines, Iowa, April 13, 1970.

Alderman, L. R. College and University Extension Helps in Adult Education, Bulletin No. 3, Department of the Interior, Bureau of Education. Washington: Government Printing Office, 1928.

Alkin, Marvin C. "The Use of Behavioral Objectives in Education: Relevant or Irrelevant?" Paper presented to the Annual Western Regional Conference on Testing Problems, San Francisco, May 9, 1969. Los Angeles: University of California Center for the Study of Evaluation, 1969. [ERIC ED 035 067, 1970].

Allen, Herman R. Open Door to Learning. Urbana: University of Illinois Press, 1963.

Allen, James E., Jr. "James E. Allen, Jr., on Education." Washington: U.S. Office of Education, Office of Information, May, 1969. (a) [ERIC ED 031 804, 1970].

_____. "The Community College and the Office of Education's Goals." Speech given at the Annual Meeting of the National Council of State Directors of Community-Junior Colleges, Williamsburg (Virginia), November 10, 1969. (b) [ERIC ED 034 535, 1970].

Allen, Lucille, et al. "The Nature and Functions of Higher Education," College and University, 35:29-33, Fall, 1959.

American Association of Junior Colleges. The Privately

Bibliography

Supported Junior College: A Place and Purpose in Higher Education. Washington: American Association of Junior Colleges, 1963. (a)

_____. A New Social Invention: The Community College, What It Is. Edmund J. Gleazer, Jr. Washington: A.A.J.C., 1963. (b)

_____. To Work In A Junior College. Washington: American Association of Junior Colleges, 1966.

_____. An Introduction to American Junior Colleges. Washington: American Association of Junior Colleges, 1967.

_____. Preparing Two-Year College Teachers for the 70's. Washington: American Association of Junior Colleges, 1969.

The American College. A Series of Papers Setting Forth the Program, Achievements, Present Status, and Probable Future of the American College. New York: Henry Holt and Company, 1915.

American College Testing Program. College Student Profiles: Norms for the ACT Assessment. Iowa City: The American College Testing Program, 1966.

_____. The Two-Year College and Its Students: An Empirical Report, Monograph Two. Iowa City: The American College Testing Program, 1969. (a)

_____. ACT Guidance Profile. Manual. Iowa City: The American College Testing Program, 1969. (b)

_____. A Guide for Using ACT Services in 2-Year Institutions. Iowa City: The American College Testing Program, 1970. (a)

_____. The Two-Year College and Its Students: An Empirical Report. Iowa City: The American College Testing Program, 1970. (b)

American Council on Education. An Introduction to American Junior Colleges (A Reprint). Washington: American Association of Junior Colleges, 1967.

Analysis of State Programs In Community-Centered Post-High School Education. Denver: Education Commission of the States, October, 1968.

Anderson, John E., Jr. "Research in the Junior College: Anethma or Anodyne?" Junior College Journal, 35:15-16, November, 1964.

Angell, James R. "The Junior-College Movement in High Schools," The School Review, 23:289-302, May, 1915.

_____. "Problems Peculiar to the Junior College," The School Review, 25:385-397, June, 1917.

Annual Report - 1968. A Report to the Governors, the Legislators, and the People of the 13 Western States. Boulder (Colorado): Western Interstate Commission for Higher Education, January, 1969.

Arnstein, George E. "Vocational Education," Bulletin of The National Association of Secondary School Principals, 48:56-72, November, 1964.

Arrowsmith, William. "The Future of Teaching," Campus 1980, Alvin C. Eurich (ed.), pp. 116-33. New York: Dell Publishing Co., Inc., 1968.

Assembly on University Goals and Governance. "Assembly Lists 85 Theses for Reforming Higher Education," The Chronicle of Higher Education, January 18, 1971, pp. 5-9.

Astin, Alexander W. The College Environment. Washington: American Council on Education, 1968.

_____. "Open Admissions and Programs for the Disadvantaged." Address presented at the 26th National Conference on Higher Education, Chicago, March 16, 1971.

_____, and J. L. Holland. "The Environmental Assessment Technique: A Way to Measure College Environments." Journal of Educational Psychology, 52:308-16, 1961.

_____, et al. "National Norms for Entering College Freshmen--Fall, 1966." ACE Research Reports. Washington: American Council on Education, 1967.

Bibliography

Axelrod, Joseph, et al. Search for Relevance. San Francisco: Jossey-Bass Inc., 1969.

Barham, Virginia Z. "Curriculum in the Associate Degree Nursing Program--Some Unanswered Questions," California Education, 3:18-19, February, 1966.

Barry, Ruth, and Beverly Wolf. Modern Issues in Guidance-Personnel Work. New York: Bureau of Publications, Teachers' College, Columbia University, 1958.

Battle, Jean Allen. The New Idea In Education. New York: Harper and Row, Publishers, 1968.

Beatty, H. Russell. To What Do The Technical Programs of The Two-Year Colleges Lead? Boston: Wentworth, 1963.

Becker, Howard S., et al. Making the Grade: The Academic Side of College Life. New York: John Wiley and Sons, 1968.

Beeler, Kent D., and August W. Eberle. "Paradoxes in Higher Education," School and Society, 99:217-18, April, 1971.

Behm, H. D. "Characteristics of Community College Students: A Comparison of Transfer and Occupational Freshmen in Selected Midwestern Colleges." Doctoral dissertation, (University of Missouri) Ann Arbor: University Microfilms, 1967.

Bell, Daniel. "The Post-Industrial Society." Background paper prepared for forum discussion, The Impact of Technology and Social Change. Boston: Liberty Mutual Insurance Co., June 14, 1962.

Bennett, G. Vernon. "A State Two-Year College of Technology," California Quarterly of Secondary Education, 5:77-81, October, 1929.

Berdie, Ralph F. "Characteristics of Students Today." Paper presented at Seminars on the Social Psychology of the Future State Metropolitan Campus. Minneapolis: The University of Minnesota, February 10, 1966. [ERIC ED 038 090, 1970].

Berth, Donald F., and John T. Henderson. "Community College and Engineering College Interaction in New York State," Engineering Education, 59:223-226, November, 1968.

Besvinick, S. L., and T. W. Fryer, Jr. "Miami Begins the Diplomate in Collegiate Teaching," Junior College Journal, 39:48-56, February, 1969.

The Bethlehem (Pa.) Globe-Times, April 10, 1967.

Birenbaum, William M. "Cities and Universities: Collision of Crises," Campus 1980, Alvin C. Eurich (ed.)., pp. 43-63. New York: Dell Publishing Co., Inc., 1968.

_____. Overlive. New York: Dell Publishing Co., Inc., 1969.

_____. "Who Should Go To College?" Paper presented at the 25th National Conference on Higher Education, Chicago, March 2, 1970. [ERIC ED 040 670, 1970].

_____. "Equal Access to What?" Junior College Research Review, 5:10-11, May, 1971.

Birnbaum, Robert. "Background and Evaluation of Faculty in New York," Junior College Journal, 37:35, November, 1966.

Bissiri, August. "Disqualified Students Admitted to the Fall 1965 Semester." Los Angeles: Los Angeles City College, 1966.

Blackburn, Robert T. "Changes in Faculty Life Styles," Research Report Number 1. Washington: American Association for Higher Education, 1970.

_____. The Professor's Role in a Changing Society, Report 10. ERIC Clearinghouse on Higher Education. Washington: The George Washington University, June, 1971.

Blocker, Clyde E. "Dissent and the College Student in Revolt," School and Society, 98:20-22, January, 1970.

_____, and H. A. Campbell, Jr. Administrative Practices in University Extension Centers and Branch

Colleges. Austin: University of Texas Press, 1963.

_____, et al. The Two-Year College: A Social Synthesis. Englewood Cliffs: Prentice-Hall, Inc., 1965.

Bock, Joleen. "Improvement of Instruction in Junior College Through Utilization of Auxiliary Personnel." Seminar paper, December, 1968. [Reported in ERIC ED 031 212, 1969].

Bode, B. H. "Our Great American Tradition," School and Home Education, 41:91-99, March, 1922.

Boggs, John R. "Studies of Student and Staff Attitudes," Junior College Research Review, April, 1971.

Bogue, Jesse Parker. The Community College. New York: McGraw-Hill Book Company, Inc., 1950.

_____. The Development of Community Colleges. Washington: American Association of Junior Colleges, 1957.

_____, and Joanne Waterman (eds.). Junior College Directory, 1957. Washington: American Association of Junior Colleges, 1957.

Bolman, Frederick deW. "New Opportunities in Articulation," Junior College Journal, 36:20-23, March, 1966.

Bolton, Frederick E. "What Should Constitute the Curriculum of the Junior College or Extended High School?" School and Society, 8:726-727, December 1918.

_____. "Some Probable Effects Upon Higher Education Due to the Development of Junior Colleges," Educational Administration and Supervision, 5:85-93, February, 1919.

_____. "Accreditation in Democratic Education," University of Washington College of Education Record, 8:34, January, 1942.

_____. "Suggestions for the Post-War Development of Junior Colleges," University of Washington College of Education Record, 10:91-92, April, 1944.

Bonner, Thomas, et al. The Contemporary World.

Englewood Cliffs (New Jersey): Prentice-Hall, Inc.,
1960.

Bossen, Doris S. "A Follow-Up Study of the Junior College
Withdrawal Student." Ph.D. Dissertation, Ohio State
University, 1968.

Bossone, Richard M. "Understanding Junior-College Students," Journal of Higher Education, 36:279-83, May,
1965. [ERIC ED 017 242, 1968].

Boucher, Chauncey Samuel. The Chicago College Plan.
Chicago: The University of Chicago Press, 1935.

Bowen, Howard R. "Finance and the Aims of American
Higher Education." Paper presented to the 25th National Conference of the American Association for Higher
Education, Chicago, March 2, 1970. [ERIC ED 038
085, 1970].

Bowles, Frank. "The Democratization of Education--A
World-Wide Revolution," College Board Review, 63:11,
Fall, 1969.

Bowles, Roy T., and Walter L. Slocum. Social Characteristics of High School Students Planning to Pursue Post
High School Vocational Training. Final Report No. 17.
Seattle: Washington Research Coordinating Unit for Vocational Education, June, 1968. [ERIC ED 021 148,
1968].

Boyer, Marcia. "Teacher Evaluation: Toward Improving
Instruction," Junior College Research Review, Vol. 4,
No. 5, January, 1970. [ERIC ED 035 408, 1970].

Branscomb, Bennett H. Teaching With Books: A Study of
College Libraries. Chicago: Association of American
Colleges, American Library Association, 1940.

Brawer, Florence B. Personality Characteristics of College
and University Faculty: Implications for the Community
College. Washington: American Association of Junior
Colleges, 1968.

_____. "Student Studies: Comparative and Remedial
Populations," Junior College Research Review, March,
1971.

Bibliography 289

Bremer, Fred H. "Philanthropic Support for Public Junior Colleges." Ph.D. Dissertation, 1965. [Reported in ERIC ED 035 388, 1970].

Brennan, Michael J. "A Cannibalistic View of Graduate Education." Address to the Ninth Annual Meeting of the Council of Graduate Schools in the United States, Washington, D.C., December 4-6, 1969. Washington: Council of Graduate Schools, 1969. [ERIC ED 036 252, 1970].

Brick, Michael. Forum and Focus for the Junior College Movement: The American Association of Junior Colleges. New York: Bureau of Publications, Teachers College, Columbia University, 1964.

Briggs, Thomas H. "Articulation: Some Fundamental Purposes and Its Ideals," California Quarterly of Secondary Education, 31:213-18, April, 1930.

Brouillet, Frank B. "The Development of Financial Support for Washington State Community Colleges," University of Washington College of Education Record, 31:23, January, 1965.

Brown, J. Stanley. "Present Development of Secondary Schools According to the Proposed Plan," The School Review, 13:15-17, January, 1905.

Browne, Richard G. "Standards for Upper Division Colleges, With Special Reference to Joplin and St. Joseph, Missouri," February, 1966. [Reported in ERIC ED 033 648, 1970].

Brubacher, John S. Bases for Policy in Higher Education. New York: McGraw-Hill Book Company, 1965.

_____. "Theory of Higher Education," Journal of Higher Education, 41:98-115, February, 1970.

_____, and Willis Rudy. Higher Education In Transition. New York: Harper and Row, Publishers, 1968.

Brue, Eldon J., et al. How Do Community College Transfer and Occupational Students Differ? A.C.T. Research Report, No. 41. Iowa City: American College Testing Program, February, 1971.

Brumbaugh, A. J. Establishing New Senior Colleges. S. R. E. B. Research Monograph No. 12. Atlanta: Southern Regional Education Board, 1966.

Buckels, Marvin W. "Coordination Means Progress in California," Compact, August, 1970.

Burns, Norman. "Some Basic Problems of Accrediting," The North Central Association Quarterly, 35:193-197, October, 1960.

_____. "Association Notes and Editorial Comments," The North Central Association Quarterly, 36:309-313, Spring, 1962.

_____. "Changing Concepts of Higher Education," The North Central Association Quarterly, 38:296-300, Spring, 1964.

Burt, Samuel M. Industry and Vocational-Technical Education. New York: McGraw-Hill Book Company, 1967.

Bush, Ralph H. "Curricular Problems in the Junior College," California Quarterly of Secondary Education, 5:87-92, 1929-30.

Butler, Nathaniel. "The Six-Year High School," The School Review, 12:22-25, 1904.

Butler, Nicholas Murray. "A Two-Year College Course," Educational Review, 19:411, April, 1900.

California Commission for the Study of Educational Problems. Report, Vol. 1. Sacramento: California Commission for the Study of Educational Problems, 1932.

California Coordinating Council for Higher Education. Academic Tenure in California Public Higher Education, Report No. 69-5. Sacramento: California Coordinating Council for Higher Education, May 6, 1969. [ERIC ED 032 837, 1970].

_____. The Undergraduate Student and His Higher Education: Policies of California Colleges and Universities in the Next Decade. Report No. 1034. Sacramento: California Coordinating Council for Higher Education, June, 1969. [ERIC ED 032 836, 1970].

Bibliography

California High School Teachers' Association. Report of the Committee of Fifteen on Secondary Education in California, 1923. San Francisco: California High School Teachers' Association, 1924.

California State Department of Education. A Guide for California Public Junior Colleges. Sacramento: Bureau of Junior College General Education, 1967.

Calkins, Hugh. "Vocational Education is Designed for Somebody Else's Children," The Personnel and Guidance Journal, 49:339, December, 1970.

Campbell, Doak S. Higher Education and a Democratic State. Gainesville: University of Florida, 1942.

Capper, Michael R. "Instructional Objectives for Junior College Courses." ERIC Clearinghouse for Junior College Information. Los Angeles: University of California, Los Angeles, November, 1969. (a) [ERIC ED 033 679, 1970].

_____. "Junior College Students On Academic Probation," Junior College Research Review, December, 1969. (b)

_____, and Dale Gaddy. "Faculty Participation in Junior College Governance," Junior College Research Review, February, 1969.

Carnegie Foundation for the Advancement of Teaching. A Chance to Learn: An Action Agenda for Equal Opportunity in Higher Education. A Special Report and Recommendations by The Carnegie Commission on Higher Education. New York: McGraw-Hill Book Company, March, 1970.

_____. The Open Door Colleges: Policies for Community Colleges. A Special Report and Recommendations by The Carnegie Commission on Higher Education. New York: McGraw-Hill Book Company, June, 1970.

_____. Less Time, More Options. A Special Report and Recommendations by The Carnegie Commission on Higher Education. New York: McGraw-Hill Book Company, January, 1971.

Carter, Barbara. "Junior Colleges are Blooming in the

Sunshine State," N. E. A. Journal, 56:24, May, 1967.

Cashin, H. John. "Some Attitudes Toward Instructor Preparation," Junior College Journal, 39:31-34, March, 1969.

Castell, Aubrey. "Wanted: A New Deal for the Liberal Arts College," University of Washington College of Education Record, 22:18, January, 1956.

Castle, Drew W. "Terminal Engineering Courses in the Junior College," Industrial Education Magazine, 31:77-79, September, 1930.

Cervantes, Lucius. The Dropout: Causes and Cures. Ann Arbor: University of Michigan Press, 1966.

"Changing Patterns In Education Beyond the High School," Part III in The Changing West: Implications for Higher Education. Papers presented at a Symposium held in Boulder, Colorado, August 7-9, 1964. Boulder: Western Interstate Commission for Higher Education, February, 1965.

The Changing West: Implications for Higher Education. Papers presented at a Symposium held in Boulder, Colorado, August 7-9, 1964. Boulder: Western Interstate Commission for Higher Education, February, 1965.

Charters, Alexander N. "Pressures on Higher Education for Adult Education Services," Current Issues in Higher Education. Washington: National Education Association, 1965.

Chase, Edward T. "Learning to be Unemployable," Harper's Magazine, 226:33-40, April, 1963.

Chase, Harry W. Twenty Years of Higher Education. Report of the Chancellor of New York University for the Year 1938-1939.

Christian, Floyd T., and James L. Wattenbarger. "Ten Years--A Plan Evolves in Florida," Junior College Journal, 38:44-47, September, 1967.

The Chronicle of Higher Education. [Selected issues as noted in text during the period from February 26, 1968

Bibliography

to May 24, 1971].

City University of New York, University Commission on Admissions. Report and Recommendations to the Board of Higher Education of the City of New York. New York: City University of New York, October 7, 1969. [ERIC ED 035 373, 1970].

Clark, Burton R. "The 'Cooling-Out' Function in Higher Education," The American Journal of Sociology, 65:569-576, May, 1960. (a)

―――. The Open Door College: A Case Study. New York: McGraw-Hill Book Company, 1960. (b)

Clark, Kenneth E. "The Graduate Student as Teacher." Speech presented to the meeting of the American Historical Association, Washington, D. C., December 28-30, 1969. Washington: American Historical Association, 1969. [ERIC ED 035 374, 1970].

Clayton, Howard. "The Scholiast," The Library-College Journal, 3:14-15, Spring, 1970.

Cleveland, Harlan. Closing address to the 50th National Convention of the American Association of Junior Colleges, Honolulu, February 28-March 4, 1970.

Coffman, L. D. "What Part Shall the Colleges and Universities Play in the American Program of Education?" School and Home Education, 41:1-5, September, 1921.

Cohen, Arthur M. "Developing Specialists in Learning," Junior College Journal, 37:21-23, September, 1966.

―――. "ERIC and the Junior College," Junior College Research Review, February-March, 1967; Junior College Journal, 38:17-19, November, 1967.

―――. "The Junior College Curriculum," Course Syllabus, University of California, Los Angeles, 1968. [Reported in ERIC ED 015 760, 1968].

―――. "Who Is Talking To Whom?" Junior College Research Review, 3:2-8, April, 1969. (a)

―――. "The Relationship Among Student Characteristics,

Changed Instructional Practices, and Student Attrition in Junior College," Final Report. Washington: Office of Education, Bureau of Research, June, 1969. (b) [ERIC ED 032 074, 1970].

_____. Dateline '79: Heretical Concepts for the Community College. Beverly Hills: Glencoe Press, 1969. (c)

_____, and Florence B. Brawer. Focus on Learning--Preparing Teachers for the Two-Year College. Junior College Leadership Program, Occasional Report No. 11. Los Angeles: University of California, March, 1968. [ERIC ED 019 938, 1968].

_____, _____. Measuring Faculty Performance. Washington: American Association of Junior Colleges, 1969.

_____, and Edgar A. Quimby. "Trends in the Study of Junior Colleges: 1970," Rationale and Recommendations for Fifteen Essential Research Projects. Junior College Research Review, September, 1970.

Cohen, Martin J. "College of the Whole Earth," Junior College Research Review, 5:8-9, May, 1971.

College Admissions Handbook. Lansing (Michigan): Michigan Department of Education, 1969.

College Entrance Examination Board. "Willingham Studies Free-Access Higher Education," C.G.P. Reports. The Comparative Guidance and Placement Program, June, 1970.

Collins, Charles C. Junior College Student Personnel Programs: What They Are and What They Should Be. Washington: American Association of Junior Colleges, 1967.

_____. "Exporting the Junior College Idea," Junior College Journal, 38:10-14, April, 1968.

_____. "A Proposal for Financing Higher Education," October, 1969. (a) [Reported in ERIC ED 038 128, 1970].

_____. "A Different Perception of the Community in

Bibliography

Community College," October 28, 1969. (b) [Reported in ERIC ED 034 532, 1970].

_____. Financing Higher Education: A Proposal. Topical Paper No. 10. ERIC Clearinghouse on Higher Education. Washington: The George Washington University, February, 1970. [ERIC ED 037 206, 1970].

Collins, John J. "Accreditation Aims and Perceptions," Junior College Journal, 38:19-23, December, 1967-January, 1968.

Colvert, C. C. "Development of the Junior College Movement," Chapter 2 in American Junior Colleges (Fourth Edition), Jesse P. Bogue (ed.). Washington: American Council on Education, 1956.

_____, and M. L. Baker. Junior College Directory, 1955. Washington: American Association of Junior Colleges, 1955.

"Comment--The Arizona Job College," Change Magazine, 2:10, January-February, 1970.

Commission on Higher Education. "Equalizing Opportunity Through Adult Education," Higher Education for American Democracy. A Report of the President's Commission on Higher Education. Washington: Government Printing Office, 1947.

Committee on Higher Education, "The Professional Preparation of College Teachers," National Society of College Teachers of Education, History of Education Journal, 4:25-40, Autumn, 1952.

Committee on Labor and Public Welfare. Selected Education Acts of 1963. United States Senate Committee, 88th Congress, 1st Session. Washington: Government Printing Office, 1963.

Committee on Preparation of Junior College Teachers. Master Plan Phase III. A Report to the Illinois Board of Higher Education. Carbondale: Illinois Board of Higher Education, June, 1969.

Committee on Standards of the American Council on Education. "The Junior College," Educational Record,

2:68-69, April, 1921.

_____. "Standards and Principles for Accrediting Junior Colleges," Educational Record, 5:202-204, July, 1924.

Committee on the Student in Higher Education. The Student in Higher Education. A report. New Haven (Conn.): The Hazen Foundation, January, 1968.

"Community and Junior Colleges," Improving College and University Teaching, Vol. 17, No. 2, Spring, 1969.

"The Community College," The Nation, 185:82, August 31, 1957.

"Community College Model for Review," The Sun, Baltimore, December 8, 1968.

Conant, James B. The American High School Today. New York: McGraw-Hill Book Company, 1959.

"Conference Activities," Academe. Newsletter of the A.A.U.P. Washington: American Association of University Professors, March, 1968.

Cook, Joseph H., et al. The Search for Independence. Belmont (California): Brooks/Cole Publishing Company, 1968.

Cook, Samuel D., et al. Dilemmas of American Policy: Crucial Issues in Contemporary Society. Notes and Essays on Education for Adults, No. 62. Syracuse: Syracuse University Press, November, 1969.

Cooley, W. W., and S. J. Becker. "The Junior College Student," Personnel and Guidance Journal, 44:464-69, January, 1966.

Coombs, Philip H. "The Technical Frontiers of Education." The Twenty-seventh Annual Sir John Adams Lecture at the University of California, delivered March 15, 1960. Los Angeles: University of California, 1960.

Corbally, John E. "Some Critical Issues in Secondary Education," University of Washington College of Education Record, 12:18-19, December, 1945.

"Correspondence," The New Republic, 152:36, February 20, 1965.

Cory, Arthur F. "Universal Educational Opportunity Beyond the High School," Current Issues in Higher Education. Washington: National Education Association, 1964.

Cosand, Joseph P. "The Community College in 1980," Campus 1980, Alvin C. Eurich (ed.), pp. 134-48. New York: Dell Publishing Co., Inc., 1968.

Cosby, Betty. "Professional Preparation for Student Personnel Work in Higher Education," Journal of the National Association of Women Deans and Counselors, 24:14-18, Fall, 1965.

Coursault, Jesse H. "Standardizing the Junior College," Educational Review, 49:59-62, January, 1915.

Cowen, Philip A. A Study of the Factors Related to College Attendance in New York State. Albany: New York State Education Department, 1946.

Cowley, William H. "European Influences in American Higher Education," Educational Record, 20:165-90, April, 1939.

_____. "A Student of Higher Education Views Junior College Administration," in Symposium: Need for Administrative Leadership in Junior Colleges. Los Angeles: University of California, July, 1960.

_____. "Critical Decisions," Twenty-Five Years 1945-1970, G. Kerry Smith (ed.). Washington: American Association for Higher Education, 1970.

Cox, Miriam. "The College Is for Everyone Cult," Junior College Journal, 37:37-39, September, 1966.

Creamer, Don G. "An Evaluation of Mid-Semester Deficiency Grading Practices," 1969. [Reported in ERIC ED 034 543, 1970].

Cremin, Lawrence A. The Transformation of the School: Progressivism in American Education, 1876-1957. New York: Alfred A. Knopf, 1961.

Cresci, Gerald D., and Carl G. Winter. "The Junior College As A Partner in Higher Education," *California Schools*, 34:31-40, February, 1963.

Crockett, Thompson S., and James D. Stinchcomb. *Guidelines for Law Enforcement Education Programs in Community and Junior Colleges.* Washington: American Association of Junior Colleges, 1968.

Cross, K. Patricia. "Beyond Ability," *The Research Reporter*, Vol. 2, No. 1. Berkeley: The Center for Research and Development in Higher Education, 1967.

_____. "Higher Education's Newest Student," *Junior College Journal*, 39:38-42, September, 1968. (a)

_____. "College Women: A Research Description," *Journal of the National Association of Women Deans and Counselors*, 3:12-21, 1968. (b)

_____. *The Junior College Student: A Research Description.* Princeton: Educational Testing Service, 1968. (c)

_____. "The Quiet Revolution," *The Research Reporter*, Vol. 4, No. 3. Berkeley: Center for Research and Development in Higher Education, 1969. [ERIC ED 036 249, 1970].

_____. "Occupationally Oriented Students," *Junior College Research Review*, November, 1970.

_____. "Access and Accommodation in Higher Education," *The Research Reporter*, Vol. 6, No. 2, pp. 6-8. Paper presented to White House Conference on Youth. Berkeley: The Center for Research and Development in Higher Education, 1971.

Crouch, L. M., Jr. *A Summary of Missouri Constitution and Laws as Affecting Higher Education for Use of the Commission on Higher Education and Its Staff.* Jefferson City (Missouri): Missouri Commission on Higher Education, May, 1968.

Cummiskey, J. Kenneth. "Community College Outreach Programs: Who is Being Reached?" *Community Services Forum*, Newsletter of the Community Services

Project of the American Association of Junior Colleges, Vol. 1, No. 4, April, 1969.

Darley, John G. Promise and Performance: A Study of Ability and Achievement in Higher Education. Berkeley: University of California, 1962.

Davis, Bertram H. "The AAUP and the Junior College," Reprint from the Junior College Journal, December, 1968. [March 4, 1969].

Davis, Calvin O. "Reorganization of Secondary Education," Educational Review, 42:270-301, October, 1911.

Davis, J. A. Great Aspirations: The Graduate School Plans of America's College Seniors. Chicago: Aldine Publishing Company, 1964.

Davis, William E. "When A University Offers Vocational Education, Too," College Management, 5:24-25, July, 1970.

Day, James P. "Three Presidents Fear More Than State Control," The Evening Sun, Baltimore, November 20, 1970.

Delaware Technical and Community College, Second Report. Dover: Board of Trustees of the Delaware Technical and Community College, January, 1969.

DeNevi, Don. "'Retreading' Teachers the Hard Way," Community College Programs for People Who Need College, pp. 78-81. Washington: American Association of Junior Colleges, 1970.

Denton, Clifford. "Community Colleges Pioneer The Open Door Policy," Pennsylvania Education, 2:18-23, May-June, 1970.

Department of Labor (Women's Bureau). Continuing Education Programs and Services for Women, Pamphlet 10. Washington: U.S. Department of Labor, January, 1968.

Devall, W. B. "Community Colleges: A Dissenting View," Educational Record, 49:168-172, Spring, 1968.

Deyo, Donald E. "Three Cliches," Junior College Journal,

34:6-7, September, 1963.

Digest of Educational Statistics, 1969. National Center for Educational Statistics. Washington: Government Printing Office, September, 1969.

Donzaleigh, Turman P. "Articulation of Admissions and Curricular Practices in Junior and Senior Colleges." Doctoral dissertation, Indiana University, 1969.

Doran, Kenneth T. "Relevancy of the Community College." Speech given before the New York State Personnel and Guidance Association, November 18, 1969. [ERIC ED 035 399, 1970].

Dotson, George E. "Advantages to the Junior College of 'Common Administration' School Districts," Journal of Secondary Education, 38:148-150, March, 1963.

Doyle, Walter. "Community-College Concept in Higher Education," Catholic Educational Review, 64:251-262, April, 1966.

Dressel, Paul L., and Lewis B. Mayhew. General Education: Explorations in Evaluation. Washington: American Council on Education, 1954.

Dublin, Robert, and Thomas C. Taveggia. The Teaching-Learning Paradox: A Comparative Analysis of College Teaching Methods. Eugene: University of Oregon Press, 1968.

Duke, Christopher. The London External Degree and the English Part-Time Degree Student. Leeds Studies in Adult Education, No. 2. Leeds (England): Leeds University Press, 1967. [ERIC ED 032 459, 1970].

Dungan, Ralph A. "Facts About New Jersey Higher Education." Trenton: Department of Higher Education, August, 1969. (Mimeographed).

Dunlap, E. T. "Oklahoma Looks to 1970," Junior College Journal, 39:29-32, February, 1969.

Dykes, Archie R. Faculty Participation in Academic Decision Making. Washington: American Council on Education, 1968.

Bibliography

Ebbsen, James A. "Junior College Board Members: Their Personal Characteristics and Attitudes Toward Junior College Functions, State of Illinois, 1968-1969." Doctoral dissertation, June, 1969. [Reported in ERIC ED 032 033, 1970].

Eble, Kenneth E. "Teaching," The Chronicle of Higher Education, April 12, 1971, p. 8.

Eckert, Ruth E., and Thomas O. Marshall. When Youth Leave School. New York: McGraw-Hill Book Company, 1938.

Edelman, Edward. "Junior Colleges Discover New Ways to Raise Capital," American Education, 5:22, December 1968-January 1969.

"Editorial Notes," The School Review, 14:609, October, 1906.

"Education Adjusted to Needs," Higher Education for American Democracy, 1:67, December, 1947.

Education Commission of the States. The Compact for Education. Denver: Education Commission of the States, 1967.

_____. State-Federal Relationships: The ECS Role. Report No. 16. Denver: Education Commission of the States, December, 1968.

_____. Higher Education in the States, Vol. 1, No. 1. Denver: Education Commission of the States, February, 1970.

Education Research Bulletin. Pasadena (California): Board of Education, May, 1926.

"Educational Events," School and Society, 41:328, March, 1935.

Educational Policies Commission. The Purpose of Education in American Democracy. Washington: National Education Association, 1938.

_____. Universal Opportunity for Education Beyond High School. Washington: National Education Association, 1964.

Eells, Walter Crosby. The Junior College. New York: Houghton Mifflin Co., 1931; Cambridge: The Riverside Press, 1931.

_____. "Abolition of the Lower Division: Early History," Junior College Journal, 6:194-95, January, 1936.

_____. American Junior Colleges. First Edition. Washington: American Council on Education, 1940.

_____. Present Status of Junior College Terminal Education. Washington: American Association of Junior Colleges, 1941.

_____. "The Bachelor's Degree at the Sophomore Level," A. A. U. P. Bulletin, 28:327-51, June, 1942.

_____. "Status of the Junior College in the United States," School and Society, 59:412-15, June 10, 1944.

_____. "The Associate's Degree." Chapter 7 in Degrees in Higher Education. Washington: The Center for Applied Research in Education, Inc., 1963.

_____, and Harold A. Hasiwell. Academic Degrees. Office of Education, Bulletin No. 28. Washington: Government Printing Office, 1960.

Eiss, Albert F. (ed.). Science Education in the Junior College. Commission on the Education of Teachers of Science. Washington: National Science Teachers Association, 1966.

Elliott, Lloyd H. "Limits of Relevance and Choice." Address presented to the Annual Meeting of the Middle Atlantic Association of Colleges of Business Administration, Washington, D. C., October, 1969. [ERIC ED 035 346, 1970].

Elsner, Paul A. "The Presidential Prism: Four Views; A State Officer's View of the Community College President." Address given at the Junior College Leadership Program Presidents' Institute, Scottsdale (Arizona), May 6, 1969. [Reported in ERIC ED 032 059, 1970].

Emerson, Lynn A. "Changing Technology Requires Planning for Occupational Education in the Future Community

College," Technical Education News. New York: McGraw-Hill Book Company, March, 1965.

Ericksen, Stanford C. "Pass-Fail Grading." Memo to the Faculty, No. 22. Ann Arbor: Center for Research on Learning and Teaching, the University of Michigan, 1967.

Erickson, Clifford G. "Illinois Balances Statewide Planning and Local Autonomy," Junior College Journal, 38:23-26, March, 1968.

──────. "Trends and Tangents," Journal of Higher Education, 41:151-55, February, 1970.

Eurich, Alvin C. (ed.). Campus 1980. New York: Dell Publishing Co., Inc., 1968.

──────. High School 1980: The Shape of the Future in American Secondary Education. New York: Pitman Publishing Corporation, 1970. (a)

──────. "Reforming American Education," The Library-College Journal, 3:11-24, Winter, 1970. (b)

Evans, Arthur H., Jr. "The 'Dead' Faculty Member: Prevention and Cure," 1969. [Reported in ERIC ED 037 214, 1970].

The Evening Sun, Baltimore, December 6, 1967; March 9, 1971.

"Events," School and Society, 59:150, February 26, 1944; 61:117-18, February, 1945.

Facing Facts About the Two-Year College. Newark: The Prudential Insurance Company of America, 1968.

The Federal Investment in Higher Education. Washington: American Council on Education, 1967.

Federal Programs for Higher Education: Needed Next Steps. Washington: American Council on Education, 1969.

"Fees, Charges and Deposits in California Public Schools," California Schools, 11:25, May, 1940.

Ferrari, Michael R., and Neal R. Berte. "American Junior Colleges: Leadership and Crucial Issues for the 1970's," 1969. [Reported in ERIC ED 035 398, 1970].

Ferrier, William W. Ninety Years of Education in California, 1846-1936. Berkeley: Sather Gate Book Shop, 1937.

Fields, Ralph R. The Community College Movement. New York: McGraw-Hill Book Company, 1962.

Final Report: Missouri Public Junior College Study. Jefferson City (Missouri): Missouri Commission on Higher Education, July, 1968.

Financial Requirements of Public Four-Year Colleges and Universities and Public Community Colleges (1969-70). Lansing: Michigan Department of Education, June, 1969.

Financing Public Education. Federal Security Agency, Leaflet No. 78. Washington: U.S. Office of Education, 1947.

Finch, Robert H. "Education for Tomorrow." Address delivered to Annual Conference of National Industrial Conference Board, New York City, November 20, 1969. [ERIC ED 035 347, 1970].

Fine, Benjamin. "Open Admissions is Working," The Sun, Baltimore, July 18, 1971, p. K11.

Fitch, Robert J. "An Analysis of the Courses Failed by Freshman Students on Academic Probation," Cerritos College (California), 1968.

Fitzwater, C. O. State School System Development: Patterns and Trends. Report No. 5. Denver: Education Commission of the States, March, 1968.

Flanders, Russell B. Jobs With A Future For High School Graduates. Washington: Bureau of Labor Statistics. (Department of Labor), February, 1968.

Flax, Roger E. "The Improvement of Articulation for Transfer from Maryland Junior Colleges to the State University." Ph.D. Dissertation, Catholic University,

1968.

Florida Community Junior College Inter-institutional Research Council. Where Are They Now? A Follow-Up of First Time College Freshmen in Florida's Community Junior Colleges in Fall, 1966. Gainesville: Florida Community Junior College Inter-institutional Research Council, 1969. [ERIC ED 035 396, 1970].

Folwell, W. W. University Addresses. Minneapolis, Minnesota: H. W. Wilson Company, 1909.

──────. A History of Minnesota, Vol. 4, pp. 119-120. St. Paul: Minnesota Historical Society, 1930.

──────. Autobiography and Letters. Minneapolis, University of Minnesota Press, 1933.

Fox, Raymond B. "Improving Relations Between High Schools and Colleges," Education Digest, 27:49-51, May, 1962.

Fredenburgh, F. A. "Does the Community College Threaten Higher Education?" School and Society, 69:289-93, April 23, 1949.

French, Joseph L. Employment Status and Characteristics of High School Dropouts of High Ability. University Park: Pennsylvania State University, September, 1966. [ERIC ED 010 648, 1967].

Fretwell, E. K. "Issues Facing Community Colleges Today," Today's Education, 57:46-47, October, 1968.

Friedman, Norman L. "Comprehensiveness and Higher Education: A Sociologist's View of Public Junior College Trends," American Association of University Professors Bulletin, 52:417-423, December, 1966.

──────. "Task Adaptation Patterns of New Teachers," Improving College and University Teaching, 17:103-107, Spring, 1969.

Fullerton, Bill J., et al. "The Identification of Common Courses in Paramedical Education." Tempe (Arizona): Arizona State University, College of Education, July, 1966. [ERIC ED 010 190, 1967].

Gaddy, Dale. "Faculty Recruitment," Junior College Research Review, Vol. 4, No. 1, September, 1969. [ERIC ED 032 864, 1970].

_____. The Scope of Organized Student Protest in Junior Colleges. Washington: American Association of Junior Colleges, 1970.

Gagne, Robert M. "Some New Views of Learning and Instruction," Phi Delta Kappan, 51:468-472, May, 1970.

Gardiner, Glenn N. "The Adult School: Trends In Course Offerings," The Clearinghouse, 45:15-17, September, 1970.

Gardner, John W. "Quality in Higher Education," Current Issues in Higher Education. Washington: National Education Association, 1958.

_____. Excellence. New York: Harper and Row, Publishers, 1961.

_____. "Agenda for the Colleges and Universities," Campus 1980, Alvin C. Eurich (ed.), pp. 1-8. New York: Dell Publishing Co., Inc., 1968. (a)

_____. No Easy Victories. New York: Harper and Row, Publishers, 1968. (b)

_____, et al. The Pursuit of Excellence: Education and the Future of America. Panel Report 5 of the Special Studies Project. New York: Doubleday & Co., 1958.

Garrison, Roger H. "Professional Teacher or Dedicated Amateur?" School and Society, 93:390-392, October, 1965.

_____. Junior College Faculty: Issues and Problems. Washington: American Association of Junior Colleges, 1967. (a)

_____. "Unique Problems of Junior Colleges," National Education Association Journal, 56:30-32, November, 1967. (b)

_____. Teaching In A Junior College: A Brief Professional Orientation. Washington: American Association of Junior Colleges, 1968.

General Education in a Free Society. Report of the Harvard Committee. Cambridge: Harvard University Press, 1945.

General Laws and Procedures Relating to Collegiate Authority. Boston: Massachusetts Board of Higher Education, 1969.

Getty, Ronald. "European Influences That Affected the Early Development of the Junior College." Seminar paper dated February, 1970. [ERIC ED 037 200, 1970].

Giles, Frederick, and Harris C. McClaskey. "The Library Technician and the American Junior College." Seattle: Washington University, Center for Development of Community College Education, January, 1968. [ERIC ED 028 764, 1969].

Gillie, Angelo C. "New Jersey Community Colleges: A Report and Prognosis," Junior College Journal, 38:34-37, November, 1967.

_____. Essays in Occupational Education in the Two-Year College. University Park (Pennsylvania): Pennsylvania State University, Department of Vocational Education, January, 1970. [ERIC ED 037 210, 1970].

Gleazer, Edmund J., Jr. A New Social Invention: The Community College, What It Is. Washington: American Association of Junior Colleges, 1962.

_____. Junior Colleges: An Introduction. Washington: American Council on Education, 1963.

_____. "AAJC Approach," Junior College Journal, 37:5, September, 1966. (a)

_____. "Junior College and Technical Education," School and Society, 94:340-341, October, 1966. (b)

_____. "Concerns and Cautions for Community Colleges," Junior College Journal, 38:18-21, March, 1968. (a)

_____. This Is the Community College. Boston: Houghton Mifflin, 1968. (b)

_____. "Junior College Explosion," American Education, 5:12-13, December, 1968-January, 1969.

_____. "The Community College Issue of the 1970's," The Educational Record, 51:47, Winter, 1970.

Glenister, Carl E. "Comparison of Values: Two-Year vs. Four-Year Students," Junior College Research Review, October, 1969.

Gombar, William. "From Business School to a Modern Junior College," Education, 88:241-244, February-March, 1968.

Graham, Robert. "Politics and Higher Education," Occasional Paper No. 2. Denver: Education Commission of the States, December, 1969.

Graham, Walter A. "It May Happen in Alabama, Too!" Junior College Journal, 35:28-29, November, 1964.

Grant, Sherman. Call to Action: A Committee Progress Report with Recommendations for Action. Sacramento: California Junior College Association, Committee on the Disadvantaged, June, 1968. [ERIC ED 032 040, 1970].

Gray, A. A. "The Junior College in California," The School Review, 23:465-473, September, 1915.

Green, Thomas F. "Post-Secondary Education: 1970-1990," Dilemmas of American Policy, Notes and Essays on Education for Adults, No. 62, pp. 59-84. Syracuse: Syracuse University Press, November, 1969.

Guide For Evaluating State Programs in Community-Centered Post High School Education. Denver: Education Commission of the States, 1968.

Guidelines for the Establishment of Public Community Colleges in Pennsylvania. Harrisburg: Department of Public Instruction, April, 1965.

Gunn, Henry M., and Everett V. O'Rourke. "California Legislature Terminates Department's Role in Accrediting Secondary Schools," California Education, 3:5-7, June, 1966.

Bibliography

Gustad, John. "Comparison of Rank Orders of Information Employed in the Evaluation of Teaching (TABLE)" in "Evaluation of Teaching Performance: Issues and Possibilities," Improving College Teaching, pp. 265-81, Calvin B. T. Lee (ed.). Washington: American Council on Education, 1967.

Hakanson, John W. Selected Characteristics, Socioeconomic Status, and Levels of Attainment of Students in Public Junior College Occupation-Oriented Education. Berkeley: University of California, School of Education, April 30, 1967. [ERIC ED 013 644, 1968].

Hancher, Virgil. "The Challenges We Face," Vision and Purpose in Higher Education, Harold Howes (ed.), p. 83. Washington: American Council on Education, 1962.

Handbook For The Establishment and Operation of Community Junior Colleges In Oklahoma. Oklahoma City: Oklahoma State Regents for Higher Education, October, 1968.

Harbeson, John W. Classifying Junior College Students. Pasadena: Pasadena City Schools, 1932.

Harlacher, Ervin L. Effective Junior College Programs of Community Services: Rationale, Guidelines, Practices. Junior College Leadership Program, Occasional Report No. 10. Los Angeles: University of California, Los Angeles, 1967.

_____. The Community Dimension of the Community College. Englewood Cliffs: Prentice-Hall, Inc., 1969.

Harper, William A. "West Florida's New Two-Year University," Junior College Journal, 37:13-15, September, 1966.

_____. "Public Relations Problems Discussed by Practitioners," Junior College Journal, 38:42, October, 1967.

Harper, William Rainey. "The High School of the Future," The School Review, 11:1-3, January, 1903.

_____. The Trend In Higher Education. Chicago: University of Chicago Press, 1905.

Harper's Magazine, 234:4+, February, 1967.

Harrington, John C. "Academic Rank in the Community College," Junior College Journal, 35:24-26, March, 1965.

Harris, Chester W. (ed.). Encyclopedia of Educational Research. New York: The MacMillan Co., 1960.

Harrisburg Area Community College. Meeting The Changing Needs of Students: Curriculum Development, Monograph 2. Harrisburg: Harrisburg Area Community College, February, 1970. [ERIC ED 038 136, 1970].

Harvey, L. D. "The True Ideal of a Public School System That Aims to Benefit All." First Address to the National Society for the Promotion of Industrial Education. First Annual Meeting, Chicago, May, 1908.

Hayden, Shelden. "The Junior College as a Community Institution," Junior College Journal, 10:70-73, October, 1939.

Hayes, Glenn E. "Junior College Work Experience Education." Seminar paper, December, 1969. [Reported in ERIC ED 035 397, 1970].

Hedgepeth, Victor W. B. "The Six-Year High School Plan at Goshen, Indiana," The School Review, 13:22, January, 1905.

Heiner, Harold. "Community College: Counselor to the Community?" The Education Digest, 34:50-52, May, 1969.

Henry, Nelson B. (ed.). The Public Junior College. The Fifty-fifth Yearbook of the National Society for the Study of Education. Chicago: The University of Chicago Press, 1956.

Hickman, Marmette, and Gustave R. Lieske. "The Current Status of Community College Organization, Control, and Support," July, 1969. [Reported in ERIC ED 032 041, 1970].

Hickok, Helen. "Ask the Junior College Parents What They Think!" Junior College Journal, 35:24-27, November, 1964.

Higgins, Milton P. "The Type of Trade School to Meet American Needs." National Society for the Promotion of Industrial Education, Bulletin No. 6, pp. 20-25. Proceedings of First Annual Meeting, Chicago, May, 1908.

"High School Terminology," The School Review, 23:491-492, September, 1915.

Higher Education for American Democracy. A Report of the President's Commission on Higher Education. Vol. 1, Establishing the Goals. Washington: Government Printing Office, 1947; New York: Harper & Brothers, 1948.

Hillsborough Junior College. "Staff and Program Development Plan 1969-1970." Tampa (Florida): Hillsborough Junior College, 1969. (Mimeographed). [ERIC ED 032 882, 1970].

Hillway, Tyrus. The American Two-Year College. New York: Harper and Brothers, 1958.

Hodgkinson, Harold L. "The Next Decade of Higher Education," Journal of Higher Education, 41:16-28, January, 1970. (a)

──────. "Campus Governance: The Next Decade," The Research Reporter, Vol. 5, No. 1. Berkeley: The Center for Research and Development in Higher Education, 1970. (b)

Hollinshead, Byron S. "The Community College Program," Junior College Journal, 7:111-16, December, 1936.

──────. Who Should Go To College? New York: Columbia University Press, 1952.

Hollister, H. A. "The Frontiers of High School Development After A Century of Growth," School and Home Education, 41:59-65, December, 1921-January, 1922.

Hood, Wenford L. Higher Education for the Disadvantaged in New York State: A Summary Report of Programs of Higher Education for the Disadvantaged at Colleges and Universities in New York State. Plattsburgh: State University of New York, Plattsburgh College, January, 1969. [ERIC ED 031 993, 1970].

Hostrup, Richard W. Orientation to the Two-Year College. Homewood (Illinois): Learning Systems Company, 1970.

Hoyt, Donald P. The Relationship Between College Grades and Adult Achievement: A Review of the Literature. A.C.T. Research Report No. 7. Iowa City: American College Testing Program, 1965.

_____. "College Grades and Adult Accomplishment," Educational Record, 47:70-75, Winter, 1966.

_____. "The Criterion Problem in Higher Education," Learning and the Professors, Ohmer Milton and Edward Shoben (eds.). Athens (Ohio): Ohio University Press, 1968.

_____, and Leo A. Munday. "Academic Description and Prediction in Junior Colleges," A.C.T. Research Reports. Iowa City: American College Testing Program, February, 1966.

_____, _____. Your College Freshmen. Iowa City (Iowa): American College Testing Program, 1968.

Hoyt, Kenneth B. "The Community Colleges Must Change," Compact, 4:37-39. Denver: Education Commission of the States, August, 1970.

Hunter, Pauline. "Problems Influencing Articulation Between Two- and Four-Year Colleges," Conference Proceedings on Administering the Community College in a Changing World, S. V. Martorana (ed.). Published jointly by the University Council for Educational Administration and the School of Education. Buffalo: State University of New York at Buffalo, 1966.

Hurlburt, Allan S. State Master Plans for Community Colleges. Monograph 8. Washington: American Association of Junior Colleges, October, 1969. [ERIC ED 032 887, 1970].

Hutchins, Robert M. "The Confusion in Higher Education," Harper's Magazine, 173:449-58, October, 1936. (a)

_____. "What Is General Education?" Harper's Magazine, 173:602-609, November, 1936. (b)

Bibliography

Huther, John W. "The Open Door: How Open Is It?" Junior College Journal, 41:24-27, April, 1971.

Illinois Board of Higher Education. Two-Year Colleges. A Report to the Board of Higher Education. Springfield: Illinois Board of Higher Education, December, 1963.

Institute for Local Self Government (Berkeley). Some Who Dared: Community College Involvement With Public Service Aspects of the Urban Problem In California. Berkeley: Institute for Local Self Government, 1969. [ERIC ED 032 873, 1970].

Institutional Research in the Junior College--A Report of a Conference. Junior College Leadership Program, Occasional Report No. 3. Los Angeles: University of California, Los Angeles, 1962.

An Introduction to American Junior Colleges. Reprinted from American Junior Colleges, Seventh Edition. Washington: American Association of Junior Colleges, 1967.

Jacobsen, Joseph M. "The Junior College Idea in South America," Junior College Journal, 38:9-13, November, 1968.

Jacobson, Robert L. "College Board's Tests Receive Passing Grade," The Chronicle of Higher Education, November 2, 1970, pp. 1, 4.

Jencks, Christopher. "Social Stratification and Higher Education," Harvard Educational Review, 38:277-316, 1968.

_____, and David Riesman. The Academic Revolution. New York: Doubleday and Company, Inc., 1968. (a)

_____. "The Triumph of Academic Man," Campus 1980, Alvin C. Eurich (ed.). New York: Dell Publishing Co., Inc., 1968. (b)

Jennings, Frank G. "The Two-Year Stretch," Change Magazine, 2:15-25, March-April, 1970.

Johnson, B. Lamar. "Junior College Trends," The School Review, 52:606-10, December, 1944.

_____. Islands of Innovation. Junior College Leadership

Program, Occasional Report No. 6. Los Angeles: University of California, Los Angeles, 1964. (a)

_____. Starting a Community Junior College. Washington: American Association of Junior Colleges, 1964. (b)

_____. "The Two-Year College," The Journal of Higher Education, 37:409-410, October, 1966.

_____. Islands of Innovation Expanding. Beverly Hills: Glencoe Press, 1969.

_____. (ed.). New Directions for Instruction in the Junior College. Junior College Leadership Program, Occasional Report No. 7. Los Angeles: University of California, Los Angeles, 1965.

_____. Systems Approches to Curriculum and Instruction in the Open-Door College. Junior College Leadership Program, Occasional Report No. 9. Los Angeles: University of California, Los Angeles, 1967.

_____. The Experimental Junior College. Junior College Leadership Program, Occasional Report No. 12. Los Angeles: University of California, Los Angeles, 1968.

_____. The Improvement of Junior College Instruction. Junior College Leadership Program, Occasional Report No. 15. Los Angeles: University of California, Los Angeles, March, 1970.

Johnson, Paul M. "Statements of Position." Baltimore: Maryland Association of Junior Colleges, 1968.

Johnston, Charles Hughes. "High School Terminology," Educational Review, 49:228-247, March, 1915.

Jones, Twyman. "Some Comments on the Role of Junior College Counselors," 1969. [Reported in ERIC ED 034 541, 1970].

"The Junior College," Educational Review, 49:215-216, February, 1915.

"Junior College Dilemma," Harper's Magazine, 234:4+, February, 1967.

Bibliography

Junior College Education in Oklahoma. Oklahoma City: Oklahoma State Regents for Higher Education, February, 1970.

"Junior College Institutional Growth Rate Spirals in 1967," Junior College Journal, 38:60, October, 1967.

"The Junior College Menace as Seen from Within," Atlantic Monthly, 139:809-11, June, 1927.

Junior College Research Review. "Needed Research in the Junior College," Clearinghouse for Junior College Information, Vol. 2, No. 6, American Association of Junior Colleges. Los Angeles: University of California, April, 1968.

"Junior Colleges," Encyclopedia of Educational Research, Chester W. Harris (ed.). New York: The Macmillan Co., 1960, pp. 736-743.

Kane, Joseph P. "Open Admissions." Seminar Report to Higher Education 764, Syracuse University, Spring, 1970.

Kaufman, Jacob J., et al. "Role of Secondary Schools in Preparing Youth for Jobs," Bulletin of The National Association of Secondary School Principals, 52:112-113, February, 1968.

Keats, John. The Sheepskin Psychosis. New York: Dell Publishing Co., Inc., 1965.

Kellogg, Frazier. Computer Based Job Matching Systems-- An Exploration of the State of the Art and the Proposed Nationwide Matching System. Cambridge: Massachusetts Institute of Technology, 1967.

Kelly, M. Francis, and John Connolly. Orientation for Faculty in Junior Colleges. ERIC Clearinghouse for Junior Colleges. Washington: American Association of Junior Colleges, June, 1970.

Kelly, Win, and Leslie Wilbur. "Junior College Development in the United States," School and Society, 97:485-498, 520, December, 1969.

_____, _____. Teaching In The Community Junior College.

New York: Appleton-Century-Crofts, 1970.

Kelsey, Roger B. "Independent State and Local Boards for Higher Education in Maryland." A Discussion with Senator Royal Hart [Md.], A.A.U.P. Chapter, Catonsville Community College [Md.], May 9, 1968.

Kemp, Barbara H. The Youth We Haven't Served: A Challenge to Vocational Education. Washington: U.S. Department of Health, Education, and Welfare, 1966.

Kemp, W. W. "The Junior College in California," California Quarterly of Secondary Education, 5:188-94, January, 1930.

Kilpatrick, Gordon. "A Consideration of Teaching Load In American Junior Colleges." Los Angeles: University of California, Los Angeles, June, 1967. [ERIC ED 036 297, 1970].

King, Spencer B., Jr. "The Junior College in Defense of Liberal Education," School and Society, 60:17-19, July 8, 1944.

Kintzer, Frederick C. "Articulation is an Opportunity," Junior College Journal, 37:16-19, April, 1967.

_____. "What University and College Admissions Officers Should Know About Two Year Colleges," College and University, 42:459-478, Summer, 1967.

_____. "The California Plan of Articulation," College and University, 43:155-161, Winter, 1968.

Klein, Arthur J. "Survey of Negro Colleges and Universities." Department of the Interior, Bureau of Education, Bulletin No. 7. Washington: Government Printing Office, 1928.

Knoell, Dorothy M. "How Can Two- and Four-Year Colleges Provide Articulation in the Face of Rapid Change?" Current Issues in Higher Education. Washington: National Education Association, 1964.

_____. Toward Educational Opportunity for All. Albany: The State University of New York, 1966.

Bibliography

    _____. "Articulation and Liaison Between Colleges." Paper presented to the National Conference of the American Association for Higher Education, Chicago, March 4, 1968.

    _____. "Potential Student Clienteles," Junior College Research Review, 4:2-5, October, 1969.

    _____. "Are Our Colleges Really Accessible to the Poor?" Community College Programs for People Who Need College, pp. 87-89. Washington: American Association of Junior Colleges, 1970. (a)

    _____. Black Student Potential. Washington: American Association of Junior Colleges, 1970. (b)

    _____. People Who Need College: A Report on Students We Have Yet To Serve. Washington: American Association of Junior Colleges, 1970. (c)

    _____. "Alternative Enrollment-Attendance Patterns," Junior College Research Review, 5:12-13, May, 1971.

    _____, and Leland L. Medsker. Factors Affecting Performance of Transfer Students from Two-to-Four-Year Colleges: With Implications for Coordination and Articulation. Berkeley: Center for the Study of Higher Education, 1964.

    _____, _____. Articulation Between Two-Year and Four-Year Colleges. Berkeley: Center for the Study of Higher Education, 1964.

Knoll, Erwin. "The Maturing of the Junior College," National Education Association Journal, 50:27-29, February, 1961.

Knowles, Malcolm S. Higher Adult Education in the United States. Washington: Committee on Higher Adult Education, American Council on Education, 1969.

Koch, Moses S. Digest, Master Plan for Higher Education in Maryland: Phase I. Baltimore: Essex Community College, February 20, 1969. (Mimeographed.)

Kohler, Mary C. "Vocational Education: A Way of Life." Report, California State Conference on Vocational

Education. Sacramento: California State Department of Education, 1965.

Koos, Leonard V. "Where to Establish Junior Colleges," The School Review, 29:413-33, June, 1921. (a)

_____. "Current Conceptions of the Special Purposes of the Junior College," The School Review, 29:520-29, September, 1921. (b)

_____. The Junior College. Research publications of the University of Minnesota, Education Series, 2 Vols. Minneapolis, Minnesota: University of Minnesota, 1924.

_____. The Junior College Movement. Boston: Ginn and Company, 1925.

_____. "Conditions Favoring Integration of Junior College with High Schools," School Life, 12:161-164, May, 1927.

_____. "A Danger and an Opportunity," The School Review, 51:2-3, January, 1943.

_____. "Junior College Administrators and Their Scope of Function," The School Review, 52:143-50, March, 1944. (a)

_____. "Opinions of Administrators on Organizing the Junior College," The School Review, 52:215-27, April, 1944. (b)

_____. "How to Democratize the Junior-College Level," The School Review, 52:271-84, May, 1944. (c)

_____. "Local Versus Regional Junior Colleges," The School Review, 52:525-31, November, 1944. (d)

_____. "The Junior College in Illinois." Report to the Commission to Study Higher Education Facilities, No. 8. Springfield (Illinois), November, 1944. (e)

_____. Integrating High School and College: The Six-Four-Four Plan at Work. New York: Harper and Bros., 1946.

_____. "Rise of the People's College," The School Review, 55:138-49, March, 1947. (a)

Bibliography

_____. "A Junior College Plan for Maryland," The School Review, 55:336, June, 1947. (b)

_____. "Essentials in State-wide Community College Planning," The School Review, 57:341-52, September, 1949.

_____. "Preparation for Community-College Teaching," Journal of Higher Education, 21:309-17, June, 1950.

_____. The Community College Student. Gainesville (Florida): University of Florida Press, 1970.

Kreps, Juanita M. Lifetime Allocation of Work and Leisure. Research Report No. 22. Durham (North Carolina): Duke University, 1967.

Krug, Edward A. The Shaping of the American High School. New York: Harper and Row, 1964.

Kruger, W. Stanley. "They Don't Have to Drop Out," American Education, 5:6-8, October, 1969.

Lacy, Bill N. (ed.). Ten Designs, Community Colleges. Houston: Rice University, Department of Agriculture, 1962.

Lahti, Robert E. "A Faculty Role in Policy Formulation," Junior College Journal, 37:9-12, September, 1966.

Laine, Oliver. "Interim Facilities: Blessing or Boomerang?" Junior College Journal, 39:25-26, November, 1968.

Landrith, Harold F. "Prescription for Junior College Dropouts," School and Society, 99:49-51, January, 1971.

Lauter, Paul, and Florence Howe. "How the School System is Rigged for Failure," The New York Review of Books, 14:14-21, June 18, 1970.

Laws, Statutes, and Constitutional Provisions Affecting Community Colleges in Michigan. Lansing: Michigan Department of Education, 1968.

"Letters," Junior College Journal, 36:48, February, 1966.

Lewis, Irvin G. "Junior-Senior College Articulation Plans:

Florida, Michigan, California," College and University, 43:576-586, Summer, 1968.

Liaison Committee of the State Board of Education and the Regents of the University of California. A Master Plan for Higher Education in California, 1960-1975. Sacramento: California State Department of Education, 1960.

Liberal Education Reconsidered: Reflections on Continuing Education for Contemporary Man. Notes and Essays on Education for Adults, No. 60. Publications Program in Continuing Education. Syracuse: Syracuse University Press, 1969.

Lillard, J. B "The 6-3-3-2 vs. the 6-4-4 Plan of Organization for the Public Junior College," School and Society, 32:262-264, August, 1930.

The Lincoln Library of Essential Information. "The Junior College." Buffalo: The Frontier Press Company, 1963.

Lindman, Erick L. "Paying for Junior Colleges," Junior College Research Review, April, 1970.

Linn, John Phillip, and M. Chester Nolte. Background Material on Collective Bargaining for Teachers. Report No. 8. Denver: Education Commission of the States, June, 1968; "Guide to Collective Bargaining for Teachers," Compact, 2:44-56, August, 1968.

Lins, L. J Post-Secondary Educational Preferences of High School Seniors. Project administered by Wisconsin Higher Educational Aids Board, No. CCHE-63. Madison: Wisconsin Coordinating Council for Higher Education, June, 1969. [ERIC ED 033 660, 1970].

Littlefield, Henry W. "Critical Issues Facing America's Junior Colleges," School and Society, 89:72, February, 1961.

Liveright, A. A. "Learning Never Ends: A Plan for Continuing Education," Campus 1980, Alvin C. Eurich (ed.), pp. 149-75. New York: Dell Publishing Co., Inc., 1968.

Locks, C. S. "Academic Performance of Students Transferring to Los Angeles Valley College from Two and

Bibliography 321

 Four-Year Institutions." Unpublished report, Los Angeles Valley College, 1965.

Logsdon, James D. "A Case for the Junior College," Bulletin of The National Association of Secondary School Principals, 52:62-65, December, 1968.

Lombardi, John. "California's New State Board," Junior College Journal, 38:27-31, March, 1968.

———. Student Activism in Junior Colleges: An Administrator's Views. Washington: American Association of Junior Colleges, 1969.

Long, James. "Congress and University Adult Education: An Approach to Interpreting Their Relationship," Adult Education Journal, 20:206-25, Summer, 1970.

A Longitudinal Study of the Barriers Affecting the Pursuit of Higher Education By New York State High School Seniors, Phase I. Albany: The State Education Department, Office of Planning in Higher Education, August, 1969.

Lunden, Walter A. The Dynamics of Higher Education. Pittsburgh: The Pittsburgh Printing Company, 1939.

McConaughy, James L. "The Future of the College in the Middle West," School and Society, 9:607-613, May, 1919.

McConnell, T. R. "Foreword," Junior College Student Personnel Programs: Appraisal and Development: A Report to the Carnegie Corporation, November, 1965.

———. "Campus Governance: Faculty Participation," The Research Reporter, Vol. 5, No. 1. Berkeley: The Center for Research and Development in Higher Education, 1970.

McGrath, Earl J. (ed.). Universal Higher Education. New York: McGraw-Hill Book Company, 1966.

McGuire, Ruth E. "Syracuse University Looks at Its Junior College Transfers," Junior College Journal, 20:95-98, October, 1949.

McLane, C. L. "The Junior College, or Upward Extension of the High School," The School Review, 21:161-170,

March, 1913.

MacLean, Malcolm S. "Social Forces and the Junior College," National Education Association Journal, 45:222-223, April, 1956.

McNutt, Walter S. "A New Experiment in the Democratization of Higher Education," Education, 60:48-54, September, 1939.

Magruder, William T. "The Junior College as Relief," Educational Review, 61:286-297, April, 1921.

Mallan, John P. "Commission Commitments," Junior College Journal, 36:52, May, 1966.

Manello, George. "Grades Must Go," Educational Record, 50:305-18, Summer, 1969.

Manpower for the Medical Laboratory, The National Conference on Education and Career Development of The National Committee for Careers in Medical Technology. University of Maryland, Summary Report, October 11-13, 1967. Washington: Government Printing Office, 1968. [ERIC ED 021 517, 1969].

Marsee, Stuart E. "Who Needs the Community College?" Junior College Journal, 39:8-10, September, 1968.

Marshall, Max S. "The Curse of Courses," School and Society, 99:32-35, January, 1971.

Martin, Warren Bryan. "Academic Reform: Priorities and Perspectives," The Research Reporter, Vol. 5, No. 2. Berkeley: The Center for Research and Development in Higher Education, 1970.

_____. "The Relevance of Present Educational Systems," The Research Reporter, Vol. 6, No. 2, pp. 4-5. Paper presented to White House Conference on Youth. Berkeley: The Center for Research and Development in Higher Education, 1971.

_____, and Judith Wilkinson. "Non-Differences That Make A Difference," The Research Reporter, Vol. 4, No. 3. Berkeley: The Center for Research and Development in Higher Education, 1969. [ERIC ED 036

282, 1970].

Martorana, S. V. "Progress and Plans in the Empire State," Junior College Journal, 35:10-13, May, 1965.

_____. "Stresses Among Junior College Students." Paper read at the National Conference of the American Association for Higher Education, Chicago, March 4, 1968.

_____. "Developments in State-Level Governance," Junior College Journal, 39:25-29, January, 1969.

_____, and Pauline F. Hunter (eds.). Conference Proceedings on Administering The Community College In A Changing World, A Continuation of "The University of Buffalo Studies." Published jointly by the University Council for Educational Administration and the School of Education, State University of New York at Buffalo, 1966.

_____, and Robert F. McHugh. "State Legislation: 1962-64," Junior College Journal, 36:27-31, 34, 36, March, 1966.

Maryland Standards for Two-Year Colleges. Maryland School Bulletin, Vol. 54, No. 2. Baltimore: Maryland State Department of Education, May, 1969.

Maryland State Teachers Association. Legislative Program, 1969. Baltimore: Maryland State Teachers Association: November, 1968.

_____. "A Master Plan," Digest, The Higher Education Journal of Maryland, Higher Education Council, Vol. 1, No. 1. Baltimore: Maryland State Teachers Association, February, 1969.

Masiko, Peter, Jr. "A Rebuttal to W. B. Devall's 'Community Colleges: A Dissenting View,'" Educational Record, 49:173-176, Spring, 1968.

A Master Plan for Higher Education in California, 1960-1975. Sacramento: California State Department of Education, 1960.

Master Plan for State Policy in Higher Education. Columbus

(Ohio): Ohio Board of Regents, June, 1966.

Mathies, Lorraine. "Junior College Educators Indicate Information They Need," Junior College Journal, 38:24-26, November, 1967.

Mauss, Armand L. Toward An Empirical Typology of Junior College Student Subcultures. Long Beach (California): Pacific Sociological Association, March 31, 1967.

Mayhew, Lewis B. "What's Ahead for Higher Education?" National Education Association Journal, 56:16-18, December, 1967.

_____. "The Future Undergraduate Curriculum," Campus 1980, Alvin C. Eurich (ed.), pp. 200-19. New York: Dell Publishing Co., Inc., 1968.

Meadows, Mark E., and Ronald R. Ingle. "Reverse Articulation: A Unique Function of the Junior College," College and University, 44:47-54, Fall, 1968.

Medsker, Leland L. "The Junior-College Picture," National Education Association Journal, 47:628-630, December, 1958.

_____. The Junior College: Progress and Prospect. New York: McGraw-Hill Book Company, 1960.

_____. The Junior College--A Powerful Motivating Force for Educational Advantage. Washington: American Association of Junior Colleges, 1961.

_____, and Dale Tillery. Breaking the Access Barriers: A Profile of Two-Year Colleges. A Profile Sponsored by the Carnegie Commission on Higher Education. New York: McGraw-Hill Book Company, 1971.

_____, and James W. Trent. Factors Affecting College Attendance of High School Graduates from Varying Socioeconomic and Ability Levels, and The Influence of Different Types of Public Higher Institutions on College Attendance from Varying Socioeconomic and Ability Levels. Project 438. Berkeley: Center for Research and Development in Higher Education, 1965.

Menefee, Selden. "When Junior Colleges Need Help,"

Bibliography 325

American Education, 5:23-25, December, 1968-January, 1969.

_____, and Esperanza Cornejo (eds.). Occupational Education in the Junior College. Selected Proceedings from Two Workshops on Occupational Education (Michigan State University, February, 1969; University of Florida, February, 1969), Monograph 3. Washington: American Association of Junior Colleges, March, 1969. [ERIC ED 032 067, 1970].

Merson, Thomas B. "The Crisis in Accreditation," Junior College Journal, 35:6-8, February, 1965.

Meyer, John D. "Junior College Students: Status Inconsistency " Doctoral dissertation, Stanford University, 1968.

Michigan State Board for Public Community and Junior Colleges. A Recommended Community College Districting Plan [Provisional]. Lansing: Michigan Department of Education, September, 1968.

Michigan State Board of Education. The Metropolitan Community College in Michigan. Lansing: Michigan Department of Education, October, 1968.

Miller, Sue. "Solvency By Innovation Foreseen For Hopkins," The Evening Sun, Baltimore, April 16, 1971, p. D1. (a)

_____. "Three Year Graduation Program Proposed In High Schools," The Evening Sun, Baltimore, June 11, 1971, p. C24. (b)

Mills, Kay. "Higher Education Council's Plan May Affect Thousands," The Evening Sun, Baltimore, January 10, 1969, Section C, p. 4.

Milton, Ohmer. "Teaching or Learning?" Research Report Number 6. Washington: American Association for Higher Education, May 1, 1971.

Montague v. Board of Education of Ashland Independent School District, 402 S.W. (2d), 94 (Ky.).

Moore, William, Jr. Against the Odds. San Francisco:

Jossey-Bass Inc., 1970.

Morgenstein, Melvin, and Harriet Strongin. <u>Study of Articulation Program Between Nassau Community College and Topic House.</u> Study by Nassau Community College of the State University of New York. Albany: Bureau of Occupational Education Research, July, 1969. [ERIC ED 037 646, 1970].

Morin, Lloyd H. "A Feasible Scheme for the Evaluation of Instructors." University of California, Los Angeles, 1968. [Reported in ERIC ED 024 361, 1969].

<u>The Morning Call</u>, Allentown, (Pa.), "Letters to the Editor," April 17, 1971, p. 6.

Morrisett, Lloyd N. "Educational Assessment and the Junior College," <u>Junior College Journal</u>, 37:12-14, March, 1967.

Morrison, D. G. "Articulation of the High School and the Public Community Junior College in the United States," <u>Bulletin of The National Association of Secondary School Principals</u>, 43:102-107, September, 1959.

_____. "So You Plan to Change Your Junior College to A Four-Year Institution?" <u>Phi Delta Kappan</u>, 47:442-443, April, 1966.

_____, and S. V. Martorana. <u>Criteria for the Establishment of 2-Year Colleges.</u> Office of Education, Bulletin 1961, No. 2. Washington: Government Printing Office, 1961.

_____, _____. "Are Public 2-Year Colleges Secondary or Higher Education?" <u>State Formulas for the Support of Public 2-Year Colleges.</u> Office of Education, Bulletin 1962, No. 14. Washington: Government Printing Office, 1962.

_____, et al. <u>The Two-Year Community College.</u> An Annotated List of Unpublished Studies and Surveys, 1957-61. Office of Education Bulletin 1963, No. 28. Washington: Government Printing Office, 1963.

Mosier, Richard D. "Educational Theories of the American Transcendentalists," <u>History of Education Journal</u>,

3:33-42, Winter, 1952.

Muck, Stephen J., and Jan Undem. "An Analysis of the Records of Students Entering El Camino College on Probation from Other Institutions of Higher Learning." Torrance (California): El Camino College, 1965.

Myran, Gunder A. Community Services: An Emerging Challenge for the Community College. Community Services Working Paper No. 1. Washington: American Association of Junior Colleges, 1969. [ERIC ED 032 051, 1970].

The Nation, 185:82, August 31, 1957.

National Conference on the Teaching of English in the Junior College, Arizona State University. Research and the Development of English Programs in the Junior College. Proceedings. Tempe: Arizona State University, 1965.

National Education Association. "Aligning Priorities in Junior and Community Colleges," Current Issues in Higher Education. Washington: National Education Association, 1965.

National Society for the Promotion of Industrial Education. "Principles and Policies That Should Underlie State Legislation for a State System of Vocational Education." Bulletin No. 16. Proceedings of Sixth Annual Meeting, Philadelphia, December, 1912.

Nattress, John A. "The Junior College Transition to Engineering in Florida," Engineering Education, 59:231-233, November, 1968.

Nelson, James H. "Do Junior College Transfers Make the Grade?" The National Education Journal, 54:55-57, October, 1965.

_____. "Guidelines for Articulation," Junior College Journal, 36:24-26, March, 1966.

The Nelson Report: The Future of the Community Colleges in New York State. Report for the Chancellor of the State University of New York. Washington: Peat, Marwick, and Mitchell Co., 1969.

New Challenges to the Junior Colleges: Their Role in Expanding Opportunity for Negroes. Atlanta: Southern Regional Education Board, 1970.

Newcomb, Theodore, and Kenneth Feldman. The Impact of College on Students. San Francisco: Jossey-Bass Inc., 1969, (2 vol.).

New Jersey Commission for the Higher Education Facilities Act of 1963. Meeting New Jersey College and University Facilities Needs Through 1980, A Report. Cleveland (Ohio): Robert Heller Associates, Inc., August 30, 1968.

New Jersey Department of Higher Education. Goals for Higher Education in New Jersey. New Jersey Master Plan for Higher Education, Number 1. Trenton: New Jersey Board of Higher Education, January, 1970.

Newman, Frank, et al. Report on Higher Education [The Newman Report]. Washington: Department of Health, Education, and Welfare, 1971.

The New Republic, 152:36, February 20, 1965.

"News Backgrounds," Junior College Journal, 36:50, February, 1966.

Newsletter. Baltimore: Maryland Association of Junior Colleges, December, 1968.

New York State and Private Higher Education. Report of the Select Committee on the Future of Private and Independent Higher Education in New York State/1968. Albany: State Education Department, January, 1968.

New York State Department of Education. New York State College Enrollment Simulation Model. Troy: Rensselaer Research Corporation, 1969.

Nixon, Richard M. [President's] Higher Education Message to Congress, March 19, 1970. Full text appears in Higher Education and National Affairs (American Council on Education), March 20, 1970, pp. 4-9.

O'Banion, Terry. Junior College Student Personnel Programs In Colorado. Denver: Colorado State Board for

Bibliography

Community Colleges and Occupational Education, June, 1969. (a) [ERIC ED 032 057, 1970].

_____. "Transfer Students," Junior College Research Review, 4:10-12, October, 1969. (b)

_____, et al. "Student Personnel Work: An Emerging Model," Junior College Journal, 41:7-14, November, 1970.

Occupational Program Inventory: An Inventory of Educational Programs Designed to Lead to Immediate Employment. Lansing (Michigan): Michigan Department of Education, 1969.

O'Connell, Thomas E. "After High School: The Role of the Community College," The New Republic, 152:17-20, January 30, 1965.

_____. Community Colleges: A President's View. Urbana: University of Illinois Press, 1968.

Official Bulletin, No. 1. Chicago: University of Chicago, 1891.

Ohio Board of Regents. Master Plan for State Policy in Higher Education. Columbus: Ohio Board of Regents, 1966.

Ohio's Newly Developed System of Two-Year Colleges. Columbus (Ohio): Ohio Board of Regents, 1969-1970.

Ohles, John F. "Extended Schooling Versus Higher Education," School and Society, 92:156-157, April, 1964.

Okerlund, G. M. "Junior College Graduates in the Universities," School and Society, 29:676-677, May, 1929.

Ollerenshaw, Kathleen. "Wasteful Overlapping Between Schools and Colleges," The Times Educational Supplement [London], No. 2763, May 3, 1968.

"Opinions of College Freshmen," School and Society, 98:302, Summer, 1970.

Otto, John. "Reflections on Recruitment for Educational Opportunity Programs Within the California State College

System." Paper prepared for distribution at the American Personnel and Guidance Association Convention, Las Vegas, Nevada, March 30-April 3, 1969. [ERIC ED 032 556, 1970].

Our Schools in the Post-War World. Leaflet No. 71. Washington: Government Printing Office, 1944.

Pace, C. Robert. Explorations in the Measurement of Junior College Environments. Los Angeles: University of California, January, 1967. [ERIC ED 014 972, 1968].

_____. "The Measurement of College Environments." Reprint from Organizational Climate: Explorations of a Concept. Ranato Tagiuri and George H. Litwin (eds.). Boston: Graduate School of Business Administration, Harvard University, 1968. [ERIC ED 033 668, 1970].

_____. College and University Environment Scales (Technical Manual) Second edition. Princeton: Educational Testing Service, 1969.

_____, and George G. Stern. "An Approach to the Measurement of Psychological Characteristics of College Environments." Journal of Educational Psychology, 49:269-77, October, 1958.

Packer, Herbert L. "Piling Higher and Deeper--The Shame of the Ph.D." Change Magazine, 2:49-53, November-December, 1970.

Palinchak, Robert S. "An Analysis of Selected Factors That Identify the Two-Year College As Being More Closely Related to Either Secondary Education or Higher Education." Master's Thesis, Loyola College (Baltimore), May, 1969. [ERIC ED 034 518, 1970].

_____, et al. "Survey of Requirements for a Doctoral Program in the Field of Higher Education." Higher Education Seminar Project. Syracuse University: Department of Higher Education, May, 1970. (Mimeographed). [ERIC ED 041 542, 1970].

Palola, Ernest. "Academic Reform: A Challenge for Statewide Planners," The Research Reporter, Vol. 5, No. 2. Berkeley: The Center for Research and Development in Higher Education, 1970.

Bibliography

Panos, R. J. "Some Characteristics of Junior College Students," A. C. E. Research Reports. Washington: American Council on Education, 1966.

Park, Young. "Teacher Preparation Programs and the Junior College," Junior College Research Review, January, 1971.

Parker, Franklin. "Continuity Between High School and College," Educational Leadership, 18:346-350, March, 1961.

Parker, Garland G. "50 Years of Collegiate Enrollments: 1912-20 to 1969-70," School and Society, 98:282-295, Summer, 1970.

Paschal, Elizabeth. "Organizing for Better Instruction," Campus 1980, Alvin C. Eurich (ed.), pp. 220-35. New York: Dell Publishing Co., Inc., 1968.

Pearson, Richard. "National Admissions Testing Programs --Their Value to Colleges--Their Impact on Secondary Schools," College and University, 39:488-514, Summer, 1964.

Peik, W. E. "What Better Accreditation Means," National Education Association Journal, 39:186-187, March, 1950.

Perkins, James A. "Higher Education in the 1970's," Educational Record, 51:246-52, Summer, 1970.

Perry, Charles F. "The Trade School as a Part of the Public School System." National Society for the Promotion of Industrial Education, Bulletin No. 6, pp. 6-19. Proceedings of First Annual Meeting, Chicago, May, 1908.

Pesci, Frank B., and Royal Hart. "The Question of Governance in Maryland," Junior College Journal, 38:7-9, February, 1968.

Peterson, B. H. "The Role of the Junior College in California," California Education, 1:3-8, October, 1963.

Phearman, Leo T. "Comparison of High School Graduates Who Go To College With Those Who Do Not," Journal of Educational Psychology, 40:405-14, November, 1949.

Pierce, E. C., and others. "Twenty-seventh Semi-Annual Meeting of The Michigan Schoolmasters' Club," The School Review, 5:95-128, February, 1897.

Pifer, Alan. "The Jeopardy of Private Institutions," Annual Report for 1970. New York: The Carnegie Corporation, 1970.

──────. "Is It Time For An External Degree?" College Board Review, 78:5-10, Winter, 1970-71.

Popham, W. James. "A Bank of Instructional Objectives for the Junior College," The Improvement of Junior College Instruction, B. Lamar Johnson (ed.). Junior College Leadership Program, Occasional Report No. 15, pp. 41-46. Los Angeles: University of California, Los Angeles, 1970.

"Population Trends and the Growth of the Junior College," The Elementary School Journal, 40:574-76, April, 1940.

Pratt, Arden L. Your Career and Two-Year Colleges. Washington: American Association of Junior Colleges, 1970.

President's Commission on National Goals. Goals for Americans. New York: Prentice-Hall, Inc., 1960.

Price, Hugh G. "Public Schools Through Grade 14," National Education Association Journal, 48:10, December, 1959.

Priest, Bill J. "Faculty-Administration Relationships," Junior College Journal, 34:4-8, March, 1964.

──────. "On the Threshold of Greatness," Junior College Journal, 37:6-8, September, 1966.

──────, and H. Deon Holt. "Community College Outlook for the 70's," Compact, 4:34-35. Denver: Education Commission of the States, August, 1970.

Proctor, William M. "The Junior College in California," The School Review, 31:363-75, May, 1923.

Ravekes, John E. (ed.). Role and Functions of Student Personnel Programs in Maryland Community Colleges.

Maryland Association of Junior Colleges, April, 1969. [ERIC ED 037 194, 1970].

Read, Betty. "The Community-Junior College." Albuquerque (New Mexico): Albuquerque Public Schools, February, 1969. [ERIC ED 035 394, 1970].

Regents of the University of the State of New York. Higher Education Planning. A Bulletin Concerning the 1968 Statewide Plan for the Expansion and Development of Higher Education. Albany: The State Education Department, June, 1968.

The Regents Statewide Plan for the Expansion and Development of Higher Education. Albany: The State Education Department, 1965.

Regulations Governing County Community Colleges. Trenton: New Jersey Department of Higher Education, September 19, 1969. (Mimeographed).

Reimer, Milton K. "Areas of Concern for Comprehensive Community Colleges," School and Society, 99:47-49, January, 1971.

Rever, Philip R. (ed.). Open Admissions and Equal Access. Monograph 4. Iowa City: American College Testing Program, 1971.

Reynolds, James W. "The Adequacy of the General Education Program of Local Public Junior Colleges," Journal of Educational Research, 39:272-280, December, 1945. (a)

_____. "The Adequacy of the General Education Program of Local Public Junior Colleges." Doctoral dissertation, University of Chicago, School of Education, 1945. (b)

_____. "Inadequacies of General Education Programs," Junior College Journal, 16:363-86, April, 1946.

_____. "We're Mighty Proud of Junior," National Education Association Journal, 42:212-213, April, 1953.

_____. "The Significance of the Past Twenty-Five Years of Junior College Development," Junior College Journal, 25:425-26, April, 1955.

_____. *The Comprehensive Junior College Curriculum.* Berkeley: McCutchan Publishing Corporation, 1970.

Richardson, Richard C., Jr., and Clyde E. Blocker. *Student's Guide to the Two-Year College.* Englewood Cliffs: Prentice-Hall, Inc., 1968.

Riendeau, Albert J. "Who Really Goes to Junior College?" *California Journal of Educational Research,* 18:208-18, November, 1967.

"The Right to Read," *American Education,* December, 1969, pp. 2-4.

Rislov, Sigurd. "The Community College," *The Atlantic,* 199:64-67, June, 1957.

Rogers, Carl R. "A Revolutionary Program for Graduate Education," *The Library-College Journal,* 3:16-26, Spring, 1970.

The Role and Scope of Oklahoma Higher Education. Oklahoma City: Oklahoma State Regents for Higher Education, February, 1970.

Ross, Woodburn O. "The Dome of Many-Colored Glass," *The Library-College Journal,* 3:45-51, Spring, 1970.

Roth, Audrey. *Report of a Study Project on Paraprofessionals in Junior College English Departments,* June 12, 1969. [Reported in ERIC ED 031 224, 1969].

Roueche, John E. "Gaps and Overlaps in Institutional Research," *Junior College Journal,* 38:20-23, November, 1967.

_____. "The Junior College President," *Junior College Research Review,* June, 1968.

_____. *Salvage, Redirection or Custody? Remedial Education in the Community Junior College.* Washington: American Association of Junior Colleges, 1968.

_____, and John R. Boggs. *Junior College Institutional Research: The State of the Art.* Washington: American Association of Junior Colleges, 1968.

_____, et al. Accountability and the Community College: Directions for the '70's. Washington: American Association of Junior Colleges, 1971.

Roush, Robert E. "The Carnegie Unit--How Did We Get It?" The Educational Forum, 35:71-74, November, 1970.

Rudolph, Frederick. The American College and University. New York: Vintage Books, 1962.

Sack, Saul. "The First Junior College," Junior College Journal, 30:13-15, September, 1959.

Sanford, Nevitt (ed.). The American College. New York: John Wiley & Sons, Inc., 1962.

Scannel, William J. "What Do Teachers Think About English in the Two-Year College?" Junior College Journal, 37:24-29, September, 1966.

Schinz, A. "Difference Between the Work of the High School, College, and Graduate School," Educational Review, 46:237-51, October, 1913.

Schreiber, Daniel (ed.). Profile of the School Drop-Out. New York: Random House, 1967.

Schultz, Raymond E. "Scholarships for Junior College Transfer Students," School and Society, 89:86-87, February, 1961.

_____. "A Follow-up on Honor Students," Junior College Journal, 38:9-18, December, 1967-January, 1968.

Scott, W. Wayne. "The Trichotomy of Research in the Two-Year College: Institutional, Faculty, and Student-Community," January, 1970. [ERIC ED 036 296, 1970].

Scully, Malcolm. "Faculty Members, Liberal on Politics, Found Conservative on Academic Issues," The Chronicle of Higher Education, April 6, 1970.

Seashore, H. "Academic Abilities of Junior College Students," Junior College Journal, 29:74-80, October, 1958.

Second Report to the President. President's Committee on Education Beyond the High School. Washington:

Government Printing Office, July, 1957.

Sedral, Roy, and Jim Hill. The Computer and the Junior College. Washington: American Association of Junior Colleges, 1969.

Seibel, D. W. "Follow-up Study of a National Sample of High School Seniors: Phase 2--One Year After Graduation," Statistical Analysis Report SR-65-62. Princeton: Educational Testing Service, October, 1965.

Selden, William K. "Struggles and Tensions in Accreditation of Higher Education," Current Issues in Higher Education. Washington: National Education Association, 1965.

———, and William G. Land, "The Forgotten Colleges," The North Central Association Quarterly, 35:271-273, April, 1961.

Selvidge, R. W. "What Shall We Teach?" Industrial Education Magazine, 31:43-45, August, 1929.

Semas, Philip W. "Malcolm X College's Aim: Black Community Self-Determination," The Chronicle of Higher Education, May 31, 1971, p. 5.

Sewall, J. I. "Toward Better Graduate Education," Journal of General Education, Vol. 2, No. 1, pp. 45-52, October, 1947.

Seyfert, Warren C. "Do Colleges Determine What the High Schools Teach?" Education Digest, 26:28-31, November, 1960.

Shane, Harold. "Future Shock and the Curriculum," Phi Delta Kappan, 49:67-70, October, 1967.

Shaw, Sterling L. "Knowledge Equals Credit or How to Enter College As a Sophomore," College and University, 43:534-535, Summer, 1968.

Shawl, William. "The Definition of Specific Objectives: A Program for Improving Instruction," The Improvement of Junior College Instruction, B. Lamar Johnson (ed.). Junior College Leadership Program, Occasional Report No. 15, pp. 49-54. Los Angeles: University of

California, Los Angeles, 1970.

Sheldon, M. Stephen. "Entrance and Placement Testing for the Junior College," Junior College Research Review, December, 1970.

Shores, Louis (ed.). The Library College: Contributions for American Higher Education at the Jamestown College Workshop, 1965. Philadelphia: Drexel Press, 1966.

──────. "If I Were a President of a Junior College," The Library-College Journal, 3:35-44, Spring, 1970.

──────, and Janiece Fusaro. "Innovations," The Library-College Journal, 3:55-60, Spring, 1970.

Showman, H. M. "Junior College Transfers at the University of California at Los Angeles," California Quarterly of Secondary Education, 4:319-322, June, 1929.

Shulman, Carol Herrnstadt. Open Admissions in Higher Education, Review 6. ERIC Clearinghouse on Higher Education. Washington: The George Washington University, June, 1971.

Sicuro, N. A. "University Branches: Solution for College Crush," School and Society, 94:458-459, December, 1966.

Siehr, Hugo E., et al. Problems of New Faculty Members in Community Colleges. Cooperative publication of Michigan State University (East Lansing) and the American Association of Junior Colleges. Washington: American Association of Junior Colleges, 1963.

Sievert, William A. "College Life Begins Two Years Earlier at Simon's Rock," The Chronicle of Higher Education, February 15, 1971, p. 4.

Simon, Lora S. "The Cooling Out Function of the Junior College," Personnel and Guidance Journal, 45:973-978, June, 1967.

Skaggs, Kenneth G. "Report from St. Louis," Junior College Journal, 37:40-43, Sep. 1966; Menefee & Cornejo, 1969.

Skinner, B. F. The Technology of Teaching. New York:

Appleton-Century-Crofts, 1968.

Smith, Alden W. "S.E.T.: Students Evaluate Teaching," 1969. [Reported in ERIC ED 035 392, 1970].

Smith, G. Kerry (ed.). Twenty-Five Years: 1945-1970. San Francisco: Jossey-Bass Inc., 1970.

Smith, Lawrence G. "Non-Punitive Grading in California Junior Colleges," 1969. [Reported in ERIC ED 035 049, 1970].

Smith, Lewis W. "Counseling and Guidance Problems in the Junior College," California Quarterly of Secondary Education, 5:343-48, June, 1930.

Smith, Virginia B. "College Finances: Ills and Remedies," Research Report Number 4. Washington: American Association for Higher Education, February 15, 1971.

Snyder, Patricia. Summary of State Legislation Affecting Education in the West: 1969. Boulder (Colorado): Western Interstate Commission for Higher Education, November, 1969. [ERIC ED 035 372, 1970].

Snyder, William H. "The Real Function of the Junior College," Junior College Journal, 1:76, 1930.

Sorrells, Daniel J. "Students in Revolution." Proceedings of the Maryland Student Personnel Conference, Williamsburg, October, 1968.

Southern Regional Education Board. New Challenges to the Junior Colleges: Their Role in Expanding Opportunity for Negroes. Atlanta: Southern Regional Education Board, 1970.

Spencer, Lyle M. "A Publisher Looks at Innovation," B. Lamar Johnson, Islands of Innovation Expanding: Changes in the Community College. Beverly Hills: Glencoe Press, 1969.

Stanley, James W. "The Oldest Junior College," Junior College Journal, 36:37-38, November, 1965.

State of Illinois Board of Higher Education. A Master Plan --Phase II. Springfield (Illinois): Board of Higher

Education, December, 1966.

──────. Admission and Retention of Students. Springfield (Illinois): Board of Higher Education, June, 1969.

State Plan for Higher Education in Michigan. Lansing (Michigan): Michigan State Department of Education, 1969.

Statistical Supplement to the 1969-70 Report to the Legislature on Financial Requirements of Public Four-Year Institutions and Community Colleges. Lansing (Michigan): Michigan Department of Education, June, 1969.

The Status and Direction of Oklahoma Higher Education. Guidelines for Policy Decisions. Oklahoma City: Oklahoma State Regents for Higher Education, May, 1968.

Stern, George G. "Higher Education in the Mass Society," Current Issues in Higher Education. Washington: National Education Association, 1964.

──────. "The Failure of Ideology," Dilemmas of American Policy, Notes and Essays on Education for Adults, No. 62, pp. 37-58. Syracuse: Syracuse University Press, November, 1969.

Stern, Milton R. "Continuing Education," Journal of Higher Education, 41:74-77, January, 1970.

Stewart, L. H. "Characteristics of Junior College Students In Occupationally Oriented Curricula," Journal of Counseling Psychology, 13:46-52, 1966.

Stewart, W. Blair. "Liberal Arts Colleges As Glorified High Schools," School and Society, 87:325, June, 1959.

Stokes, Carl B. Junior College Journal, April, 1969.

Stratton, Alan G. "Needed: The Doctor of Arts in College Teaching," Junior College Journal, 39:19-23, May, 1969.

Strawbridge, James R., and James L. Wattenbarger. "Articulation--Florida Style," Junior College Journal, 37:50-52, March, 1967.

The Student in Higher Education. Report of the Committee on the Student in Higher Education. New Haven: The Hazen Foundation, 1968.

Sulkin, Sidney. "The Challenge Summarized," Bulletin of The National Association of Secondary School Principals, 50:74-90, Summer, 1966.

Summerskill, John. "Dropouts from College," The American College, Nevitt Sanford (ed.), p. 627. New York: John Wiley and Sons, 1962.

Sykes, Abel B., Jr. "Junior College Boards of Trustees," Junior College Research Review, June, 1970.

Symposium: Need for Administrative Leadership in Junior Colleges. Based upon the Western Conference of Junior College Administration. Los Angeles: University of California, Los Angeles, July, 1960.

Syracuse Herald-Journal, "Futurologists Gain Stature As Problem Solvers," August 27, 1970, p. 52.

Talbott, John E. "The History of Education," Daedalus, 100:133-50, Winter, 1971.

Tanner, Laurel L., and Daniel. "The Role of Paraprofessionals in the Schools: A National Study." Paper presented at the California Educational Research Association Conference, Los Angeles, March 15, 1969. [ERIC ED 027 896, 1969].

Teaf, H. M., Jr. "What Price Grades?" The Journal of Higher Education, 35:100-103, February, 1964.

Thomas, Barbara. "Student Assessment," Junior College Research Review, 4:6-7, October, 1969.

Thomas, Charles L., and Julian C. Stanley. "Effectiveness of High School Grades for Predicting College Grades of Black Students: A Review and Discussion," Journal of Educational Measurement, 6:203-15, Winter, 1969.

Thornton, James W., Jr. The Community Junior College. New York: John Wiley & Sons, Inc., 1966.

Time, October 19, 1970.

Toews, Emil O. "The Role of the Bureau," California Education, 1:33-39, September, 1963. (a)

Bibliography

_____. "The Accreditation of Junior Colleges in California," California Education, 1:19-20, December, 1963. (b)

_____. "California Leads with Many 'Firsts' in Junior College Education," California Education, 1:19-20, January, 1964. (a)

_____. "Nursing Education--A Community Service," California Education, 1:19-20, 30, March, 1964. (b)

_____. "Janus Looks at the Junior College," California Education, 1:7-8, 10, June, 1964. (c)

_____. "The Present Status of Junior College Education in California," California Education, 2:13-15, May, 1965.

Toward A Long-Range Plan for Federal Financial Support for Higher Education. A Report to President Johnson. Washington: U.S. Department of Health, Education, and Welfare, January, 1969. [ERIC ED 038 102, 1970].

Toynbee, Arnold. "Higher Education In A Time of Accelerating Change," Preface to Campus 1980, Alvin C. Eurich (ed.), pp. xix-xxiv. New York: Dell Publishing Co., Inc., 1968.

Trent, James W. "Circle of Evaluation," Junior College Research Review, 4:13-15, October, 1969.

_____, and Leland L. Medsker. Beyond High School: A Psycho-sociological Study of 10,000 High School Graduates. San Francisco: Jossey-Bass, Inc., 1968.

_____, and J. H. Ruyle. "Variations, Flow, and Patterns of College Attendance: The High School Graduate Study," College and University Business, 42:61-76, Fall, 1965.

Tressler, A. W., and others. "Twenty-seventh Semi-Annual Meeting of The Michigan Schoolmasters' Club," The School Review, 5:95-128, February, 1897.

Trow, Martin A. Preliminary Findings From National Surveys of American Higher Education. New York: The Carnegie Commission on Higher Education, January 15, 1971.

Troyer, Maurice E. "Some Background Information Pertinent to the Preparation of College Teachers," Syracuse University, January 5, 1948. (Mimeographed).

Turnbull, W. W. "Relevance In Testing," Science, 160: 1424-1429, June 28, 1969.

Turner, Hugh J., Jr. The Half That Leaves: A Limited Survey of Attrition in Community Colleges. Gainesville: Florida University Institute of Higher Education, March, 1970. [ERIC ED 038 127, 1970].

Tuthill, Richard L., et al. "Commencement Procedures and Degree Terminology," College and University, 38: 494-496, Summer, 1963.

Twenty-Five Technical Careers You Can Learn in Two Years or Less. Washington: U.S. Office of Education and the National Industrial Conference Board (Undated).

"Two-Year Colleges," School and Society, 98:206-07, April, 1970.

Tyler, Henry T. "Full Partners in California's Higher Education," Junior College Journal, 35:4-7, March, 1965.

Tyler, Ralph W. Basic Principles of Curriculum and Instruction. Chicago: The University of Chicago Press, 1949.

U.S. News and World Report. Vol. 70, No. 6, February 8, 1971.

University Commission on Admissions. Report and Recommendations to the Board of Higher Education of the City of New York. New York: City University of New York, October 7, 1969. [ERIC ED 035 373, 1970].

University of Chicago. Official Bulletin No. 1. Chicago, 1891.

The University of the State of New York. Major Recommendations of the Regents for Legislative Action, 1970. Albany: The State Education Department, November, 1969.

Urban Government Manpower and the American Junior College.

Report of the American Association of Junior Colleges. Washington: American Association of Junior Colleges, 1968.

Usdan, Michael, et al. The Politics of Elementary-Secondary and Higher Education. Report No. 11. Denver: Education Commission of the States, November, 1968.

Utah System of Higher Education. Utah's Master Plan for Higher Education. Salt Lake City: Utah Coordinating Council of Higher Education, 1968.

Vaccaro, Louis C. "The Two-Year College and the Federal Government--Issues and Directions," 1968. [Reported in ERIC ED 034 525, 1970].

Vail, Curtis C. D. "Adult Education," University of Washington College of Education Record, 11:49-55, February, 1945.

Vaizey, John. The Economics of Education. New York: The Free Press of Glencoe, 1962.

Valien, Preston. "The Office of Education and the Improvement of Junior College Instruction," The Improvement of Junior College Instruction, B. Lamar Johnson (ed.), Occasional Report No. 15. Los Angeles: University of California, Junior College Leadership Program, March, 1970.

Venn, Grant. Man, Education and Work: Postsecondary Vocational and Technical Education. Washington: American Council on Education, 1964.

Virginia State Council of Higher Education. The Virginia State Plan for Higher Education. Richmond: Virginia State Council of Higher Education, December, 1967. [ERIC ED 033 661, 1970].

"Vocational Education," School and Society, 98:136-37, March, 1970.

Vocational-Technical Education: Changing the Contexts in Which Occupational Education Takes Place. Report No. 1. Denver: Education Commission of the States, November, 1967.

Vocolo, Joseph M., and Douglas C. Sheppard. "High School-College Intervisitation," The Modern Language Journal, 50:477-478, November, 1966.

Walters, Raymond. "Statistics of Registration in American Universities and Colleges, 1931," School and Society, 34:784, December, 1931.

──────. "Statistics of Registration in American Universities and Colleges, 1934," School and Society, 40:787, December, 1934.

Warren, James R. "Comprehensiveness May Depend on Public Relations," Junior College Journal, 38:24-25, April, 1968.

Warren, Jonathan R. Patterns of College Experience. U.S.O.E. Cooperative Research Project S-327. Claremont (California): College Student Personnel Institute and Claremont Graduate School and University Center, October, 1966.

──────. College Grading Practices: An Overview. Report No. 9. ERIC Clearinghouse on Higher Education. Washington: The George Washington University, March, 1971.

Warriner, E. C., and others. "Twenty-seventh Semi-Annual Meeting of The Michigan Schoolmasters' Club," The School Review, 5:95-128, February, 1897.

Wattenbarger, James L. "Changing Patterns of Control," Junior College Journal, 38:9-11, May, 1968.

Wayland, Francis. An Introductory Address ... The American Institute of Instruction. Boston: Hilliard, Gray, Little, and Wilkens, 1830.

──────. Report to the Corporation of Brown University on Changes in the System of Collegiate Education. Providence: George H. Whitney, 1850.

Weeks, I. D. "Getting Better Teachers," College Management, 5:32, August, 1970.

Weersing, F. J., and L. V. Koos. "Guidance Practice in Junior Colleges," California Quarterly of Secondary

Education, 5:93-104, 1929-30.

Weidenthal, Bud. The Community College Commitment to the Inner City--Implications for Facilities. Washington: American Association of Junior Colleges, 1967.

Weiss, R. D. "The Effect of Education on the Earnings of Blacks and Whites." Cambridge: Program on Regional and Urban Economics, Harvard University, April, 1969. (Mimeographed).

Weisz, Vern C. A Junior College's Approach to Training Auxiliary Personnel in Education. Washington: Office of Economic Opportunity, Community Action Program, June, 1968. [ERIC ED 024 356, 1969].

Welden, J. Eugene. "30 Million Adults Go To College," American Education, 5:11-13, November, 1969.

Wheatly, Michael. "State Would Assume Power Along With Cost of Schools," The Evening Sun, Baltimore, January 30, 1971, p. 16.

Whipple, James B. Community Service and Continuing Education: A Literature Review. Occasional Papers, No. 21. ERIC Clearinghouse on Adult Education. Syracuse: Publications in Continuing Education, June, 1970.

_____, et al. Liberal Education Reconsidered: Reflections on Continuing Education for Contemporary Man. Notes and Essays on Education for Adults, Number 60. Syracuse: Syracuse University Press, January, 1969.

"Who Needs College?" C. G. P. Reports, The Comparative Guidance and Placement Program. Princeton: The College Entrance Examination Board, May, 1970.

Wilbur, R. L. "The Junior College--A Message," Sierra Educational News, 23:147, 1926.

Williams, Richard C. "Tenure Practices--Redefined," Junior College Journal, 39:26-29, May, 1969.

Willingham, Warren W. "The Importance of Relevance in Expanding Postsecondary Education," Trends in Postsecondary Education. Washington: U.S. Office of Education, 1969.

———. Admission of Minority Students In Midwestern Colleges. Higher Education Surveys Report M-1. Evanston (Illinois): College Entrance Examination Board, May, 1970.

Wilson, Logan. "Higher Education and the National Interest," Campus 1980, Alvin C. Eurich (ed.), pp. 23-42. New York: Dell Publishing Co., Inc., 1968.

Wilson, Robert C., and Jerry G. Gaff. "Faculty Supporters of Change," The Research Reporter, Vol. 5, No. 4. Berkeley: The Center for Research and Development in Higher Education, 1970.

Wireman, Billy O. "Letters: End of the Bull Market," Change Magazine, 2:4, 63, January-February, 1970.

Wise, John E., S. J., et al. Methods of Research In Education. Boston: D. C. Heath and Company, 1967.

Wisgoski, Alfred E. "Attitudes of Community College Presidents, Chief Student Personnel Officers, and Faculty Toward The Student Personnel Point of View in Selected Illinois Community Junior Colleges, 1967-1968." Doctoral dissertation, 1968. [Reported in ERIC ED 032 047, 1970].

Wood, Wenford L. Higher Education for the Disadvantaged in New York State: A Summary Report of Programs of Higher Education for the Disadvantaged at Colleges and Universities in New York State. Plattsburgh: S. U. N. Y., Plattsburgh College, Jan., 1969. [ERIC ED 031 993, 1970].

Wood, William R. "Professional Personnel for Community Colleges," Junior College Journal, 20:513-22, May, 1950.

———. "The Community College," National Education Association Journal, 44:16-17, January, 1955.

Woodring, Paul. The Higher Learning in America: A Reassessment. New York: McGraw-Hill Book Co., 1968.

Wortham, Mary. "The Case for the Doctor of Arts Degree: A View from Junior College Faculty," A. A. U. P. Bulletin, 53:372-77, December, 1967.

Wright, Stephen J. *Faculty Participation in Academic Governance.* Washington: American Association for Higher Education, 1967.

Wurster, Stanley R. "Community Junior College Faculty: Needs, Characteristics, and Sources," 1969. [Reported in ERIC ED 036 294, 1970].

Yarrington, Roger (ed.). *Junior Colleges: 50 States/50 Years.* Washington: American Association of Junior Colleges, 1969.

Yelon, Stephen. "An Alternative to Letter Grades," *The Educational Forum,* 35:65-70, November, 1970.

Yeo, Richard D. "Departmentalization--Solution or Problem?" *The Educational Forum,* 35:39-44, November, 1970.

Young, Raymond. "Critical Times for North Central Area Junior College Development," *The North Central Association Quarterly,* 36:323-327, Spring, 1962.

Ziegler, Warren L. (ed.). *Essays on the Future of Continuing Education Worldwide.* Notes and Essays on Education for Adults, No. 66. Publications in Continuing Education. Syracuse: Syracuse University Press, July, 1970.

Zook, George F. "The Junior College," *The School Review,* 30:574-76, October, 1922.

_____. "The Junior College in the State's Program of Education," *National Education Association Proceedings,* Vol. 68, June 28-July 4. Washington: National Education Association, 1930.

INDEX

Abbas, Robert D., 192, 193
Academic aptitude, 203, 204
Academic probation, 204-207
Academy, 22, 70
Accreditation, 93, 178
Administrators, 143, 163, 176, 192, 211, 213, 222, 232
Adult education, 121, 127, 141, 157-163, 259
Agnew, Spiro T., 154, 155
Aims and functions, 40
Alabama Association of Junior Colleges, 25
Allen, James E., Jr., 76, 106, 113, 122, 123, 127, 161
All-purpose college, 144
American Association for Higher Education, 232
American Association of Community and Junior Colleges, 16, 20, 21, 24, 27, 68, 74, 95, 126, 132, 134, 159, 162, 207, 212, 213, 229
American Association of State Colleges and Universities, 229
American Association of University Professors, 210, 253
American College Testing Program (A.C.T.) 62, 63, 64, 77, 106, 188-189, 191, 192, 199, 200, 203, 204
American Library Association, 172
Angell, James R., 38, 43, 44, 58, 59, 69
Anti-university college, 113
Arrowsmith, William, 246
Articulation, 191
Ashby, Sir Eric, 13, 101
Assembly on University Goals and Governance, 148, 223
Associate Degree Completion Program, 67
Associate's Degree, 64-67, 83, 122, 189
Association of Colleges and Secondary Schools, 65
Astin, Alexander W., 62, 119, 154, 193, 203, 242
Attendance patterns, 117, 118, 207, 208
Axelrod, Joseph, 19

Bachelor of Medicine programs, 170
Bachelor of Technology programs, 171

Baltimore, 162
Bard, Harry, 131
Barzun, Jacques, 122
Becker, Howard S., et al., 241
Beeler, Kent D., 104, 105
Behavioral objectives, 236, 248
Behm, H. D., 202
Bell, Daniel, 252
Bennett, G. Vernon, 30
Berdie, Ralph F., 181
Besvinick, S. L., 230
Bifurcation, 58
Birenbaum, William M., 67, 102, 114, 158, 228, 240, 254
Birnbaum, Robert, 225-227
Bisection movement, 60
Bissiri, August, 206
Blackburn, Robert T., 120
Blacks, 130, 131-135, 153, 158, 183, 195-198, 204, 208, 258
Blanchard, B. E. 72, 73
Blocker, Clyde E., 72
Bock, Joleen, 167, 171, 172, 248
Bode, B. H., 10
Bogue, Jesse Parker, 20
Bolton, Frederick E., 43, 47, 78, 80
Bonner, Thomas, 14
Bossen, Doris S., 191, 206
Bossone, Richard M., 200
Boston English High School, 34
Boston Latin School, 34
Bowen, Howard R., 125
Bowles, Frank, 123
Bowles, Roy T., 188
Boyer, Marcia, 236, 237, 238
Bradley Polytechnic Institute, 25
Brawer, Florence B., 211, 215, 220, 222, 223, 234, 235, 237
Brennan, Michael J., 225
Briggs, Thomas H., 10, 36
Brown, J. Stanley, 15
Browne, Richard G., 108, 114, 144
Brubacher, John S., 25, 50, 74, 158
Brue, Eldon J., et al., 183, 194, 202, 203
Brumbaugh, A. J., 94, 126
Buckels, Marvin W., 177
Bucknell University, 61
Bureaucracy, 110, 111, 115, 163, 213

Burns, Norman, 94
Burt, Samuel M., 18, 53
Bush, Ralph H., 48
Butler, Nicholas Murray, 47, 65

Calendar, 117
California, 17, 27, 28, 29, 39, 48, 57, 60, 61, 78-84, 91, 92, 95, 96, 109, 122, 125, 152, 157, 168, 172, 174, 215, 218, 221, 225, 226, 233
California High School Teachers' Association, 69
California Junior College Association, 81, 82
Calkins, Hugh, 104
Campbell, Doak S., 10, 13, 30
Canfield, Albert A., 110
Capper, Michael R., 206, 236
Career education, 17, 57, 76, 140, 165-179, 208, 258, 260
Carnegie, Claretha, 197, 198
Carnegie unit, 31-33
Cartter, Allan, 228
Cashin, H. John, 212, 220, 221
Castle, Drew W., 45, 73
Center for Research and Development in Higher Education (Berkeley), 228, 244
Cervantes, Lucius, 102
Chase, Edward T., 102
Chase, Harry W., 9, 12, 37, 75, 223
Chicago, University of, 27, 42, 46, 51, 59, 60, 65
Chickering, Arthur W., 187, 204-205
Christian, Floyd T., 84
Cicero, 234
Civil War, 12
Clark, Burton R., 3, 76, 143
Clark, Kenneth E., 233, 234
Clayton, Howard, 114
Clearinghouse on Community Services, 161
Cleveland, Harlan, 20, 124, 132
Clinton, DeWitt, 23
Coffman, L. D., 11, 36, 37
Cohen, Arthur M., 1, 73, 119, 206, 211, 215, 220, 222, 223, 234, 235, 237, 247, 254, 265
Collective negotiations, 232, 233, 248, 263
College Characteristic Index (C.C.I.), 62, 63
College Entrance Examination Board, 129, 130
College of the Pacific, 46
Collins, Charles C., 107, 135-137
Colorado, 129, 169

Colvert, C. C., 66
Commenius, 234
Commission on Higher Education, 38, 55, 211, 224
Committee on College Entrance Requirements, 32
Committee on Education Beyond the High School, 96, 161
Commission on National Goals, 76, 125
Committee on Preparation of Junior College Teachers, 223
Committee on the Student in Higher Education, 184
Community college misunderstanding, 14, 21, 68, 70, 72, 90, 97, 113, 122, 139-141, 179, 181, 205, 209, 212
Community dimension, 135-137, 141, 156, 157
Community service, 156-165, 259
Comprehensiveness, 126, 141, 144-147, 164, 257
Compulsory education, 56
Conant, James B., 75
Conference on Youth, 161
Continuing education, 74, 251, 259
Cooling-out function, 143
Coombs, Philip H., 121
Coordination, 168, 177, 197
Corbally, John E., 48
Cornejo, Esperanza, 19, 105, 138, 168, 170, 171, 175, 176
Cosand, Joseph P., 105, 113
Council of Graduate Schools, 225, 228, 229
Counseling, 141, 180-183, 195, 262
County college, 19
Cowley, William H., 184, 249
Creamer, Don G., 246
Credentials, 114, 115, 119, 217, 250, 259
Cross, K. Patricia, 17, 113, 124, 194, 195, 199, 200, 203, 207, 208, 211, 212, 213
Cummiskey, J. Kenneth, 164
Curriculum, 28, 31, 35, 45, 47, 51, 52, 53, 57, 59, 70, 73, 83, 84, 106, 135, 164, 169-177

Davis, Calvin O., 35, 188
Davis, J. A., 299
Dearing, Bruce, 229
Degree dilemma, 223-230, 253
Democratic education, 10, 12, 30, 36, 38, 55, 56, 75, 105, 119, 124, 149, 156
Democratic Party Platform (1964), 56
DeNevi, Don, 214
Denton, Clifford, 24, 90, 134
DePaul University, 72, 73
Detroit Junior College, 93

Devall, W. B., 71
Deyo, Donald E., 76
Diplomate in College Teaching, 230
Disadvantaged, 127, 128, 135, 169, 173, 186, 222, 258
Doctor of Arts, 224, 226, 229, 230
Doctor of Education, 225
Donzaleigh, Turman P., 113
Doran, Kenneth T., 22, 23, 68, 70, 99, 124
Dotson, George E., 74
Downward extension, 74
Draper, Andrew, 22
Dressel, Paul L., 51
Dropouts, 102, 175, 204-207, 252, 260
Dual status, 68-78, 82, 84, 87, 92, 249
Duke University, 169
Dunham, E. Alden, 225
Dunlap, E. T., 17
Dykes, Archie R., 232, 233

Ebbsen, James A., 136
Eberle, August W., 104, 105
Education Professors Development Act, 222
Educational aspirations, 200, 201
Educational paradox, 78
Educational Policies Commission (1966), 55, 119
Educational Resources Information Center (ERIC), 247, 266
Eells, Walter Crosby, 21, 24, 30, 64, 65, 66, 67, 233
Elitism, 9, 34, 90, 103, 105, 134, 178, 180, 204, 205, 213, 260
Elliott, Lloyd H., 113
Emerson, Lynn A., 53, 54
Encyclopedia of Educational Research, 19
Environmental Assessment Technique (E.A.T.), 62, 190
Equal opportunity, 124, 133
Ericksen, Stanford C., 241
Erickson, Clifford G., 211, 222
Etzioni, Amitai, 153, 155
Eurich, Alvin C., 98, 122, 234, 235
Evaluation, 178, 236-239, 240, 260, 262
Evans, Arthur H., Jr., 214
Excellence, 137-141, 214, 233, 253, 258, 260
Extended secondary education, 43, 45, 55, 87, 155
Extension programs, 71

Faculty, 120, 121, 123, 131, 164, 182, 205, 209, 210-248, 253, 261-263

Faculty problems, 230-233
Faculty recruitment, 215-220
Fairleigh Dickinson University, 60
Fashion Institute of Technology, 175
Feeder institution, 61
Ferrier, William W., 25, 29, 96
Financial barriers, 207, 208
Finch, Robert, 106, 158, 165
Fine, Benjamin, 153
Finishing schools, 49, 105
Fitch, Robert J., 206
Flax, Roger E., 191
Florida, 84, 85, 91, 109, 125, 189, 196, 197, 215, 226
Folwell, William Watts, 23, 41, 42, 43, 58, 70
Four-year status, 93-97
French, Joseph L., 192
Fresno (California), 48, 79
Fretwell, E. K., 77
Friedman, Norman L., 69, 70, 210, 219
Fryer, T. W., 230
Fullerton, Bill J., 169
Funding, 54, 76, 79, 82, 85, 90, 91, 92, 107-112, 145, 167, 178, 181, 263
Futurologists, 252

Gaddy, Dale, 192
Gaff, Gerry G., 244
Gardner, John W., 121, 138, 167, 246
Garrison, Roger H., 70, 221
General education, 18, 36, 50, 51, 57
Georgia, 108
German influence, 41, 58
Getty, Ronald, 15, 21
Giles, Frederick, 171
Gleazer, Edmund J., Jr., 16, 21, 68, 70, 95, 127, 128, 150, 151, 166, 167
Glenister, Carl E., 200
Glorified secondary schools, 72
Goals, 114
Goldberg, Arthur N., 56
Goldman, Freda, 3, 142
Gore, Harold, 161, 162
Grades 13 and 14, 48, 53, 55, 58, 80, 83, 95
Grading, 154, 191, 203, 204, 206, 239-244
Graham, Robert, 15
Graham, Walter A., 25

Grand Rapids Junior College, 89
Grant, Sherman, 128, 183
Gray, A. A., 38, 69
Guidance, 50, 195, 222
Gustad, John, 237
Gymnasium, 41

Hakanson, John W., 175
Halfway house, 113
Hancher, Virgil, 211
Harlacher, Ervin L., 157, 160
Harper, William Rainey, 25, 38, 42, 43, 45, 58, 59, 65, 70
Harris, Chester W., 19
Harvard University, 8, 22, 66, 77, 149
Harvey, L. D., 10, 12, 34
Hayden, Sheldon, 20
Hayes, Glenn E., 168
Hedgepeth, Victor W. B., 46
Heiner, Harold, 183
Heiss, Ann, 228
Henry, Nelson B., 27, 31, 51, 175, 192
Higgins, Milton P., 51
High school, 12, 32, 34, 35, 40, 41, 42, 47, 49, 50, 52, 55, 58, 68, 75, 167, 177, 204, 234
High school college, 19, 32, 43
High school department, 24
High school stigma, 210
Higher education, 14, 15, 16, 33, 34, 68, 77, 179, 249, 263
Higher education confusion, 1, 13, 14, 15, 16, 19, 21, 33, 36, 50, 51, 54, 65, 68, 70, 104, 105, 180, 209
Hillsborough Junior College (Florida), 147
Hillway, Tyrus, 25
Hodgkinson, Harold L., 98, 121, 159, 228
Holland, J. L., 62
Hollinshead, Byron S., 20
Hood, Wenford L., 196
Howe, Florence, 241
Howe, Harold, 137-138
Hoyt, Donald P., 203, 241
Hoyt, Kenneth B., 178
Hunter, Pauline, 220
Hurlburt, Allan S., 144
Hurst, Charles, 131-134
Hutchins, Robert M., 13, 45, 50, 60, 101, 249
Huther, John W., 150, 151

Identity, 47, 56, 77, 101, 126, 138, 181, 210, 254
Illinois, 45, 58, 88, 91, 92, 95, 108, 109, 125, 144, 217, 229
Illinois Institute of Technology, 25
Illiteracy, 103, 127
Industrial arts, 18
Inservice education, 221-222, 262, 264
Institute for Local Self-Government, 173-174
Institutional characteristics, 61, 129, 255-258
Institutional research, 224-246, 263
Interests, attitudes and self-estimates, 199-200
Intermediate colleges, 70

Jacksonian era, 37
Jacobsen, Joseph M., 93
Jacobson, Robert L., 129-130
Jennings, Frank G., 144
Johnson, B. Lamar, 31, 56, 74, 144, 236, 244
Johnson, Paul M., 77
Joliet Junior College, 25, 27, 45, 88
Jones, Twyman, 182
Junior college department, 79
Junior college growth, 27-28, 30, 43, 46, 50, 57, 67, 79-93, 105, 110, 125, 161, 187-189
Junior College Leadership Program, 222
Junior College of Kansas City, 66
Junior college principal, 80
Junior college purposes, 28, 29, 30, 37, 38, 39, 46, 48, 49, 51, 54, 56, 60, 76, 80, 93, 99, 141, 143, 146-147, 174
Junior division, 57
Junior Federal Assistant Examination, 171
Junior high school, 43

Kane, Joseph P., 153
Kansas, 27
Kastner, Harold, 196-197
Kaufman, Jacob J., 52
Kellogg, Frazier, 171
Kelly, Win, 22, 25, 26, 27, 215
Kelsey, Roger B., 68
Kemp, W. W., 28, 37, 44, 49, 51, 69, 181
Kennedy, John F., 138
Kentucky, 108
Kerner, Otto, 131

Kerr, Clark, 121
King, Spencer B., Jr., 30
Knoell, Dorothy M., 117-118, 163, 245-246
Knowles, Malcolm S., 159
Kohler, Mary C., 175
Koos, Leonard V., 11, 23, 28, 29, 30, 38, 39, 40, 43, 44, 49, 50, 54, 57, 97, 181, 189, 215, 233, 273
Krug, Edward A., 39, 59
Kruger, W. Stanley, 205

Land-grant institution, 1, 12, 54, 59, 121, 127, 148, 249, 255
Landrith, Harold F., 205, 211, 212
Lange, Alexis F., 37, 39, 48, 225
Lasell junior college and seminary, 24-25
Latin grammar school, 9
Lauter, Paul, 241
League for Experimentation and Innovation, 147
Learning, 217, 233-236, 248, 252
Legal definitions, 19
Legislative-legal influence, 78-93, 108, 111, 160-161, 167-168, 172, 230, 257
Leisure, 141-142, 259
Lewis Institute, 25, 66
Liberal arts, 71, 95, 142, 178, 206
Lins, L. J., 188-189, 207
Literature, related, 265-281
Littlefield, Henry W., 17
Lombardi, John, 81-82
Long, James, 159
Lower colleges, 58
Lower division, 59, 60
Lunden, Walter A., 8, 9, 13
Lyceum, 42

McClaskey, Harris C., 171
McConaughy, James L., 59
McConnell, T. R., 179
Machlup, Fritz, 155-156
McLane, C. L., 38
McNutt, Walter S., 60
Magruder, William T., 69
Malcolm X College, 130-133
Mallan, John P., 91
Manello, George, 240

Marion Institute, 25
Marsee, Stuart E., 183
Marshall, Max S., 206
Martin, Roscoe, 213
Maryland, 33, 97, 98, 178, 217
Maryland Association of Junior Colleges, 77
Masiko, Peter, Jr., 72
Massachusetts, 166
Master of Philosophy, 224, 226, 229
Master plans, 80, 89, 90, 99, 108, 144, 146
Mauss, Armand L., 193
Mayhew, Lewis B., 51, 122, 266
Medsker, Leland L., 74, 76, 165, 190, 193, 194, 203, 213
Menefee, Selden, 19, 105, 113, 138, 168, 170, 171, 175, 176
Meyer, John D., 205
Miami-Dade Junior College, 147, 230
Michigan, 27, 39, 41, 45, 57, 58, 59, 89, 91, 125
Millet, Fred B., 224
Milton, Ohmer, 245
Minnesota, 27, 39, 41, 59, 108
Minnesota plan, 42
Minorities, 130, 140, 154, 184, 195-198
Missouri, 27, 57, 66, 97
Modern Language Association, 229
Moore, William Jr., 122, 128, 153, 211, 220
Morgenstein, Melvin, 164
Morin, Lloyd H., 237-238
Morrisett, Lloyd N., 73
Morrison, D. G., 68, 94, 96
Morrissey, Kermit C., 110, 131
Mortorana, S. V., 68
Moynihan, Daniel, 149
Muck, Stephen J., 206
Munday, Leo A., 203
Myran, Gunder A., 157

NEA Committee of Ten, 32
Nation-campus, 71
National Advisory Council on Vocational Education, 167
National Conference Committee on Standards of Colleges and Secondary Schools, 46
National Conference on the Teaching of English in the Junior College, 214
National Council of Independent Junior Colleges, 147
National Faculty Association of Community and Junior

Colleges, 226
National Science Foundation, 217
National Society for the Promotion of Industrial Education, 11, 51
National Society for the Study of Education, 50
New Jersey, 86-87, 97, 125, 166
New York, 70, 85, 91, 93, 96, 97, 99, 109, 125, 146-147, 151-153, 162, 166, 189, 195-196
Newman Report, 114-116, 120, 121
Nixon, Richard M., 16, 98, 107, 124, 207
North Carolina, 141

O'Banion, Terry, 181, 185
Occupational education, 165-179, 201-203
O'Connell, Thomas E., 123, 136, 151
Ohio, 86, 94, 144
Okerlund, G. M., 69
Oklahoma, 17, 27, 89, 94
Open Door, 3, 106, 126, 132, 141, 148-156, 168, 198, 209, 252
Ordinance of 1787, 8
Organization of the past, 71

Pace, C. Robert, 62, 190
Packer Collegiate Institute, 25
Packer, Herbert L., 224
Palinchak, Robert S., 181
Panos, R. J., 203
Parallel function, 76
Paramedical education, 168-170
Paraprofessionals, 67, 166, 173
Park, Young, 213, 214
Parker, Garland G., 22, 27, 60, 98
Pasadena, 20, 48
Paschal, Elizabeth, 122
Pennsylvania, 23, 75, 85, 90, 97, 145, 172
People's vocational college, 69
Perkins, James A., 125
Perry, Charles F., 35, 51
Ph.D., 55, 58, 61, 120, 131, 143, 156, 223-230, 248, 263
Pherman, Leo T., 195
Pierce, E. C., 45
Pifer, Alan, 106
Political climate, 255
Popham, W. James, 71

Postsecondary education, 14, 34, 52, 53, 76, 107, 119, 151, 188-189, 258
Price, Hugh G., 74
Princeton, 138, 156
Principles for action, 255-263
Prisoners, 132
Private junior college, 213
Proctor, William M., 28, 43, 48, 76, 225
Professional preparation, 220-223
Professors (teachers), 72, 73, 120, 122, 135, 180, 204, 210-248, 261-263
Programs, 258-259
Proprietary schools, 71
Prussian influence, 13, 41, 58
Public confidence, 5, 10, 71, 140-141, 256, 260
Public service careers, 162, 173

Quimby, Edgar A., 254

Racial imbalance, 131-134, 162, 204, 259
Ravekes, John E., 185
Read, Betty, 108, 109, 171, 190, 207, 220
Remedial courses, 84, 128, 133-134, 143, 262
Reorganization, 42
Research, 61, 121, 144, 156, 178, 222, 223, 224, 244-247, 262, 263-264
Rever, Philip R., 149
Reverse articulation, 143, 201
Revolving door, 148
Reynolds, James W., 50, 51, 151
Richardson, Richard C., Jr., 23, 139-141
Riendeau, Albert J., 203
Right vs. privilege, 120
Rislov, Sigurd, 37, 141, 244
Rockefeller, John D., 22
Rogers, Carl R., 151, 223
Roosevelt, Franklin D., 74
Ross, Woodburn O., 13, 14, 98
Roth, Audrey, 173
Roueche, John E., 235
Roush, Robert E., 32, 33
Rudolph, Frederick, 37, 60
Rudy, Willis, 25, 50

St. Petersburg, Junior College, 84
Salvage function, 143, 260
San Diego, 48
San Jose, 48
Sanford, Nevitt, 55, 73, 77, 205, 215
Sanford, Terry, 141
Schoenfeldt, L. F., 194
Science Research Associates, 17
Scott, W. Wayne, 245
Scully, Malcolm, 120
Seashore, H., 203
Secondary education, 43, 46, 47, 50, 51, 53, 55, 59, 68, 69, 72, 74, 102
Second-class status, 186
Seibel, D. W., 203
Seidlin, Joseph, 211
Semas, Philip W., 131
Sewal, J. I., 225
Seward, William H., 23
Shawl, William, 235, 238
Shores, Louis, 103, 123, 127
Shugrue, Michael, 229
Siehr, Hugo E., et al., 212, 230-232
Sievert, William A., 110
Six-four-four plan, 43, 44, 48
Six-year high school junior college, 25, 45, 46
Skaggs, Kenneth G., 52, 169, 171
Skinner, B. F., 235
Slocum, Walter L., 188
Smith, Lawrence G., 243
Smith, Lewis W., 50
Smith-Hughes Act (1917), 54
Snyder, William H., 51
Social issues, 124-125, 133, 136, 234, 248
Social mobility, 102-103, 163, 183
Social promotion, 98
Socioeconomic background, 193-195
Sorokin, P. A., 102-103
Sorrells, Daniel J., 96
Southern Regional Education Board, 134, 185, 197-198
Spencer, Lyle M., 106
Stanford, Leland, 22, 57, 60
Stanley, James W., 25
Stanley, Julian C., 204
Stephens College (Mo.), 66
Stern, George G., 62
Stern, Milton R., 159

Stewart, L. H., 202
Stewart, W. Blair, 72
Stinchcomb, James, 159
Stokes, Carl B., 162, 163
Stratton, Alan G., 211, 226
Street academy, 132
Strongin, Harriet, 164
Student clientele, 126, 142, 143, 153, 163, 180-181, 183-184, 186-209, 239, 251
Student government, 260-261
Student personnel service, 179-185, 254, 261
Student protest, 192
Subversive influences, 120
Summerskill, John, 205
Superior high school, 92

Tanner, Laurel L., and Daniel, 172
Tappan, Henry Phillips, 23, 41, 58, 70
Teaching, 211, 215, 219-222, 229, 233-236, 244, 252, 262
Teaf, H. M., Jr., 240
Tests, 130, 182, 196, 197
Texas, 27, 88, 91, 93, 246
Thomas, Barbara, 193
Thomas, Charles L., 204
Thornton, James W., Jr., 26, 127
Toews, Emil O., 16, 27, 39, 79, 81
Toynbee, Arnold, 235
Tradition, 101, 251, 258
Transfer status, 137, 165, 176, 186, 191-192
Trent, James W., 190, 193, 194, 203
Troyer, Maurice E., 224
Truxal, Andrew, 154
Tuition, 56, 150, 260
Turnbull, William W., 201
Turner, Hugh J., Jr., 122
Two-year thinking, 255
Tyler, Henry T., 83-84
Tyler, Ralph, 121, 221, 236

Undem, Jan, 206
Underemployment, 166
U.S. Office of Education, 20, 111, 173, 230
Universal higher education, 55, 56, 118-119, 125, 150, 155
Universal National Service, 71
Universal postsecondary schooling, 155

Universities, 11, 15, 40, 57, 59, 98, 121, 134, 153, 158, 159, 163, 220, 222, 225, 233, 234
University branch campus (center), 144-145, 189, 253
University Commission on Admissions (CUNY), 152
University junior-college, 19, 61
University of California, Los Angeles, 60, 147, 220, 247
University of Miami, 230
Upper division, 144, 239, 263
Upward extension, 38, 48, 56, 73
Urban crisis, 159, 162-163

Vaccaro, Louis C., 168
Vail, Curtis C. D., 74
Vaizey, John, 12
Valien, Preston, 196, 205
Venn, Grant, 3, 166
Vincennes University, 25-26
Virginia, 125
Vocational education, 17, 18, 22, 28, 36, 48, 50, 51, 52, 53, 54, 83, 91, 103, 165-179, 250, 258

Walters, Raymond, 27, 37
Warren, Jonathan R., 239-242, 243
Warriner, E. C., 46
Washington, State of, 48, 57, 87, 91, 97
Wasteful education war, 145
Wattenbarger, James L., 84, 90, 215
Wayland, Francis, 11, 233
Wayne State University, 93, 122
Weeding-out institution, 61, 73
Weekend college, 132
Weeks, I. D., 215
Weis, Vern C., 173
Weisinger, Herbert, 223
Welden, J. Eugene, 160
Wheatly, Michael, 108
Whipple, James B., 4, 158
Wilbur, Leslie, 22, 25, 26, 27, 215
Wilkes College, 61
Willingham, Warren W., 195
Wilson, Logan, 105
Wilson, Robert, 244
Wireman, Billy O., 98, 105, 113
Wisconsin, 108
Wisgoski, Alfred E., 222

Women, 158, 160, 189, 200, 202
Wood, William R., 220
Woodring, Paul, 241-242
World War I, 12, 30
World War II, 30, 31, 55, 88
Wortham, Mary, 223
Wrenn, C. Gilbert, 238
Wright, Stephen J., 232
Wurster, Stanley R., 215-218, 226-227

Yale, 149
Yarrington, Roger, 85-90, 162
Yelon, Stephen, 239
Yeo, Richard D., 102

Zook, George F., 46, 47, 48